THE JEW WITHIN

THE JEW WITHIN

Self, Family, and
Community in America

Steven M. Cohen and Arnold M. Eisen

INDIANA UNIVERSITY PRESS   BLOOMINGTON & INDIANAPOLIS

THIS BOOK IS A PUBLICATION OF

INDIANA UNIVERSITY PRESS
601 NORTH MORTON STREET
BLOOMINGTON, IN 47404-3797 USA

HTTP://WWW.INDIANA.EDU/~IUPRESS

Telephone orders 800-842-6796
Fax orders 812-855-7931
Orders by e-mail IUPORDER@INDIANA.EDU

THE PAPER USED IN THIS PUBLICATION MEETS THE MINIMUM REQUIREMENTS OF AMERICAN NATIONAL STANDARD FOR INFORMATION SCIENCES—PERMANENCE OF PAPER FOR PRINTED LIBRARY MATERIALS, ANSI Z39.48-1984.

MANUFACTURED IN THE UNITED STATES OF AMERICA

LIBRARY OF CONGRESS CATALOGING-IN-PUBLICATION DATA

COHEN, STEVEN MARTIN
THE JEW WITHIN : SELF, FAMILY, AND COMMUNITY IN AMERICA /
STEVEN M. COHEN AND ARNOLD M. EISEN.
P.   CM.
INCLUDES BIBLIOGRAPHICAL REFERENCES AND INDEX.
ISBN 0-253-33782-8 (CL : ALK. PAPER)
1. JUDAISM—UNITED STATES. 2. JEWISH WAY OF LIFE. 3. JEWISH FAMILIES—UNITED STATES—RELIGIOUS LIFE. 4. JEWS—UNITED STATES—INTERVIEWS.   I. EISEN, ARNOLD M., DATE   II. TITLE.

BM205 .E47 2000
296'.0973'09051—DC21
00-037000

1   2   3   4   5   05   04   03   02   01   00

FOR ADAM, EDEET, SHULIE, AND NATHANIEL

CONTENTS

ACKNOWLEDGMENTS

This has been a collaborative effort in more ways than our co-authorship. We have accumulated an especially large number of debts along the way to completion of the study, and can acknowledge only some of them here.

Our first thanks go to the sixty individuals who agreed to speak with us at length about the patterns and meanings of their Jewish activity, whether in one-on-one interviews or in focus groups. We were repeatedly astonished by and appreciative of the candor, thoughtfulness, and passion of their responses to our queries. No less, we were grateful for their patience in the face of questioning which in many cases went on for several hours.

No less, we are grateful to the interviewers whom we engaged to help us ask these questions in diverse corners of America and Israel: Esther Benjamin, Daniel Groper, Nadia Hoffmann, Liz Kraut-Nahar, Julie Lebenson, Rachel Levy, Dana Rawitsch, Heni Schwartz, and Kathy Simon.

The project could not have gotten under way without the warm encouragement and generous support provided by the Wilstein Institute of Jewish Policy Studies, which assisted us from the very earliest stages of the planning process through the completion and evaluation of our qualitative materials, and will help us reach several of our target audiences following publication with conferences bringing together scholars, communal professionals, and lay leaders. We owe special thanks to David Gordis, the institute's director, and to its former associate director, Yoav Ben-Horin. Our quantitative study of a representative sample of American Jewish adults was made possible by the generous support of the Jewish Community Centers Association. We are grateful to the JCCA's executive vice president, Allan Finkelstein, and his associates.

A number of colleagues provided helpful critiques of and responses to our methods and findings during various stages of the study at conferences convened by the Wilstein Institute for that purpose. They include Aryeh

Davidson, Leonard Fein, David Gordis, Bethamie Horowitz, Paula Hyman, Charles S. Liebman, Deborah Dash Moore, Wade Clark Roof, Carl Sheingold, Jonathan Sarna, Barry Shrage, Ann Swidler, and Jonathan Woocher. Several of these colleagues also read all or part of the manuscript and offered invaluable suggestions for its improvement. Steven M. Cohen wishes to express a special note of gratitude to Charles S. Liebman and Riv-Ellen Prell for their years of friendship, professional and personal. Both contributed directly (by reading the entire manuscript) as well as indirectly to this work.

Diane Herman in Jerusalem offered research assistance on the survey and invaluable editorial assistance on the manuscript. David Albertson, Joel Astman, and Mitchell Kimbrough in Palo Alto also assisted with preparation of earlier drafts.

Our spouses, Susan Wall and Adriane Leveen, contributed numerous insights to our analysis, bore with numerous phone calls at all hours of the day and night, and generously assumed added family responsibilities while we spent many pleasant hours poring over our data in Jerusalem cafés.

We have dedicated the book to our children, who in more ways than we can name both inspired our work and guided our reflection. It is our hope that they will in some measure benefit from what the research has taught us.

THE JEW WITHIN

1

INTRODUCTION

The American Jewish community, rocked by reports of soaring inter-marriage rates, rampant assimilation, and diminishing population, has been more concerned of late than ever with issues of Jewish identification and "continuity." Anxiety about the Jewish future has led to increased interest among scholars, communal leaders, and laypeople alike in the factors which shape, nourish, and sustain Jewish commitment. How does one nurture, engage, and mobilize actively involved Jews? What leads some Jews to place Jewish commitment at the very center of their lives, while others are content—or driven—to leave it at the margins? Are experiences during childhood the most critical in preparing the ground for Jewish commitment—or can adolescent or adult experiences prove of greater or equal value? And—last but surely not least—to what degree are American Jews similar to or different from other American ethnic and religious groups in regard to these issues? Are Jews as distinct as they sometimes claim or wish to be—or as typical as they claim or wish to be at other times, for other purposes?

These questions, we believe, are urgent. They have long engaged both of us not only professionally but personally, Cohen as a sociologist of American Jewish attitudes and behavior, Eisen as a student of American Jewish religious belief and modern Jewish thought and practice. However, we have suspected for some time that the answers generally proposed to these and similar questions are off the mark. American Jews at century's end, we believe, have come to view their Jewishness in a very different way than either their parents or they themselves did only two or three decades ago. Today's Jews, like their peers in other religious traditions, have turned inward in the search for meaning. They have moved away from the organizations, institutions, and causes that used to anchor identity and shape behavior. As a result, scholars too must revise their thinking. New research questions and new methods of pursuing these questions are required.

Three convictions guide and shape the present study. We shall argue that the discovery and construction of Jewish meaning in contemporary America (as of ultimate significance to life more generally) occur primarily in the private sphere. American Jews, we believe, enact and express their decisions about Judaism predominantly in the intimate spaces of love and family, friendship, and reflection. These are the spaces in which late-twentieth-century American individuals—Jewish or Gentile, religious or secular—are in their own eyes "most themselves" and least the creatures of roles and obligations imposed from the outside. "Faith is considered a private matter" in America, writes Robert Wuthnow in a recent study. "It is practiced mostly in the quiet recesses of personal life" (1998, p. vii). That is certainly true for the Jews we interviewed. By contrast, the importance of the public sphere—the organizational life which previously nourished and molded Jewish identity in this country, whether focused on philanthropy, social causes, support for Israel, or the fight against antisemitism—has severely diminished. The institutional arena is no longer the primary site where American Jews find and define the selves they are and the selves they want to be. Roles played in public settings, and the behavior on display there, are often regarded as just that: roles and displays that do not reveal, and certainly do not constitute, their true selves, the essence of who they are.

The principal authority for contemporary American Jews, in the absence of compelling religious norms and communal loyalties, has become the sovereign self. Each person now performs the labor of fashioning his or her own self, pulling together elements from the various Jewish and non-Jewish repertoires available, rather than stepping into an "inescapable framework" of identity (familial, communal, traditional) given at birth. Decisions about ritual observance and involvement in Jewish institutions are made and made again, considered and reconsidered, year by year and even week by week. American Jews speak of their lives, and of their Jewish beliefs and commitments, as a journey of ongoing questioning and development. They avoid the language of arrival. There are no final answers, no irrevocable commitments. The Jews we met in the course of our research reserved the right to choose anew in the future, amending or reversing the decisions made today, and defended their children's right to do so for themselves in turn. Personal meanings are sought by these Jews for new as well as for inherited observances. If such meanings are not fashioned or found, the practices in question are revised or discarded—or not undertaken in the first place.

In order to get at behavior which takes place in the private sphere, and probe attitudes buried deep within the self, one must turn to a research method capable of taking us beyond the reports of public behavior and unreflective attitudes which are generally reflected in the results of questionnaires. Existing survey research into American Jews, which we shall draw upon extensively in the present work, along with studies of American religious behavior generally, has established that Jewish adults vary significantly in the extent and nature of their involvement. Survey data have provided an operational definition of Jewish identity and some sense of how to measure it. Adult involvement has been convincingly correlated with factors such as Jewish schooling, camp, and Israel experiences.

But research to date has not provided systematic knowledge of the complex ways in which Jews express and enact their Jewish identities. The highly personal factors that lead Jews to opt for serious Judaism have yet to be clarified. We know, for example, how often American Jews come to synagogue or visit Israel, but have not yet clarified the sense that Jews make of what transpires in these visits or how these experiences of being in synagogue or in Israel fit into the larger fabric of their personal Jewish meanings. Quantitative methods alone cannot grasp the ways in which contemporary American Jews follow and depart from the attitudes, behaviors, and conflicts that they witnessed as children. They cannot measure how being Jewish impinges on and reflects the ways they rear their own children, work out the division of household roles with their spouses, consider the ultimate matters of existence, express their love. Social scientists who work in this field would be the first to admit that such nuances and subtleties, critical to the understanding of American Jewish identity in its many varieties as well as to effective intervention in the formulation of identity, have yet to be adequately explored.

Understanding these matters is precisely our aim in the present study, and so we have followed in the footsteps of other scholars of contemporary American religion, most notably Wade Clark Roof (1993) and Robert Wuthnow (1989, 1994, 1998, 1999), a group which now includes feminist scholars of the Jewish experience who have stressed the importance of first-person narration (Davidman 1991; Kaufman 1991). All these researchers have integrated survey data with case studies based on extensive personal interviews. We have had their example very much in mind as we sought to document and explicate the habits of American Jewish hearts.

OUR METHOD

With the help of several associates, we conducted almost fifty in-depth interviews around the country over the past few years, most taking place over two sessions. Interviews of this length gave us access to meanings and motivations rarely uncovered through quantitative methods. No less important, they gave each respondent the opportunity to describe his or her Jewish development in some detail, and to do so in his or her own words.

Our interview subjects were suggested by contacts in synagogues, Jewish Federations, Jewish community centers, or other agencies. For reasons discussed below, the contacts were asked to recommend names of articulate men and women between the ages of about thirty and fifty who were members but not activists in their own or other organizations, or had become active only recently. We met with women and men in equal numbers, took care to interview Jews living in major centers of Jewish population as well as those in smaller cities and in suburbs, and conducted conversations in a wide variety of locales throughout the United States, from the Bay Area and Los Angeles on the West Coast through Chicago and Detroit in the Midwest, to Boston, New Haven, Manhattan, and suburban New York in the Northeast. Jews living in or around large urban centers predominate in our sample, as they do in the American Jewish population as a whole. In several cases we intentionally interviewed individuals whose involvement fell "over the line" of moderate affiliation on either side. We also interviewed three individuals who had come to study for a year at the Pardes Institute in Jerusalem.

The use of interview data has obvious advantages, affording insight into meaning, motivation, and conflict not easily attained through yes and no questions or rating scales that run from one to five. At the same time, we should be aware that the past may not have been exactly as our informants describe it. Grandparents in particular seem to be idealized in memory, while parents are recalled no less selectively but with significantly less positive valence. Our interviewees sometimes lend to their own thoughts or events in their lives a degree of clarity in describing them to us that was not present when the thoughts or events actually transpired. At other moments, precisely the opposite occurred: lacking the ability to articulate thoughts or feelings, even the most thoughtful people in our sample became tongue-tied, stumbling where one would have expected them to be sure-footed. Interviews, as Wuthnow warns, do not constitute "a portal through which we can view the past as it actually happened." Nor do they offer "a peephole into the inner consciousness of those giving the accounts." Indeed, "the language of spiritual journey" to which our subjects naturally gravitated in response to our questioning has itself "become a kind of genre," causing the speaker to "emphasize changing conceptions and experiences of faith" while downplaying the importance of that which is inherited, static, or routine (1999, pp. xxxiii–xxxiv).

Our focus on the baby boomer generation (with the exception of several individuals selected intentionally in order to explore generational differences) follows recent research into patterns of Christian belief and practice in this country. The demographic significance and societal influence of this cohort in the Jewish community are comparable to its significance and influence in America generally. Baby boomers make up nearly half of the adult population of American Jewry. What is more, comparison has been part of our purpose in this study from the outset. We wanted to test the degree of uniqueness in American Jewish attitudes and behavior vis-à-vis other American ethnic and religious groups that likewise find themselves on the boundary between "modern" and "postmodern" forms of commitment.

Recent scholarship on religion in the United States, for example, has demonstrated a steep decline in the membership of liberal churches, the erosion of denominational boundaries, the privatization of religious impulse, and a pervasive consumerism when it comes to church membership and attendance. Would we find these developments among moderately affiliated Jews? Recent scholarship on ethnicity has shown a decline in the social bases for ethnic loyalties along with the persistence of a superficial, noncompelling affiliation motivated in large part by nostalgia. Would Jews, too, exhibit such patterns? The answer in both cases turned out to be yes—though not without important nos, qualifications, and complications that we shall seek to elucidate. We want to give full weight to the uniqueness of the American situation and the Jewish beliefs and practices it has called forth, as well as to the "rules" of modern life that have limited Jewish options in every modern Western diaspora, and continue to do so to no small extent in America.

We concentrated on the "moderately affiliated Jews" who make up the great bulk of American Jewry, in large measure because they *are* so significant numerically. The "core group" comprising those who are most active Jewishly is estimated to constitute about 20 percent of the American Jewish population, while those who are completely uninvolved in organized Jewish life, hardly ever setting foot in a Jewish communal setting throughout the entire course of their lives, account for another 20 percent. Operationally, we have defined "moderately affiliated Jews" as those who belong to a Jewish institution (a Jewish community center, synagogue, or organization) but are not as involved, learned, or pious as the most highly engaged 20–25 percent of American Jews. (We employed scales of ritual observance, institutional participation, and belief in order to identify members of this target group [Cohen 1991b].) Our aim was to get to know the average members of Reform and Conservative congregations, Hadassah chapters, and the like. These individuals, for at least a significant portion of their lives, are at least somewhat involved with Jewish institutions and traditions. And precisely because they are neither firmly committed to active Jewish life nor firmly ensconced in non-involvement, they are for our purposes the most interesting, exhibiting both thoughtfulness and fluidity as they chart their way to Jewish attitudes and behaviors with which they feel comfortable.

The National Jewish Population Survey (NJPS), the authoritative study of American Jewry sponsored by the Council of Jewish Federations in 1990, provides several parameters which support this choice of subject (Kosmin et al. 1991; Goldstein 1992). Of married Jewish adults between the ages of thirty-five and fifty, our target generation in this study, fully three-quarters identify as Reform or Conservative Jews, as do the bulk of our sample. Just over one-quarter reported that they attend worship services monthly or more often than that: those who do so would tend to be numbered among the "activists" rather than the moderately affiliated, and thus would fall outside our target population. About a quarter of the NJPS sample were married to non-Jews, and most of this group belong to the unaffiliated segment of American Jewry, who fall outside our sample on the other end. Only a handful of our respondents are intermarried.

All our subjects, as well as their spouses or significant others, are cited or described in this study with fictitious names meant to protect the privacy we promised them. All the interviews were taped, and then either transcribed verbatim or extensively summarized. The interview protocol is presented in appendix A. One-on-one conversations were supplemented at the outset by two focus groups that followed the same protocol but allowed for collective give-and-take.

The survey data on which we shall draw derive from a mail-back questionnaire (also reprinted in appendix B) which was completed by 1,005 Jewish respondents throughout the United States. The survey was carried out in June and July 1997 (after interviewing for our study had been completed) by the Washington office of Market Facts, Inc., a national survey research company. Respondents belong to the company's Consumer Mail Panel, consisting of about 368,000 Americans who have agreed to be surveyed from time to time on a variety of concerns. Of those, about 8,400 individuals were potentially eligible for sampling for this study. Questionnaires were sent to the Jewish members of 1,400 households.

Market Facts drew the sample so as to approximate the demographic characteristics of the NJPS. Eligible households contained at least one Jewish adult, as previously reported in responses to questions on religious identity posed in an annual screening questionnaire that collected information on a variety of basic socio-demographic variables from each panel member. NJPS determined that approximately 80 percent of adults who are Jewish also said that their *religion* is Jewish (Kosmin et al. 1991, pp. 5–6). Jews who did not identify as Jewish for purposes of religion (so-called secular or ethnic Jews) reported lower levels of Jewish involvement (e.g., observance, affiliation, in-marriage). Hence, a survey such as this one, based upon a sample who claim to be Jewish by religion, underrepresents the Jewishly less involved. As a consequence, our survey slightly overestimates the overall population's levels of Jewish identification, making it appear that American Jews are more ritually observant, organizationally affiliated, socially cohesive, and emotionally engaged in being Jewish than they are in reality.

OUR FINDINGS

The single most important finding of our study is decidedly double-edged. On the one hand, the American Jews we interviewed overwhelmingly follow the pattern explained fifteen years ago by Bellah and his co-authors in *Habits of the Heart*. The "first language" that our subjects speak is by and large one of profound individualism. Their language is universalist, liberal, and personalist. Community—though a buzzword in our interviews, a felt need, even a real hunger for some—is a "second language," subordinate to the first. Our subjects, like Americans more generally today, do not speak it as often or as well.

Indeed, to a surprising degree, we found that that first language remains predominant among moderately affiliated American Jews even after the second language has found expression and enactment. Community and commitment, in fact, are repeatedly redefined and apprehended by our subjects in terms acceptable to sovereign and ever-questing selves. Only in those terms is commitment possible and community permitted to obligate the self. The more committed and active among our sample told us repeatedly that they decide week by week, year by year, which rituals they will observe and how they will observe them. They also repeatedly reconsider which organizations and charities they will join or support, and to what degree; which beliefs they will hold, which loyalties they will acknowledge. The self is and must remain autonomous and sovereign.

The decline of communal obligations, the rise of sovereign individuals, is of course the modern story par excellence, one that has been told and retold by countless scholars of religion in the modern world. Individuals newly liberated from inherited identities and obligations seize hold with a vengeance of the autonomy afforded them, and are driven as a result to reject or recast traditional beliefs and behaviors. Religious life, if it survives at all in a "disenchanted world," transpires "in pianissimo," as Max Weber put it: in personal relations selected by each person. The "sacred canopy" (Peter Berger's famous term) no longer overarches existence, and so the demand to choose and re-choose identity (which Berger called the "heretical imperative") is inescapable (Berger 1969, 1980). Nowhere have these processes been more evident than among Jews. Their move "out of the

7

ghetto" and into major achievement in many areas of modern life has often been chronicled. The continuing effects of this transformation in America have also been the subjects of much scholarly attention, including our own.

Yet here the postmodern story weighs in: the labor of fashioning a Jewish self remains deeply significant to moderately affiliated American Jews. We can state with confidence that the quest for Jewish meaning is extremely important to our subjects, just as the search for meaning is important to contemporary Americans more generally (Bellah et al. 1996; Wuthnow 1994; Roof and McKinney 1987). Middle-range American Jews seek an abiding significance in their lives that goes beyond the activities of daily life and the limits of their own mortality. They readily discussed their highly personal searches for transcendent meaning, and confessed (to a degree that surprised us) to belief in God. Our subjects reported a strong desire to find a sense of direction and ultimate purpose, and the wish to find it largely or entirely in the framework of Jewish practices and beliefs. The fact that decisions concerning Judaism are inextricably wrapped up in the search for personal meaning to life is perhaps the reason that our subjects most often expressed their Judaism in the private sphere, where transcendent purpose is most readily discovered and located by contemporary Americans of whatever tradition. Judaism "happens" at home, with family or good friends. It transpires in the place within the self given over to reflection, longing, faith, and doubt.

This development marks in several crucial respects a veering away from the modern story: the "grand narratives" of emancipation and enlightenment in which the rejection of religion has figured prominently. Far from leaving faith behind in favor of secular national or communal loyalties, as many of their parents and grandparents did, the Jews we interviewed are dissatisfied with secular affiliations and are in search of personal spiritual meaning. Where previous generations abandoned ritual practice almost entirely, believing it outdated or superstitious, Jews today are returning to ritual observance and making it a major locus of personal meaning. Avowed discontent with the disruptive and alienating aspects of modern life has led many of them to seek out religious communities that hold the promise of personal meaning as well as of enriched and enduring family relations. Finally, where the parents and grandparents of those we interviewed had in many cases lost faith in God and lost interest in all but the ethical and historical aspects of the Jewish tradition, moderately affiliated Jews today are not abandoning tradition but refashioning it. They have no wish to sacrifice the particularity of ethnic and religious loyalty in the name of America or of humanity.

Quite the opposite: the Jews who speak in the pages that follow take the existence of "multiple life-worlds" and "local narratives" for granted, and value them as precious goods. They aim to make Jewish narratives part of

8

their own personal stories, by picking and choosing among new and inherited practices and texts so as to find the combination they as individuals can authentically affirm. This attempted synthesis of disparate commitments, including the commitment to an unending journey, does not leave moderately affiliated Jews untroubled. Almost all our subjects, including the most Jewishly active among them, knowingly and unknowingly betrayed enduring ambivalence toward the organizations, institutions, commitments, and norms which constitute Jewish life: families of origin, synagogues, federations, God. Ambivalence continues to be felt and expressed, even after the decision has been made to be a serious Jewish self; freedom to choose is retained even after the recognition that one has been "chosen" and is obligated. This is, perhaps, inevitable given the close association between Jewish identity and the family ties that are the source of intense and conflicting emotion. But the combination of modern and postmodern patterns at work inside these selves also plays its part. Our aim in chapter 2 is to set out these complexities of self-conception, drawing as always upon other research into these matters, including our own. The kinds of selves Jews are and want to be go a long way toward explaining the eclectic, idiosyncratic, and nearly always ambivalent patterns of behavior and belief that we will examine in succeeding chapters of the book.

Our focus in chapter 3 is the family: the single most important source of Jewish identity, and the site at which it is most frequently enacted and contested. Childhood relations with grandparents were consistently recalled by our subjects as key positive influences upon their later adult decisions on behalf of more active Jewishness. Reaction to parents, as we would expect, was far more equivocal. We heard stories about parental pressures toward observance which our subjects resented and resisted. We heard too—and perhaps more often—of childhood homes that were indifferent to Jewish observance, a heritage likewise rejected (with full appreciation of the irony involved) but this time in *favor* of the tradition. Spouses, the individuals who exercise the most immediate influence on what adult Jews will decide to do or believe, likewise have a complex impact: at times supportive of Jewish activity and involvement, at other times antagonistic, and in still other cases—remarkably so, perhaps— indifferent.

Family has this impact, in large measure, because it is the stimulus to and location of ritual observance, our subject in chapter 4. Ritual practice is without doubt the most important way in which moderately affiliated Jews express their Jewish commitments, the means through which "the Jew within" steps outside the self, in the company of family, into times and spaces hallowed by centuries of tradition. Our subjects spoke warmly and with great enthusiasm about their holiday observance, describing at length the choices they have made from among the repertoire available to them thanks to the Jewish calendar. The reason given for those choices was almost always the satisfaction provided by enhanced connection to family. Again and again, as the holidays approach, moderately affiliated Jews—whatever their denomination or past practice—are impelled to reflect on whether and how Jewish sacred time should affect them. Year by year, in the framework of the holidays, they discover, adapt, and construct Jewish meaning, inserting it into the course of everyday life.

Holidays thus serve as a major marker of Jewish ethnic and religious difference, our subject in chapter 5. In part, the observance of ritual occasions, distinctive to Jews, has the effect of marking and heightening ethnic difference. When Jews take off from work on the High Holidays, eat matzo rather than bread during Passover, or avoid the celebration of Christmas, they are departing from the American majority in ways that are noticed by children, co-workers, spouses, and themselves. No less importantly, however, their observance may testify to the *erosion* of ethnic attachment. The Passover seder, as sociologists Marshall Sklare and Joseph Greenblum pointed out several decades ago, may be such a popular observance precisely because it takes place in private space and leisure time (at home in the evening), is child-centered, carries a universalist theme (liberation), and occurs only once a year. It and other holidays might well be witnessing to the triumph of "symbolic ethnicity," partaking more of nostalgia than commitment.

Our concern was to find out what moderately affiliated Jews make of their own Jewish distinctiveness: how they calculate the balance of their obligation to Jews as opposed to Gentile Americans (or humanity as a whole); whether and how much they worry about antisemitism; the ways in which "vertical" connection to the Jews of past generations translates into "horizontal" connection with other Jews in the present. We were surprised by the degree of "tribalism" exhibited by our subjects: the oft-expressed conviction that they were Jews, period, because one or both of their parents had been Jews, regardless of what they believed or observed, and regardless of whether they ever had appeared or would appear on the membership list of any Jewish organization. Their children would be Jewish in turn, for the same reasons of blood, and their children after them. Yet these same Jews took pains at other moments to play down particularist loyalties, insisting that Jews are no more obligated to other Jews than to the human family as a whole. They showed signs of far less ethnic commitment than was common a decade or two ago.

This pattern is new; all three of the major pillars on which Jewish identity in the United States has rested in recent decades—as we shall see in chapter 6—have been considerably undermined. The Jews we studied betrayed little interest in or knowledge of the organized Jewish community. They drew universalist lessons from the Holocaust far more than they related to it as a Jewish tragedy with consequences for the survival of the Jewish people; they exhibited far less attachment to the state of Israel than was the case only a few years ago. The implications of these developments for the future of Jewish ethnic distinctiveness in America seem to us to be profound.

American Jews' relation to God and synagogue, our subject in chapter 7, also has serious implications. The Jews we interviewed overwhelmingly believe in God, far more so than we would have expected or that survey data about American Jews led us to believe. They are also surprisingly content with, and even fondly attached to, their synagogues. But they rarely make any straightforward connection between the two. God for them is a Being or Force who/which they encounter as individual human beings rather than as Jews. They overwhelmingly do not believe in special divine commandments to the Jews, or special divine providence watching over Jews. When they come to synagogue, it is to enjoy the pleasures of Jewish community and of attachment to Jewish tradition. God is rarely sought or found there, and is certainly not brought near by the words of the prayer book, which—to our subjects at least—rarely carry personal significance. We were repeatedly struck by the salience of faith to our respondents—and by their unease with it. They revealed a significant degree of both devotion and disquiet, sometimes in the very same sentence. This pattern of alienation and belonging is not easily unraveled, and—we expect—will not soon be reversed.

In the conclusion to the study we shall review the patterns of American Jewish selfhood and attachment that we have examined, and compare them with trends discerned by other researchers in America generally. Belief in God, for example, plays far less of a role among Jews in motivating involvement than it does among American Catholics and Protestants; home observance and attachment to primordial community, by contrast, are both far more important.

We will then take up the question of what brought the Jews we encountered to make the sort of commitments which now characterize them, and will consider the likely consequences of these commitments both for American Jewish selves and for the community as a whole.

Our findings, in sum, are complex—in part because the present moment is one of striking personal and communal transition, but principally because the many voices of our subjects, heard clearly and at length in the pages which follow, are rich with diversity, thoughtfulness, and ambivalence. Marshall Sklare and Joseph Greenblum, introducing their landmark study of American Jews a generation ago, warned that the temptation to bias is strong among scholars in the field. "Frequently the Jewish social scientist is in conflict: he prides himself on accepting his group identity but he wishes to separate himself from a community which does not seem to honor his values." For example, we confess at the outset that the attitudes and behaviors we encountered in the course of our research occasioned no little perplexity on our part, and much unease. The sovereign Jewish self, in its search for personal fulfillment, may turn out to be the stimulus for personal growth and fulfillment in a Jewish context and may even prove the stimulus to Jewish communal renewal and creativity as yet unimagined in America. Or—more likely, in our view—it will contribute to the dissolution of communal institutions and intergenerational commitment, thereby weakening the very sources of its own Jewish fulfillment and making them far less available to succeeding generations. Our understanding of this issue draws upon both our personal Jewish commitments and the analytical tools we bring to bear. We have tried to lend a sympathetic but not uncritical ear to moderately affiliated American Jews as they told us what matters most to them about Judaism, and why.

"The most important thing a Jew should do as a Jew," we were told by one person who could have been speaking for nearly all those we interviewed, "is to pursue a Jewish journey . . . not to ignore Judaism or to give up on it . . . to be open to it." That has been our task as well, as we set out to study this generation's journey. We have sought to go inside, to listen carefully, and to reckon with the contradictions we encountered as well as with our subjects' attempts to live with or get around these contradictions —part of their search, and ours, for Jewish meanings in America.

THE SOVEREIGN SELF

I remember at my bat mitzvah having a thought, a prayer, and saying:
Let me never leave this. I also remember being surprised, because that
was a time when I couldn't imagine Judaism *not* being important to
me—it was almost like knowing what was coming. I remember thinking
it and being surprised I was thinking it.

—MOLLY

Molly is a physician in her forties who lives in suburban Boston: thoughtful, soft-spoken, and extremely articulate—reason enough to take careful
note of what she has to say about the formative experiences which led to
her current commitments as a Jew. We begin with her, however, for another reason as well: because the key words in this passage from our
conversation, "I remember," are repeated no less than three times—
reflecting their importance to our interview sample as a whole. It would
not be too much to say that *what* Molly and the other Jews we interviewed
remember of their Jewish journeys, and—more importantly—*how* they
remember it, provide the clues to a new sort of Jewish self emerging in the
United States in recent decades. Our purpose in this chapter is to provide
a sketch of that Jewish self and to begin to ponder the implications of its
emergence.

The first thing that Molly remembers is a key moment in her development as a person and a Jew, her bat mitzvah, which is still vivid in her mind
despite the passage of three decades. Similar events or experiences from
childhood or adolescence figured prominently in almost every interview

we conducted. Time and again we heard details of family gatherings decades earlier, or reports of conversations with a grandparent long since departed, or descriptions of a moment of high emotion that proved formative of later growth. The Judaism practiced by adult American Jews is almost always bound up in key family relationships and rites of passage, nourished by a stock of memories which are marked by passion and ambivalence. Our subjects did not offer us dry "remembrances of things past" tucked safely away. Rather, their memories were tokens of present commitments and signals of the future they hoped to build. The individuals we met all care deeply about their Jewishness—even when, or perhaps especially when, they are rejecting it. Indifference concerning Jewish identity was nonexistent. The memories associated with the fact of being Jewish are far too precious for indifference, too powerful, too charged.

Molly recalls "a thought, a prayer" that crossed her mind on the day of her bat mitzvah: a reflection on how important her Judaism was to her at that moment, a desire that it remain that way, and an awareness, even then, that it might not remain important. Molly recalled these things as a person who has come full circle in her relation to Judaism. She has moved successively from childhood attachment, to alienation as a young adult, to renewed commitment as she raises her own children. In this too Molly is not alone; the pattern she articulated holds true, as previous studies have documented, for a great many American Jews, and not only for the moderately affiliated among them.

Strongly Jewish childhoods, for all that a Jew may wander from them for a time, are a very good predictor of actively Jewish adulthoods. The memories of those childhoods, and in particular of observant parents, grandparents, or teachers, are crucial to the beliefs and behavior adopted later in life. Molly has returned to a Jewish commitment that is very different in its content from the one she knew as a child. She does not believe or practice as her parents did. But the salience and intensity of that commitment are very similar to the Judaism in which she was raised. Molly is very much aware of this, and seems to take quiet satisfaction in her return. The circle she has traveled carries a measure of rightness, of grounding, that is itself no small part of the meaning Judaism now holds for her.

The return in her case and others may be all the more satisfying because the path leading from childhood upbringing to adult commitment is so indirect. Molly took pains to stress the degree to which she had stepped out of any path prepared for her by parents and teachers. The course her life has taken over the years would likely surprise them. It has certainly surprised her. Like other American Jews of her generation, Molly has had to make a great many choices concerning Jewish belief and practice along the way. The Judaism to which she is currently attached is not one that she has simply grown into or inherited, but one that she herself has fashioned from the large repertoire of possibilities available, just as she has chosen to highlight the particular memories she related to us, rather than others. What is more, Molly is still choosing from among possibilities, self-consciously so. She told us that her attachments to Judaism may well change further in coming years. Molly encourages her children to find their own path in a similar fashion, knowing they will likely not choose the exact same pattern of beliefs and practices which she finds meaningful. She seems to have no firm expectations about what they are likely to choose.

Molly views her Jewish life, in a word, as a journey. That is true of virtually every one of the Jews we interviewed. The pasts they remember, the places they have been, are in their view indispensable to their own understanding of where they are right now, and so are indispensable to our understanding as well. We could not get at what matters to them about Judaism by simply marking organizational affiliations or counting charitable donations or ticking off synagogue visits. Only by hearing personal stories can one comprehend the Judaism wrapped up in those stories. These Jewish memories, we believe, are also the key to imagining the possibilities which lie ahead, both for the individuals concerned and for the American Jewish community they make up.

To some degree, of course, we prompted Molly's construction of her Jewish past by interviewing her about it. Recall Robert Wuthnow's comment that the reporting of such journeys has already "become a kind of genre" in its own right, recognizable to "seekers" and scholars alike. We solicited the memories just noted and all the others in this book. Every conversation we conducted began by asking our respondents to tell us something about who they were and how they spent their days. They talked about family and work, hobbies and politics, the books and magazines they read, the charities and politicians they supported. The interview continued with a brief autobiography, followed in turn by a brief *Jewish* autobiography intended to fill in details of schooling and camp, formative experiences and influential family members, dating and friendships, marriage and divorce that might have been omitted from the first recital. An additional round of questions, normally posed in a second interview a week or two later, concerned present beliefs and observances, and these questions as well often stimulated memories of the events and individuals which helped to form them. Our subjects could not but engage in an organized act of Jewish remembering. Some of them told us afterward that when they did so at our prompting, it was for the very first time.

We are convinced, however, that—more than ever before—personal stories are basic to who American Jews are, as Jews and as human beings. That is so in part because Jews such as Molly, compared to predecessors a generation or two ago, define themselves far less by denominational boundaries (Reform, Conservative, Orthodox) or institutional loyalties (Hadassah, Jewish community centers, synagogues). Their Jewish identities are not constituted by organizational activity, do not center on concern for the state of Israel, and do not arise out of anxiety about anti-semitism. The communal quest for "sacred survival" that animated many American Jews a generation ago is simply not what motivates the Jews whom we studied (Woocher 1986). Nor do they manifest any traditional sort of Jewish religious commitment. We rarely met individuals who said they came to Jewish commitment (which we shall label their "Judaism," regardless of the presence or absence of strictly "religious" content) because of particular beliefs in God or revelation or the chosenness of Israel. Nor did we meet many individuals who expressed their Jewish commitment primarily by performing a fixed set of behaviors.

What matters to the Jews we interviewed, rather, are powerful individual memories and experiences, the personal stories in which these figure, the personal journeys that they mark, and the people who share the most meaningful moments on these journeys with them—primarily the members of their families. In this they bear a strong resemblance to Christians in late-twentieth-century America, among whom, Wuthnow argues, "a traditional spirituality of inhabiting sacred places [e.g., churches] has given way to a new spirituality of seeking," characterized—as it is among the American Jews we encountered—by negotiation among competing glimpses of the sacred, experiences of partial knowledge, and a preference for practical wisdom (1998, pp. 3–4). Personal journeys and experiences, especially if shared with other family members, are the stuff out of which their Judaism is now imagined and enacted, a Judaism constructed and performed by one individual at a time. The spaces in which it transpires are predominantly intimate and private—homes and families, friendships and romances—and some of the most important Jewish action transpires deep inside the self, where meaning is registered, reflected on, and imposed.

We can only probe these spaces, within the self or outside it, with the help of the individuals who inhabit them. We begin, therefore, with fairly lengthy sketches of two particularly articulate individuals who shared their stories with us.

TWO JOURNEYS

David, married to a therapist and the father of two college-age daughters, is an administrator and adjunct member of the faculty at a major West Coast university. He reads widely and voraciously on a number of subjects that include politics, history, Jewish issues, and science fiction. David subscribes to *Commentary* and *The Nation*, among other journals. His politics are liberal. "I give money to anybody running against Jesse Helms," he says. Are his political convictions linked to his Judaism? "I never really thought of the origins of it. I was clearly brought up in a liberal agnostic Jewish family where I was aware of being Jewish but without Jewishness being an issue very much, in fact not at all, but where sympathy for the underdog [was expected]." David's maternal grandfather, descended from a long line of rabbis in Prague and Berlin, was born in Palestine; his father's family was Orthodox until his father's generation, and conservative Republican in their politics. "My father rejected all of that."

Judaism as a result did not figure prominently in David's home as a child, though Jewish ethnic consciousness was strong: his father served for many years on the medical staff at a Jewish-sponsored hospital, and his mother worked as a volunteer for the local Jewish Federation. (Throughout this work, "federation" refers to the central Jewish philanthropic agency found in almost every Jewish community in the United States.) But there was "no Hebrew school, no Sunday school," and there was a tree at home every Christmas. His brother requested a bar mitzvah, which took place at the largest Reform temple in San Francisco, but David was not interested in having one, and his parents did not care.

David said that he first became acutely aware of being Jewish at the New England prep school he attended during high school. However, as far as his Jewish commitment is concerned, the truly transformative events came later, beginning with a trip to Germany in the context of overseas study during college. "I went to Munich. I didn't know quite why, what I was supposed to see or what I was supposed to do. I didn't speak German, I needed to go to Dachau. I didn't know anything about Dachau . . . I didn't know the word for concentration camp. People pointed me in the right direction. It blew my mind. It absolutely blew my mind. Not that I learned something factually . . . but just the experience of seeing it . . . that really affected me. I came back and I now knew I was Jewish. I was connected to that part of modern Jewish history in some way." The "next significant event" was the Six-Day War. "I remember watching the news and seeing those arrows sweeping through [a map of] the Sinai, and those arrows were my arrows."

After David described his graduate work in history and his first teaching position, our conversation turned to his wedding. At his wife's insistence, the ceremony was performed by a rabbi. "I could've married a Gentile very, very easily. The fact that M was Jewish, however, by that time was an appealing feature, though I didn't know much about what that meant, to be Jewish." The couple's Jewish observance was at first limited to attending Passover seders to which they had been invited and going to High Holiday services at the campus Hillel Foundation. "I liked seders. The seder was my introduction to Judaism as a tradition. . . . It didn't involve a profession of faith." At the time, David's father-in-law, a committed Reform Jew, complained that "I wasn't Jewish enough, and that didn't appeal to me." Synagogue did not appeal to him then either. The couple did eventually join the local Reform temple when their older daughter turned five. That affiliation, David said, was "the key thing" in his adult Jewish identity. "It gave me a formal membership in the Jewish community. It was a public statement of being a Jew. Slipping in and out of a Jewish service on High Holidays was not. My body could be there but not my heart. Now I was paying good money to do this."

David still has trouble finding meaning in the liturgy, but over the years he has grown more and more involved in Jewish life. He serves on the boards of the local Jewish Community Relations Council and of Hillel, takes classes on various aspects of Jewish history and thought, and finds meaning in holiday and life-cycle rituals, particularly when they involve his family. "I had this revelation last year while taking the cantor's class, that Hanukkah was actually rather ambiguous in Jewish history, that it was about certain kinds of Jews killing other kinds of Jews and other people, and actually I would have been one of the secularized/Greek sort of Jews. That sort of changed my attitude towards Hanukkah. . . . My kids will say, 'Dad, chill out.' My kids are great. But we do light the candles; my kids have always enjoyed the different colors of the candles and that we were using some menorah that they made in Sunday school. I get pleasure out of the fact that my children know the blessing and can say it as they light the candles. I don't know the blessings but I enjoy it." David now goes to synagogue regularly on High Holidays and on several other occasions in the course of the year. Passover, however, continues to be the holiday he likes most, "because it's not synagogue-based, it's family-based, you do it in the home."

What does David want Jewishly for his children? Had we asked a few years ago whether it mattered to him that his children marry Jews, David replied that he would have said, "All I want is for [them] to be happy." Now, he is not certain about his indifference to the religion of their spouses, though he knows he would object to an intermarriage with a "religious Christian." David draws lines between Jews and non-Jews in other ways as well, sometimes unequivocally. For example, David reacts differently toward the persecution of Jews than toward the persecution of other groups. "Those are my people. Those killed in Argentina [in a bombing of the Jewish community center]: those are my people. It could happen here." David has never been to Israel, though he has thought about going. He follows news reports about it carefully. The only thing he dislikes about being Jewish is the internal borders erected by Jews who insist that there is only one right way to be Jewish. "The notion that there is a good Jew and a bad Jew . . . the fact that people would judge other people and use Judaism as a boundary line or something is . . . threatening to me. Right now I'm in their good graces . . . but that could change."

How might David himself change Jewishly in the future? He has been thinking about God a lot lately. "Is there somebody that spoke to Abraham on Mount Moriah? I'm not really sure about that, but there may be some pattern up there somewhere, and there may be something. So, if Judaism has a way of getting at that, of thinking about that, of articulating the experience of a group which I am a part of whether I joined it or not," he wants to be involved. "I decided to join the JCRC [Jewish Community Relations Council], but I'm a Jew whether I want to be or not. What's interesting is how Jews ask these questions." Over the past few years David has for the first time come to know Jews who take their religious tradition seriously. "I realize that you don't have to sacrifice your mind, you don't have to sacrifice your appreciation of man's labor in order to see that there is something. I'm not there . . . but I know there's a there there."

❧

Most of Molly's time at present is taken up by work (she is a physician) and family (she is married, with two sons of elementary-school age). She reads *Newsweek, Scientific American, Moment* (a Jewish monthly), and professional journals. Her volunteer activity is focused on her children's school and on their (Reform) synagogue. Molly was born in Ohio, went to public school, and moved to Michigan for college and medical school. Her parents belonged to a Conservative synagogue, and their home was kosher and "reasonably observant." A lot of her mother's family lived nearby, and they were emotionally close as well. Education was a very important value in her home. It was clear all along that Molly would go to college, though the point for her parents might well have been "to meet a guy."

Molly remembers her parents as being inconsistent where Jewish practice was concerned. She was not allowed to color or to play solitaire or pick-up baseball on the Sabbath, but her mother and aunt often spent the day shopping. "I had difficulty with what my parents would and would not tolerate." The family went to synagogue every Friday night, but on Saturdays, when Molly attended services even after her bat mitzvah, her parents did not. Molly was active as a teenager in USY (United Synagogue Youth) a group affiliated with her Conservative synagogue. The Jewish figure Molly remembers most fondly from childhood is her maternal grandfather. He was "probably the biggest influence in terms of what I wanted to be, the sweetest, kindest person I have ever met, very insightful but very nonjudgmental." Her father's father died in a transit camp in Vichy France during the Holocaust. It was clear to her as a child that "this was something we did not talk about." The story emerged, she says, only gradually.

In high school, several years after the bat mitzvah memory with which we opened this chapter, Molly unexpectedly fell in love with a non-Jewish boy. It provoked the "rote response" from her parents that "you can't do this, you can't see him, we don't approve." She is "not sure that conversation about this changed anything, but it meant I had to choose, I could be Jewish or care for him, and that was a point where I was going to care for him." The relationship precipitated further rejection of involvement with Judaism. She quit USY as well as a Jewish high school sorority. This made her mother more upset. At the same time, the Jewish teenagers of her acquaintance, who had once run around the synagogue together and noticed each other skipping the "Christ our Lord" lines when singing Christmas carols in public school, now stopped being engaged in Jewish activities. One by one they dropped out of Hebrew school and synagogue life, and drifted apart. Later in the interview we learned that Molly's grandfather also died around this time. When that happened, Molly "seriously questioned the existence of God, and no one around me was able to help me through that period." It was, she said, a real turning point.

A few years later Molly fell in love with and eventually married a man who was not Jewish. This was "a really big deal for me then." Religion was not very important to her at that point, Molly recalls, but being Jewish was. She made it clear to S before they decided to marry that she "could not deal with Christmas trees and the kids had to be Jewish." But at the same time she "could not ask S to convert, because that was important to my parents." The latter were very upset at the prospect of an intermarriage. "My mother's first comment was 'who will marry you?'" (They found a rabbi who agreed to do the ceremony.) It took five years for her parents to accept S, Molly reports, and when he converted to Judaism a few years ago "my parents went crazy in the opposite direction. They were thrilled beyond belief."

Molly for her part has mixed feelings. "He's not a different person than the day before." She couldn't bring herself to say to him at any point, "Being a Jew is important to me and I want you to share it with me." Nor did she want religion to "be a wedge between us." In fact, over the years it was S who would say, "What are we doing for seder this year?" But "it is nice" that the family can now share fully in Jewish activities, and S's conversion also "opened us up" as a couple. The conversion took Molly completely by surprise. Her husband "just announced it, it was not something we discussed." S had been doing a lot of reading about Judaism, had taken courses in Jewish history and thought along with Molly in the context of Me'ah, a high-level adult Jewish education program held at their local Reform synagogue, and had enjoyed ritual activities with the family.

The adult education program had another impact as well. A year before, Molly reported, S had been unwilling to consider sending their children to a Jewish day school. He was not interested in private schools of any kind. After a year of Me'ah, S went to see a nearby Reform day school and was impressed. Molly feels good about the way Judaism is now infusing her children's lives. They are in a Jewish environment all day long at school and feel very good about that. This year her sons were far more involved in the family seder than ever before. They wrote stories which the adults read. Molly and her family not only celebrate Passover ("my favorite") but also the High Holidays, Hanukkah, and Purim, as well as Shabbat. Friday night is a family time together at home, with occasional synagogue attendance. Saturday mornings Molly goes to services by herself. She once found the experience incredibly lonely. Now she enjoys the time it furnishes for peaceful introspection.

What does Molly like about being Jewish? Feeling part of a community, the structure given her year by the Jewish calendar, feeling the continuity of history over thousands of years, the relationship with writings that have been studied for generations "and I can read them and think about them as well." What does she not like? Intolerance toward diversity. "I feel bad for people who don't think there's anything for them in Judaism and who have let their bad experiences of Sunday school or whatever drive them away. I'm not so far from that place." What does she want for her children Jewishly? "I'd love to see them marry Jewish people because I'd like their Jewishness to stay important in their lives. But it would be hypocritical to demand it, because I didn't do it, and have a wonderful family. Our lives have taken a turn in terms of depth and breadth of Jewishness [since S's conversion, but before that] it was still a Jewish household. It matters to me more that they continue to live as Jews and their children be Jews."

The most important thing a Jew should do as a Jew, Molly concluded, is to study. "In whatever way. As the rabbis said, from study comes everything else. . . . I don't profess to know enormous amounts, I just started studying a year and a half ago, but I see the effect it's had on my life. The rabbis hit it on this one. It gave me a sense of belonging and of why being Jewish does and can fill your life with meaning. . . ."

CHOOSING JUDAISM

Molly and David live on opposite coasts, grew up in families with very different degrees and patterns of Jewish practice, work at different professions, and are of course of different genders; this last factor, as we shall see in subsequent chapters, is of some importance in shaping Jewish commitments. But the commonalties underlying the two interviews are no less striking. Molly and David are of the same generation, belong to the same socio-economic group, and have been influenced by many of the same aspects of American culture. Their Jewish choices have taken parallel paths.

Indeed, the fact of this choice is perhaps the most salient feature of their Jewish journeys. In David's case, the election of Judaism stands out because it is in stark contrast to his parents' lack of interest in religious belief and practice. They lived down the street from the synagogue, he said pointedly, and never went inside. David in effect chose against his parents when he opted as an adult for active Jewish ritual engagement, though in other respects he has very much followed in their path: his father was on the staff of a Jewish hospital and his mother did volunteer work for the local Jewish Federation. Nor is David entirely comfortable in synagogue today, largely because it speaks a language of faith in which he, like his parents, does not believe.

Molly presents the opposite case. She grew up in a fairly observant home, and chose against her parents when she rejected Judaism as a teenager. Here too, however, the situation is more complex than it seems at first. In Molly's eyes, her parents' commitment to Judaism was inconsistent, even hypocritical. Her election of consistent Jewish practice as an adult, after straying far from it, is thoroughly in accord with what her parents preached but did not practice, and goes along with their wish for her. More important still, it follows in the footsteps of Molly's most important Jewish role model, her grandfather. When she told us about her family's innovative seders, she noted that "my grandfather always said you do what you can." She craves his blessing, and believes she has it.

What is more, both David and Molly, fully aware of (and happy with) the fact that they have chosen Judaism, believe nonetheless that it was theirs all along. It is a birthright which they have voluntarily claimed, a given which they have autonomously elected to receive. Molly's memory of her bat mitzvah prayer beautifully articulates this sense of voluntary rejection and return. David expressed the same paradox when he said that he likes being an active member of a group "which I am a part of whether I joined it or not. . . . I'm a Jew whether I want to be or not."

We heard this combination of sentiments time and again from our respondents. They do not seem bothered by the paradox (or the contradiction!) involved in what some American Jewish religious thinkers have called "choosing chosenness"—freely deciding to take on commitments which one could (perhaps just as easily) have rejected, and yet which define the person one is and always was. Fully 94 percent of those we surveyed concurred with the simple declaration, "Jews are my people, the people of my ancestors"—this, despite the fact that they jealously guarded their right to choose or reject this legacy as they pleased. Dave, a freelance writer and editor in Connecticut, responded to our question "What are some of the things you like about being Jewish?" with the words "I never thought about it as something I like or dislike, it is . . . what I am." Dave does not believe in the doctrine of Jewish chosenness, has no problem with intermarriage, and reports that when he met his future wife he did not much think about whether Judaism was important to her. "Being Jewish, it really didn't come up. I kind of knew she was Jewish." That mattered, because he too is Jewish: "It is . . . what I am." Yet it is also what he chose to be.

Joshua is a young artist who lives in Berkeley, a single man who has never dated a Jewish woman and is only marginally involved with the Jewish community. But he said, "I think I identify very strongly with Judaism. I mean I always thought of myself as a Jew as something very central to who I was." The minute he is introduced to people for the first time, Joshua reported,

his obviously Jewish first and last names broadcast his identity. He cannot
fail to be aware of this, and has been for as long as he can remember. "I
think that [Jewishness] was an identification that had some . . . a lot of
meaning for me, a lot of value." Jewish identity, like his name itself, comes
from family. "I guess I'm wondering a little bit that if I had very negative
feelings about my family . . . I might also have negative feelings about
Judaism. I'm not sure."

This is an insight to which we shall return in a moment. At present we
wish to draw attention to the implications of the simultaneous conviction
held by Joshua, Dave, and many others that Judaism is (1) a *given* from
birth, identity in the strict sense of total overlap with who one is as a person,
and (2) a *choice* one makes, and is entitled to make, even if one chooses not
to choose it. Because Judaism is a given, it is fully possessed no matter what
one elects to make of it. One cannot become more Jewish by opting for
greater Jewish involvement, and cannot become less Jewish by opting for
less. No Jews are more Jewish than other Jews. One does not sacrifice any
quotient of Jewishness by marrying a non-Jew, because the identity resides
in the self and is independent of the course one's life takes. The children
of an intermarriage will automatically be Jewish for the same reason, as will
their children.

Judaism in this view is, though no one we met used the phrase, in the
blood. On hearing this conviction we were reminded of the famous and
controversial passage by one of the most important figures in twentieth-
century Jewish thought, Franz Rosenzweig, in his book *The Star of Redemption*. Rosenzweig writes that Judaism is and

> must be a blood-community, because only blood gives present warrant to
> the hope for a future. . . . While every other community that lays claim to
> eternity must take measures to pass the torch of the present on to the
> future, the blood community does not have to resort to such measures.
> (1964, p. 299)

Of course a great many Jews, including those we interviewed, often go to
great lengths to secure the Jewish future. They remain anxious about the
future of the community to which, in greater or lesser degree, they feel
attached. As *individuals,* however, those we interviewed believe their Jewishness and that of their descendants is assured, regardless of the existence
or intensity of their Jewish activity, by the fact of birth to at least one Jewish
parent. The only way to lose this Jewish birthright is to choose a different
religion for oneself—not something that anyone in our sample had ever
contemplated.

As we shall see in later chapters, this rather tribalist conception of identity goes along with beliefs and practices that are profoundly universalist
and personalist. In this, too, our subjects resembled Rosenzweig, whose
beliefs concerning God's roles as creator, revealer, and redeemer were far

from traditional. Our subjects almost all believe in God, for example, but not in a God who exercises special providence for, or gives special revelations to, Jews or any other group. Some confess to greater concern for Jewish suffering than for suffering inflicted on other human beings—but they are almost always uneasy with this sentiment. Almost all have been touched by the Holocaust directly or indirectly, but many—unlike Molly and David—see no specifically Jewish meaning in the event, no significance to their lives as Jews, and no lessons for Jewish history. Even the most observant and active of our interviewees expressed discomfort with the idea of commandment, all the more so with the notion of particular commandments issued by God to Jews alone. The Jews we encountered hold to a notion of voluntary obligation not unlike that of Rosenzweig or his friend and colleague Martin Buber. In the chapters which follow, we will have occasion to witness many expressions and repercussions of this view.

At this point, however, let us return to the suggestive linkage made by Joshua between identity and family, a theme evident as well in our interviews with David and Molly. In choosing to reject Judaism, Molly knew she was rejecting her parents. Dating non-Jewish boys caused them hurt; when she married one, she could not ask him to convert—in part because, she said, "that was important to my parents." Despite a continuing conviction of the importance of being Jewish, she married a person lacking that conviction, persuaded that this need have no effect on her own subsequent Jewish choices.

Ann, a physician in suburban Detroit, likewise linked her dating of non-Jews in college, after going out with Jewish boys exclusively in high school, to a period of rebellion. She too eventually married a non-Jew; his religion, Ann says, "wasn't an issue. . . . I think it bothered my mother, but she had learned she couldn't tell me what to do. I was twenty-seven. What could she say?" Ann was not so much determined to marry a non-Jew, she reflects, as to marry a man who was the opposite of her father, whom she characterized as "very dependent." She "felt I couldn't have anyone dependent on me. . . . Did I think a Jew could not give that to me? On some level, I probably did. I denied that part of me," i.e., her Jewishness. Ann has begun to explore it again only in the last year or two—long after divorcing her first husband, marrying a Jew (who, she says, is indifferent to his Jewishness), and giving birth to a son, now five.

David did marry a Jew, and confesses that his prospective partner's Jewishness was appealing to him. But he could just as easily have married a Gentile, he maintains—this too without cost to his own Jewish identity, already emergent at that point. Other interviewees reported that romantic relationships with non-Jews evoked a resistance in themselves to marrying outside the faith that proved crucial to later development of their Jewish identity. The patterns of response to involvement with non-Jews are many; the involvements themselves, however, are nearly universal among moder-

24

ately affiliated Jews, a change from previous decades that bears consequences and to which we shall return.

It seems that the connection between commitment to Judaism and commitment to a Jewish partner may well go deeper still. Joshua, very much a
loner in his work as well as in his leisure-time pursuits, connected the fact
that he had dated only non-Jewish women, and none of them very seriously, with the sense that "someone being Jewish opened the possibility for
it to be a much longer term relationship." Or, as he put it a moment later,
"I think I probably feel strongly attracted to Jewish women, and maybe the
strength of that attraction is something that may interfere with establishing a lighter relationship that might lead to something more serious.
Maybe, I'm not sure, it's a guess." The Jewishness of a prospective partner
"is a significant factor in altering my perception of even immediate events.
. . . Maybe it's because I don't want that," i.e., a long-term relationship.

We surmised that Joshua is a person not ready to commit in any respect
—either to a partner or to a tradition. Indeed, we believe, Joshua identifies
Judaism with commitment, not only because it is wrapped up with family—
in other words, with what he most essentially is—but because it demands
obligation. Family and obligation are in his eyes indissolubly connected.
Discussing his parents' desire that he settle down with someone, Joshua
said, "The two perspectives we need to bring in are my mother, who says,
'Find someone,' and my sister, who says, 'Do what you're doing for as long
as you want to do it. . . . trust your heart and it will lead you in a good
place.'" Freedom and obligation collide. Judaism is identified with the latter, as articulated by the Jewish mother.

Asked later on in the interview if there is anything about Judaism that
he dislikes, Joshua replied that "I think I feel a sense of responsibility to
. . . my family, which is hard to separate from Judaism for me. . . . I feel like
[I have] some sort of obligation in that sense, maybe, to have kids. I also
sort of think of the larger Jewish picture in terms of a lot of questions
we talked about before, of assimilation and the Holocaust and then also
maybe a sense of obligation in that sense to bring up Jewish children into
the world . . . these are open questions." At another point in the interview
Joshua told us, right after recounting a story about a moment in his past
when he tried to conceal his Jewish identity, that he likes "being in places
where I can completely lose track of time . . . where I just have no obligations for a few days. It's very nice." Judaism is not like that, in his view. It
involves, inevitably, weighty matters such as serious learning, activist politics, facing up to the Holocaust, participation in a community, connecting
to family, and God.

Sarah, the daughter of a rabbi, also lives in Berkeley and like Joshua is
still single, though she is currently involved with a man who is Catholic.
The linkage she made between commitment to Judaism and to men paralleled Joshua's rather exactly. Sarah recalled doing a seder once with a

non-Jewish boyfriend. "I, in some ways, thought that it was easier being with someone who wasn't Jewish, because then we could do [it] the way I thought it ought to be done, with the right amount of tradition but the right amount of levity and none of this 'oh, but my mother used to make this' type of stuff." For a while Sarah did go out with a Jew "who seemed to have that right kind of mix [in his approach to Judaism]. . . . we had a very strong basis of understanding, of humor and religious observance. I like to dip in and then dip out a little bit and he had a real similar feeling about it." Her current boyfriend, she reported, "actually has a pretty strong commitment to that [Catholicism]. It's sort of been a joke since then that he wants to have Catholic children, and I'm not sure what that means because of course my children will be Jewish, no matter what, because their mother will be Jewish."

Sometimes Sarah thinks it would be much "easier to be with somebody Jewish, and then you don't have to be the one making sure you do something Jewish. . . . I guess in general my feeling is, I'm thirty-four, I wasn't gonna have Jewish children anyway. I'm not less Jewish than I was single. . . . I guess I have more of an issue about whether I even want to have children, so worrying about what their religion is going to be doesn't seem relevant." Once again, commitment as such—this time to children—connects directly to commitment to Judaism.

Other Jews, of course, have made both sorts of commitment, and many have made one, to active Jewishness or to marriage, without undertaking the other. However, the issues which surfaced so distinctly in our conversations with Sarah and Joshua came up—albeit less pointedly—in many of the other interviews as well. Moderately affiliated Jews are aware of their degree of freedom when it comes to choosing for or against Judaism. They are aware of the choices that their parents have made in this regard. They are aware, as well, that they have been shaped by their parents' choices. The choice for or against Judaism is consciously made, in some cases, in order to choose for or against parents, ineluctably and perhaps regrettably. One is born Jewish, after all, because one is born to Jewish parents. The connection cannot be escaped—even when, as seems to be the case with Joshua and Sarah, reluctance to choose Judaism decisively is tied to a refusal to choose *anything* decisively, lest major options in life be foreclosed.

Let us look one more time at Dave's comments on this matter. He is about forty, we recall, married with two children, active in his synagogue as his parents were before him. Asked what he likes or dislikes about being Jewish, Dave replied that he never thought about Judaism "as something I like or dislike . . . it's what I am." Pressed by us to reflect on his feelings about his identity, however, Dave volunteered that he likes the "community feelings and family feelings [that] you hear coming in and coming at you in synagogue. . . . It's a very comfortable way to live your life." Dave recognizes that he likes these messages and is comforted by them because he has grown up with them. "It's a circular logic type of thing. . . . I work very hard not to believe that being Jewish makes me special because I feel one of the values that's coming at you all the time is inclusiveness. That's a hard one to balance with chosen people . . . but I think you have to do it."

Dave's difficulty finding that balance became apparent once more when we asked at the conclusion of the interview whether he would be upset if his children married Gentiles. "I want them to be caring people. I want them to be people that get involved. I don't want them to be people who sit back and let the world wash over them. Whether I'd be unhappy or not if they married non-Jews is a really difficult question, obviously it's the most difficult question for any parent." He knows children of actively Jewish families who have not "lost their integrity or what makes them special, regardless of the relation they've maintained or not maintained with the organized Jewish community." He suspects that his own children will remain active Jews because of the experiences they have had—including experiences in their synagogue of Jews in interfaith marriages who have remained committed to Judaism. Dave would prefer that his children marry Jews. "But," we pressed, "if they stayed good, caring, compassionate people, that would be the most important thing?" "Absolutely."

David, for his part, is no longer as sure as he once was that he would not care if his children married non-Jews. But he is sure that it would bother him if they married a "religious Christian"—perhaps because this would threaten his strong desire, shared by Dave, that his children remain Jews and raise Jewish children. Molly, unable to oppose her children marrying non-Jews because she did so herself, nonetheless expressed precisely this hope. She too wants Jewish children and grandchildren. Barring conversions to another faith, she and David and Dave will all have them. Their shared definition of Judaism, tribal despite their own misgivings about tribalism, holds that a Jew who does not convert to another faith is always a Jew and is always the parent of Jewish children, assuming they do not convert either. Such are the complexities of choice and birthright in late-twentieth-century America.

TRADITIONAL, MODERN, AND POSTMODERN SELVES

These dilemmas, we believe, are new. American Jews began to face them, in the particular form exhibited in our interviews, only in the current generation. The novelty in some cases is subtle, a mere variation on patterns long in evidence. In other cases, however, the change is stark: a sign, perhaps, of a significant shift in the understanding of Jewish selfhood. In order to grasp what is new in this understanding, as well as what is not, we must embark on a brief survey of previous Jewish self-conceptions.

Before the modern period Jews took for granted a conviction of *essential Jewish difference* from non-Jews. Both Jewish doctrine and Jewish ritual posited an axiomatic and dichotomous view of self and other, a distinction between "Israel" and "the nations of the world" as fundamental and self-evident as the difference between day and night. The Torah (in chapter 19 of Exodus) declares the Israelites gathered at Sinai to be God's "kingdom of priests and holy nation." God had redeemed them from Egyptian bondage in order to set them apart as a "peculiar treasure," thereby making them (and only them) a party to a unique covenant that, according to the Torah, would remain in force forever. When the Israelites were exiled to Babylonia in 586 B.C.E., the prophets interpreted the debacle as confirming rather than disconfirming the people's status as God's elect. Exile was God's punishment for their misdeeds. God took special note of their wrongdoing, and would give them a chance to make amends. Their return to the land decades later was taken as a sign of God's forgiveness, and proof that the prophetic account of God's relation with them was correct.

This self-understanding apparently remained in place during the historical vicissitudes of the centuries which followed. It survived intact the challenge posed by the second exile, this time by the Romans in 70 C.E.— a tragedy interpreted by the founders of Christianity as proof that God had abandoned the old partner to the covenant and elected a new one. The teachers and jurists who assumed national leadership in the wake of defeat by the Romans, known to us as "the rabbis," provided rites and forms which countered that thrust. Jews survived as "a people dwelling alone" for nearly two millennia, secure in the framework of Judaism still practiced by many Jews today. The covenant remained in force, despite Christian (and, later, Muslim) claims to the contrary and the periodic miseries of Jewish history. Teachings and rites encompassed nearly every aspect of daily existence with instruction in the nature of Jewish selfhood. Apartness continued to seem not only right, but also inevitable.

The lesson, to a practicing Jew, was ubiquitous. Jews thanked God daily in prayer for not making them "like the nations of the world" who bowed down to idols, "vain and empty things," rather than to the one true God. At the blessing over wine which inaugurated the Sabbath each Friday night, Jews declared (addressing God), "You have chosen us and sanctified us from among all the nations." At the blessing over wine, candle, and spices that concluded the Sabbath, Jews blessed God for distinguishing "sacred from profane, light from darkness, Israel from the nations, the Sabbath from the six days of work." The historical experience of isolation, as Jacob Katz has pointed out, seemed to confirm this ontological distinction every day, even as the fundamental difference between Jews and Gentiles made good sense out of the facts of daily apartness. Jews *were* a people apart, scattered among the nations. Each individual Jew came into this inheritance at birth as a member of the covenant people (Katz 1961a).

Three basic component elements constituted the view of self and world put forward in the doctrine of election, all three evident in the Torah and reiterated in the countless texts which reinforced it over the centuries. *Exclusivity* was one: the basic and inevitable apartness of Jews from Gentiles. The character of daily Jewish interactions with non-Jews (or the lack of interactions) confirmed a distinction as basic as the difference between Sabbath and weekday. *Covenant* was a second component: Jews were bound not only to fellow Jews but to God—and bound to each of these covenant partners by the tie binding them to the other. Religion was inseparable from nationhood. A Jew was born simultaneously into a people and a faith, both of which entailed a regimen of lifelong obligation. Third, however, chosenness involved *mission;* the separation of Jews from Gentiles served a divine purpose that would one day bring the entire human race to the worship of the one true God. Jewish particularity, then, was meant for a universal end. Universalism and particularism stood in perpetual tension. At the end of days, when the messiah came, Jewish and non-Jewish selves might not be essentially different. All would worship the same God, though they would perhaps do so in different ways.

In the meantime, however, the difference between Jews and all others was pronounced. The result of teachings and historical experience alike, reinforced by communal forms which in turn were justified by appeal to the teachings as well as to Jewish history, was a notion of the Jewish collective that we might term "historical familism" (Liebman and Cohen 1990). *Historical* expresses the extent to which the religion, the culture, the myths, and the symbols of Judaism centered on the historical memory (factually accurate or not) of one particular people. *Familism* points to the several senses in which this people regards itself as united by ties of blood, with far-reaching consequences that extend from the most abstract theological speculation to the most mundane everyday behavior.

Almost all major Jewish holidays, for example, were and still are linked to real or putative historical events that involved the entire people of Israel, and are further embellished by stories of the ancestors and their commemoration of those events. The Jewish collective consciousness contains pointed lessons from both recent and distant history. Emile Durkheim might well have been describing the motivations of his own Jewish forebears when he wrote that "native" informants, when asked by anthropologists why they performed the rites they performed, always replied, "It is because our ancestors arranged things thus. This is why we do thus and not differently." The authority of tradition, Durkheim continued, is a "social affair of the first order" (Durkheim 1915, pp. 401, 415–416). Among Jews this was certainly the case—witness the collective consciousness of descent from the same ancestors: Abraham, Isaac, and Jacob; Sarah, Rebecca, Rachel, and Leah. Jacob became known as Israel as a consequence of his "wrestle with God"—the apparent meaning of his new name; his descendants, "the children of Israel," continued that often troubled engagement.

Jews were family, bound to one another first of all by blood ties. They were all born into the same covenant with each other and with God. If—as occurred in rare cases—they had converted into the faith, they were known in the Jewish community as "children of Abraham and Sarah," adopting at the moment of conversion not only a religion but a family, a tribe. Gentiles, unwilling to intermarry with Jews over the centuries, lent still more meaning—and seeming inevitability—to the association between religion and family. So did religiously based notions of mutual responsibility and assistance among Jews. The simple fact that Jews felt more comfortable in each other's presence than in the company of Gentiles was due in part to safety from antisemitism and in part to shared experience nurtured by immersion in the beliefs and customs of their tradition.

Jewishness was, in short, a very precious birthright, confirmed over many centuries by innumerable everyday interactions with Jews and Gentiles alike.

Modernity constituted a grave challenge to this conception of the personal and collective Jewish self. Emancipation—the opening of Western societies to Jewish participation on a formally equal footing, or the promise of that opening—meant the sudden or gradual end to many elements of the social segregation that undergirded Jewish tribalism. Even before the granting of civil rights, the politically autonomous Jewish communities (*kehillot*) which had governed daily Jewish life for centuries had lost much of their authority, ceding effective control to emerging state and national governments. Over time Jews dispersed to Gentile towns, cities, and neighborhoods and integrated in lesser or greater degree into the surrounding Gentile societies.

Historians of the period have demonstrated that Emancipation entailed a contractual quid pro quo, not always left unspoken, in which Jews agreed to sacrifice exclusivity in return for civil rights and economic opportunities (Katz 1972, p. 19; Eisen 1998a, pp. 107–121). Sabbath observance, a bar to employment opportunities as well as to leisure activities, atrophied. Dietary laws, a barrier to social relations with non-Jews and so to acceptance in their society, were relaxed or abandoned. Jews increasingly worked side by side with Gentiles. Indeed, beginning with Moses Mendelssohn, arguments on behalf of Judaism itself had to be couched in the language—literal and figurative—of the non-Jewish culture which Jews had begun to internalize. Enlightenment, unlike Christianity before it, was not seen as an opposing religion to be resisted but as an achievement of human culture, a vehicle of truth and human dignity, which many Jews sought to make their own.

How then could they make the case for chosenness? Jews could no longer deny that other peoples too, personal friends and neighbors now among them, possessed equal access to divine truth. Nor could Jews propound a distinctiveness at odds with their aspirations to civic equality. It is telling that the prayer book adopted for use by the Reform congregation in Berlin in 1844 found it necessary to note in the very first section of its introduction that changes had been made in all prayers mentioning the chosenness of Israel. Enlightened Jews, many of them university graduates, could not subscribe to any "concept of tribal holiness" or of the "special vocation arising from [it]." The concept of chosenness needed to be altered, universalized. "Human character and dignity, and God's image within us—these alone are signs of chosenness" (Plaut 1963, p. 59). Reform Jewish writings in particular, but not only these, played down the exclusivity inherent in the chosen people idea, re-interpreted covenant to stress the autonomy of human beings in general and of each individual vis-à-vis God, and placed more emphasis upon Israel's "mission" to bring the highest knowledge of "ethical monotheism" to all humankind.

The existence of Reform Jewish prayer books and writings signals another dramatic change in the understanding of Jewish selfhood: the need to qualify it with an adjective such as "Reform" or "Orthodox" or, later, "secular." One could now choose what sort of Jew to be, and could in some cases choose—by conversion or assimilation—not to be any sort of Jew at all. The "plausibility structure" (to use Peter Berger's felicitous phrase) which, when intact, had made Jewish selfhood seem inevitable, gave way with Emancipation to a "structure" of Jewish community that contained many and diverse rooms, and—no less important—many exits. Jews increasingly inhabited Gentile, more than Jewish, time and space, at work as well as at play, and filled the storehouses of consciousness with Gentile rather than Jewish cultural artifacts. The two parts of the Sinaitic covenant, faith and peoplehood, were no longer inseverable. One could be a Jew by religion but of German or French nationality; one could regard oneself as a part of the Jewish people and profess no religious faith. The various adjectives now modifying Jewish identity were routinely accompanied by hyphens linking the Jewish to the non-Jewish halves of individual identity. It became a question, in fact, whether Jews were Jews first and foremost or something else: Germans or Frenchmen "of the Mosaic persuasion," for example. Would Jew remain a subject's noun, or become its adjective? It was up to each individual Jew to choose.

Nowhere was this challenge to traditional selfhood more apparent than in the United States during the decades of the "second generation" (ca. 1925–1950), a period shaped by children of immigrants who sought to take advantage of political and economic opportunities that promised unparalleled acceptance by the surrounding Gentile society. How could such Jews proclaim their essential apartness at the very same moment when they were working so hard to become a part of an ethnically and religiously diverse America? Sociologists such as Charles Liebman and Marshall Sklare have pointed to the conflicting desires of "ambivalent American Jews," in Liebman's apt term, for integration on the one hand and group survival on the other. Eisen has charted the ways in which this ambivalence was played out in re-interpretations of the doctrine of chosenness. On the one hand, the aim was to preserve Jewish particularity, and in some cases to make sense of the singling out of Jews by antisemites in America and by the Nazis overseas. On the other hand, the concept was stripped of any vestiges of exclusivity or superiority.

The sociological dilemma was straightforward. Jews who were at home in America, or wished to be, could not affirm either to themselves or to others that they were essentially "strangers in a strange land," exiles awaiting a return to Palestine, or God's one true chosen people. America was, after all, a society which, thanks to the Puritan legacy, conceived of itself as a "city on a hill," embarked on a providential mission involving all humanity. Zionism was for this reason embraced by American Jews only after Louis Brandeis and others had made it clear that the movement, in this country at least, aimed only at providing a home for Jews who lacked one —and no American Jew did. No uprooting of American Jews (or Jewish Americans) was contemplated. Brandeis urged Jews and Gentiles to see Zionism as the extension to Jewish refugees overseas of American ideals of freedom, justice, and equal opportunity. Jews could not and would not be seen as exclusivist; they were not a "holy nation" (Eisen 1983, pp. 25–52). This points as well to the theological problem with the traditional notion of chosenness. The claim to election made little sense in the absence of belief in a revealed covenant. Two centuries of experience with modernity had long since eroded belief by many Jews (and many Gentiles) in a God active enough in history to choose any people, and undemocratic enough to choose only one. Shorn of its theological base, chosenness seemed ethnic chauvinism, pure and simple. Jews were not comfortable with that, for obvious reasons. Yet if one abandoned the claim to election, what reason was there for continued apartness?

Sermons, sociological studies, and works of fiction from the period all bear witness to Jewish selves torn between the conflicting imperatives of integration and apartness. In the prewar years, still vividly recalled by many older American Jews, apartness was in many respects the dominant experience, and integration a promise yet to be realized. Occupational and residential discrimination were commonplace. Jews were denied admission to elite colleges and country clubs. Antisemitic attitudes were widespread in the United States as the specter of Nazism hovered across the ocean, all too near. Even after the war, when barriers in America began to fall and social acceptance became more and more a reality, a degree of mutual suspicion remained. Philip Roth's classic story "Eli the Fanatic" captures the alarm of assimilated Jews, newly arrived in the 1950s in Gentile suburbs, at the prospect of openly Orthodox Jews walking the streets in distinctive black garb and thereby threatening their newfound acceptance by Gentiles—and, perhaps, their sense of themselves as Americans at home in America and its suburbs.

Roth has also testified eloquently to the sense of distinctiveness that survived among Jews of his parents' generation even after physical apartness and belief in a God of revelation had either lessened or completely disappeared. "There were reminders constantly that one was a Jew and that there were goyim out there." One was special, but did not know how or why. So "one had to invent a Jew. . . . there was a sense of specialness and from then on it was up to you to invent your specialness; to invent, as it were, your betterness." His inheritance, Roth said, was a "psychology without a content, or with only the remains of a content." The psychology was perhaps no less powerful for that, and perhaps all the more so (Roth 1963, pp. 21, 39; Eisen 1983, p. 135).

As we will see, elements of this psychology remain in place even today, at century's end. In other respects, however, the Jews we met and surveyed are strikingly different from those studied by Sklare and others four decades ago—when many of the Jews examined in this book were growing up. For one thing, Jews were just making the move from urban neighborhoods, often heavily Jewish, to the suburbs. They not only married other Jews, with very few exceptions, but for the most part numbered only other Jews among their closest friends, retained a social distance from Gentile co-workers, and—by virtue of the Jewish neighborhoods in which many remained, or the new suburbs in which Jews tended to cluster—encountered other Jews on a daily basis when shopping, taking their kids to the playground, or swimming at the country club.

No less important, educational attainment—with all its implications for values fostered by the university—is much higher among this generation of Jews than any of its predecessors. Most (53 percent) of Sklare and Greenblum's suburban respondents—by no means a representative sample of American Jews—reported having finished college (including 42 percent of the women) while 24 percent (including 14 percent of the women) had earned graduate degrees, mirroring American Jewry as a whole. Nearly all of those we interviewed were college graduates, men and women alike, while significantly more than half our interviewees were employed in business, wholesale or retail. Most were working as professionals—a group that made up only about a fifth of the Sklare-Greenblum sample. Median income has risen accordingly.

Perhaps the greatest change affecting Jewish identity in the past half century is the expansion of roles available to women. They now routinely make choices of which their mothers could not conceive, just as they and their male spouses, for the most part, take for granted a level of wealth and status which to their parents' generation was a source of great anxiety and insecurity (Hartman and Hartman 1996; Prell 1999).

In the sixties—in part because of those anxieties—Jews continued to choose other Jews almost exclusively as their close friends, and even their wider friendship circles were composed overwhelmingly of other Jews. The rate of intermarriage remained in or close to single digits. Sociologist Benjamin Ringer, probing Jewish-Gentile relations, concluded in 1967 that "an aura of uncertainty and fantasy" still characterized these relations, despite "the significant contacts between Jews and Gentiles." The warmth and trust associated with close friendships were rare. Few Jews or Gentiles could gauge the position of the other with any accuracy, and so they tended instead to "consult their own underlying anxiety or complacency, as the case may be" (Ringer 1967, p. 267).

Among themselves, meanwhile, Jews built an impressive array of communal institutions. Federations of Jewish philanthropies raised unprecedented amounts of money, particularly after the events of May and June 1967 in the Middle East seemed to bring Jews face to face with renewed threat to their collective survival. Synagogues built impressive new buildings in the suburbs, even as they lost pride of place in the community to secular organizations which could claim to speak for American Jews as a whole rather than for particularist or partisan sectors of the population. Jonathan Woocher has perceptively analyzed the "civil religion" which emerged and triumphed among Jews in this period, and gained adherents in particular among communal lay leaders. The key tenets embraced by the adherents of civil Judaism included the following: that one could be a good Jew and a good American; that the separation of church and state was essential; that Jews were one people and could not permit denominational differences to divide them; that while theology was somewhat irrelevant, ensuring Jewish survival was central; that Jewish rituals were valuable, but individuals must be free to observe them or not as they chose; that every Jew was obliged to work for the survival of Israel. "To the question of what it means to be Jewish," Woocher writes, "civil Judaism responds: to be part of a people with a proud tradition and enduring values, values which can be embodied in the life of the modern Jew and the modern Jewish community" (Woocher 1986, pp. 95–96).

❧

In several crucial respects, today's Jews are very different. For one thing, they count non-Jews among their close friends (only 10 percent of our survey respondents indicated that "all or almost all" their closest friends are Jews), and marry non-Jews in ever greater numbers (recall the example of Molly). Even when they do marry Jews, they maintain that they might well have done otherwise but for the intervention of chance or circumstance. (Recall David's remarks on this point.) Our subjects remain anxious about the possibility of renewed antisemitism in America, but few reported actual experiences of such hostility in their own lives. Quite the contrary: they take for granted the opportunity for full participation in every aspect and arena of American society. They have attended some of the best universities in the country, and are not socially isolated. They know that Jews are counted among the members of the most exclusive country clubs and are represented (or overrepresented) in American political and financial elites. The people we interviewed enjoy such thorough acceptance by Gentile friends, co-workers, and in-laws that they have come to terms with the real possibility that their children may marry non-Jews. We noticed, too, that the language, literal and figurative, spoken by our subjects was almost entirely that of American culture. Few had extensive knowledge of either Hebrew or Yiddish, not having grown up in immigrant homes. Most had received no sustained Jewish education after adolescence.

Despite retention of most of the principal tenets of "civil Judaism," today's moderately affiliated Jews do not fit the previous notion of what it is to be a Jew. Their connection to Israel, for one thing, is weak, as is the connection they feel to the organized Jewish community in America. They take for granted the compatibility of being both Jewish and American; this is simply not an issue anymore. And they are even less interested in denominational differences than their parents' generation was, insisting from first to last on the right—and fact—of individual autonomy when it comes to deciding the details of Jewish practice. On the other hand, theology is far from irrelevant to these Jews. God, as we shall see, is often quite important to them; spirituality is a felt concern; ritual and texts resonate with religious meanings that they view positively. Their self-consciousness as Jews is strong, their claim to their birthright proud despite their insistence, on the basis of personal struggles with their identity, that they themselves had chosen Judaism, and could have chosen otherwise. They want to be Jewish because of what it means to them personally—not because of obligations to the Jewish group (though some felt these obligations), or the historical destiny of the Jewish group (though many wrestled with that destiny), or the need to ensure Jewish survival (this too was a widespread concern). Jewish survival is not in and of itself sacred in their eyes. Jewish life, in the private spaces of self and family, *is* held sacred—it is that which they most deeply value.

With all due respect for the varieties evident even in our relatively small interview sample, and encouraged by our quantitative survey and the evidence of other recent studies, we suggest that this pattern marks the emergence of what we with some hesitation call a postmodern Jewish self. We intend no mystification by the term "postmodern," and certainly no grandiosity; we stake out no turf in the debates over what postmodernity means or entails. We use the term rather to point to several elements of the selfhood that we discovered in our interviews, all of them elaborated further in the chapters which follow, that are consistent with major currents in the set of theories grouped together under the rubric of postmodernism. Consider the following:

• Our subjects emphasize *personal meaning as the arbiter of their Jewish involvement.* Their Judaism is personalist (to use Liebman's coinage): focused on the self and its fulfillment rather than directed outward to the group. It is voluntarist in the extreme: assuming the rightful freedom of each individual to make his or her own Jewish decisions. "Each individual has to decide the proper way to serve his religion," said Sam, a teacher in Queens. As a result, Judaism must be strictly nonjudgmental. Each person interacts with Judaism in ways that suit him or her. No one is capable of determining for others what constitutes a good Jew. "My way is not right or wrong, it's just my way," Sam continued. Irv, a salesman in Queens, put it this way: "I don't have any problem with what anybody does [as far as Jewish observance is concerned], as long as they don't tell me what I have to do. So, if you want to be involved in something that's very dear to your heart that's fine, but don't sit there and tell me about something that is clearly an option in life, that I have to be doing it, and I should be doing it, because I am this [Jewish]."

Note the interaction, in this quite typical quotation, between the primacy of individual meaning and the inviolability of individual autonomy when it comes to pursuing it. Jewish meaning must be sought and discovered one person at a time, sometimes in odd places—"whatever makes them happy in life"—and not necessarily in the conventional quarters of the synagogue, rarely in the organizational boardroom. Sam, whose sense of "extra responsibility for other Jews" is strong, on the grounds that "you have to take care of your own first," expressed little interest in the synagogue and none whatever in Jewish organizations. Judaism matters to him because "it has given me a foundation in life." Irv finds it hard to believe that the Jews' religion is right and all the others wrong. "It is what you make of it, what you want to do with it, and that is how it should be."

• *Jewish meaning is not only personal but constructed, one experience at a time.* The Jews we met exhibit unusual and diverse configurations of Jewish involvement. With the revalorization of tradition, the absolute commitment to pluralism, and the continuing assumption of individual autonomy, they feel free to borrow selectively, and perhaps only temporarily, from traditional Jewish religious and cultural sources. They also—routinely and without embarrassment—combine these Jewish elements with others drawn from the larger cultural milieu, including non-Jewish religious or spiritual traditions.

The principal arena for the construction of this meaning is the family, our subject in the chapter which follows. Judaism more and more is enacted in private space and time. Recall David's preference—echoed by many others—for Passover, because, as he put it, the seder takes place at home rather than in synagogue. The holiday happens on his turf, we might say, where he is surrounded by people who matter, i.e., are close to him personally and not merely part of the group into which he was born. The fact that these people matter so much makes the rituals they do together matter as well. At home each Jew is sovereign in relation to the tradition, assuming, of course, that the spouse agrees or acquiesces—more on this point later. In the synagogue, by contrast, one enters a space in which what is said and done is predetermined and prescribed.

Sarah likes to conduct her own seders and invite guests to them so that she can control both the guest list and the content of the ritual. "It turned out that it was just easier for me to do that myself because then I could get the haggadahs that I wanted to use." She has had trouble finding a synagogue she likes because "nothing really seemed to [suit me], either they're too much or too little. . . . It's like when I was talking about having a boyfriend who is Jewish, who doesn't want to do it the same way that you want to do it, and it's sort of the same thing. I want something where the other people really believe pretty much the same way I believe and want to do the parts of the services that I want to do. Maybe it's an impossible thing to find." In her own home, however, and given the right partner (she is still looking), it just might work.

Edward, a Chicago lawyer, put the matter still more succinctly. There is nothing annoying about Judaism as he experiences the tradition, he said, because "I elect to observe it as I elect to observe it. If something is potentially annoying, I avoid it." The key to renewed interest in ritual observance among moderately affiliated American Jews seems this recognition that one need not take on any rituals with which one is uncomfortable, or associate with anyone who will challenge the Jewish choices one has made, however idiosyncratic those might be. Seventy-four percent of our survey participants agreed that "I have the right to reject those Jewish observances that I don't find meaningful."

• A related development is the *emergence of Jews who combine great concern for issues of spirituality and meaning with severely diminished interest in the organizational life of the Jewish community.* This seems to us a further concomitant of the shift of passion from the public domain to the private sphere, from what postmodern theorists call the "grand narrative" (in this case, the exalted story of Jewish peoplehood and destiny) to the "local narratives" and "personal stories" of family and self. Not all the Jews we interviewed evinced this pattern, but many did, revealing a high degree of commitment to Judaism and concern for the continued existence of the Jewish people, accompanied by relatively infrequent participation in conventional Jewish communal activities. (We exclude rituals performed at home from this sphere of "communal activity," for reasons already explained.) The boundaries dividing the various modern Jewish ideological camps, as we have already remarked, are less salient today than they were to partisans of "sacred survival." Adjectives essential to modern Jewish self-definition seem to matter far less to postmodern Jews. Denominationalism is clearly "out."

• Finally, *identity is far more fluid than ever before.* One can change Jewish direction, and change again, at many points in life. Scott, having taken a year off from his career to study in Israel, put the matter most forcefully. "I feel like I have been in a state of flux and a state of learning. I certainly realize that I am not going to rest somewhere, [so that I could say,] 'This is the kind of Jew I am and therefore I need this kind of person.' . . . No, I'm never going to be able to articulate that necessarily in such a way that makes sense. I am always going to be in this exploration. . . ." He could have been speaking for almost all our subjects, who—without taking a break from careers or families—nonetheless saw themselves as explorers in Judaism, people in perpetual quest of Jewish meaning. They are full-fledged members of what Wade Clark Roof (1993) has termed the "generation of seekers," their credentials recertified, as it were, with each successive stage in the journey.

Life is fluid in other senses as well. The boundaries dividing Jews from non-Jews have come to seem less essential, because they have been, in the experience of our subjects, less fixed and of less consequence. Fully two-thirds of our survey participants agreed that "my being Jewish doesn't make me any different from other Americans." Intermarriage, interdating, and close friendships with non-Jews have left their mark. The self is more and more composed of multiple parts. One does not demand they hang together neatly, need not for example sacrifice particularity in the name of co-existence with the otherness in one's home or one's self. Jews rather seem content with a piecemeal approach to selfhood as to life: an interior "bricolage" to match the cultural diversity of the surroundings. And if few adults end up exactly where they started in life as Jews (in part because they never really end up anywhere, in their own minds, but always remain on the journey), nonetheless their level of commitment in the home of origin, or the commitment they remember their grandparents as having evinced, remains a good indicator of the salience of Judaism in the homes they themselves build.

There were, of course, exceptions to these generalizations, most notably among those Jews who exhibited the highest degree of activity and involvement. Ken, a filmmaker in Los Angeles, spoke movingly about his desire to serve God in all he does: "One of the deepest prayers I have when I go to shul is that the work of my hands express God's will on earth." Simon, a lawyer from Denver who brought his family to Israel for a year dedicated to exploring and deepening their Jewish commitment, expressed a sense of humility before the tradition that we found rare. He would never characterize any manifestation of Judaism as irrelevant to the Jewish people or tradition, Simon reflected, even if he found it incomprehensible or un-sympathetic. "I realize, the more I study, the more I know how much I don't know; the more I wade into the sea of Jewish knowledge, the more I realize how big it is, and how deep it is, and how wide it is. I didn't have any idea before; I was barely on the beach, let alone in the sea." He added that he "want[s] to be sure that my life is lived in a way that people would know, and I would be cognizant of the fact, that I'm Jewish. It should be some-thing that I do part of every day."

Betsy, a homemaker in Los Angeles, does not believe in the chosen peo-ple doctrine and is not sure Jews have any special obligation to help other Jews as opposed to human beings in general. She commented, when asked how her role as a Jewish parent differs from her husband's, that "I always felt family comes first, not religion." She told us how important her Jewish community has been to her own development as a Jew—and by "commu-nity" she meant not only her synagogue, though it too constitutes a com-munity she values, but her neighborhood, where families regularly cele-brate the holidays in each other's homes. "Being in the community was a turning point, giving us guidelines and [enabling us to feel] comfortable bringing up kids with other families who feel the same."

These sentiments, we repeat, were somewhat exceptional in our sam-ple—but they highlight the fact, true in nearly all cases we encountered, that we are not witnessing an extreme turn inward by Jewish selves uninter-ested in Judaism or the Jewish people or in Jewish community at the local level. Our subjects, like the Americans examined in *Habits of the Heart,* are rather "caught between ideals of obligation and freedom." On the one hand, they articulate the concern of the "therapeutic" for self-knowledge and self-fulfillment, and on the other, they cleave to ideals of responsibility that extend beyond the self or even the family (Bellah et al. 1985, p. 102). True, "for them, as for most Americans, the only real social bonds are those based on the free choices of authentic selves" (p. 107). And yes, "it is the self . . . that must be the source of all religious meaning" (p. 229).

But we did not find many examples of what Bellah and his colleagues called "Sheila-ism," named for a woman devoted to a religion of her own invention, focused on her own inner self. It would not be accurate to say that our subjects allow for "few criteria for action outside the self," that they believe in self and love and little else, or that "the love that must hold us together is [in their view] rooted in the vicissitudes of our subjectivity" (Bellah et al. 1985, p. 90). Nor do we believe that, inside their families, our subjects hold to a notion of love as the "sharing of feelings between simi-lar, authentic, expressive selves—selves who to feel complete do not need others and do not rely on others to define their own standards or desire" (p. 100). And while our subjects do evince something of the tendency toward "invisible religion" first enunciated as such by Thomas Luckmann (1967)—religion as "a private affair, something to be worked out within the boundaries of one's life experiences, each individual fashioning, from the sources available, a system of sacred values and meanings in keeping with personal needs and preferences"—they do not exhibit a religion so "privatized" that, in the words of sociologist Wade Clark Roof, it "knows little of communal support, and exists by and large independent of institutionalized religious forms" (Roof 1983, p. 132).

Our subjects remain Jews who value their membership in a people three thousand years old. No less than 94 percent of the participants in our survey agreed that "Jews have had an especially rich history, one with special meaning for our lives today." The individuals we interviewed expressed pride in their participation, real or vicarious, in the achievements of the Jewish people in the present day. Theirs is, to use Roof's terms, very much a "shared faith," one which is "likely to inspire strong group involvement" (Roof 1983, p. 132). The Jews we met celebrated Jewish community where they found it to exist in more than name only—that is, where they sensed real connection, tangible obligation—and voiced the desire for more such community. They took no pleasure in the "invisibility" of their religion; indeed they could rarely become aware of themselves as Jews, let alone sustain Jewish involvement, except in the presence of extremely "significant others" and with the help of the community and its tradition. Finally, our subjects did recognize substantive obligations that begin in the family but do not end there, a kind of love too complex and mature for the therapeutic model Bellah et al. described as "incompatible with self-sacrifice" (p. 100).

Indeed, if those we interviewed are and seek to be autonomous, sovereign selves, who carefully weigh every commitment they make and no less carefully guard their options for transferring commitments as they please, they are only exhibiting in the Jewish realm attitudes and behaviors which are demanded of them in every other realm of contemporary American life (Swidler 1999). Jewish families inculcate independence, initiative, agility, and personal drive no less than any other middle-class families, and savor the rewards these attributes bring no less than any others. Our subjects, at times, seemed to recognize that the kind of selves they have been raised to become does not always jibe with the models of self put forward by the Jewish tradition. They seemed aware as well, at least to some degree, that the demands placed upon them by their careers—and their own drive to self-fulfillment—often leave little room for the kind of family life they had hoped to enjoy as the fruit of successful careers and had expected to place at the center of their own fulfillment. The conflicts are many—this itself is an aspect of contemporary identity which is often perceived as a departure from historical patterns of traditional norms. Those we interviewed did not fault themselves for falling short of wholeness, even while seeking it with the help of Judaism.

It occurred to us as we listened to them speak that a great deal of modern Jewish thought has stressed that Jewish commitment represents precisely the fulfillment of the self rather than its denial. How else could Judaism appeal to selves who had internalized notions of autonomy and agency, and for whom submission or obedience were no longer virtues to be prized? Fulfillment by means of tradition and community is very much the message preached in the synagogues of virtually every denomination these days. Our subjects have perhaps heard that message and made it their own.

Rabbi Joseph Soloveitchik, one of the twentieth century's leading Orthodox thinkers in America, stressed in a well-known essay that for Jews repentance is always "an act of creation—self-creation . . . the creation of a new 'I,' possessor of a new consciousness, a new heart and spirit, different desires, longings, goals" (Soloveitchik 1983, p. 110). Abraham Heschel, probably the leading thinker of Conservative Judaism in the twentieth century, deplored the fact that Jews spent so much time worrying about "the community and its institutions," while "the individual has been lost sight of." Heschel believed rather that "the problem of the individual is the urgent issue of our time. . . . I mean a relatedness to the center of one's being . . . the search for meaning" (Heschel 1966, pp. 190–193). Buber, of course, stressed always and everywhere in his mature writings that fulfillment as a self came from the relation of "I" to "Thou," the ideal being a community comprising such relations and focused on a common "Living Center." But even Mordecai Kaplan, who epitomizes concern for the forms and institutions of the Jewish community, conceived of the community as an avenue to the fulfillment of the self. "No individual is spiritually self-sufficient," Kaplan wrote in *The Meaning of God in Modern Jewish Religion.* "The meanings and values that life has for him are a result of his relationship to the civilization in which he participates." Only if Judaism was an instrument of "salvation to Jews," a term Kaplan translated for his audience as "self-fulfillment," could Judaism legitimately appeal to Jewish individuals—and flourish thanks to their renewal (Kaplan 1962, p. 92).

These thinkers differed dramatically from one another in their notions of Jewish obligation and their imaginings of the ideal Jewish self. All were more demanding of themselves and others than the Jews we interviewed. Indeed the very notion of "moderate affiliation" would not be one that any Jewish thinker, by definition, could unequivocally embrace. The commitment they seek is more thoroughgoing. Not even Buber, for all his emphasis upon spontaneity, would have been entirely pleased with the notion of perpetual quest without arrival. Heschel, who championed the notion of a "ladder of observance," had a clear notion of the higher rungs to which the lower rungs were meant to lead. More *was* better, in his view. Though he did not much care for Soloveitchik's notion of "halakhic man," he too felt bound to the regimen of commandments in its entirety. He was not free in his own mind to pick and choose among them. On these matters our subjects have departed from the injunctions of the elite thinkers in every denomination, and further still from the premodern forms of belief and practice that we surveyed earlier in this chapter.

And yet our subjects have also moved beyond the modern rejection of Jewish commitment in the name of modernity, a rejection often enacted by their own parents or grandparents. They are defined as much by what they have embraced Jewishly as by what they have rejected of the tradition —and still more, as we have argued, by *how* they have embraced it, resolutely protecting their autonomy at the same time as they reach out for meaning and community they cannot attain on their own. These are selves very much in process, engaged in fashioning a relation to the Jewish past and to other Jews that is likewise only now emerging. We turn next to the principal site at which that Judaism is being constructed, and experienced: the private spaces of home and family.

3

ALL IN THE FAMILY

We joined [a synagogue] . . . our daughter got a lot of love there. . . .
There is no question that our involvement paralleled B's development
and interest in things Jewish. A couple of years before her bat mitzvah,
she expressed an interest in junior congregation. . . . So we started
attending junior congregation as a family. . . . My entree to synagogue
organizational life came when someone called looking for new blood on
the school committee. B joined United Synagogue Youth and [my son]
joined junior USY. B and I became regular members of a davening
[prayer] group. We were "on board." A lot of my involvement would
have evolved without B, but she was the catalyst.

—GIL

The families of our respondents—both families of origin and current
families—loomed large in respondents' accounts of their Jewish journeys,
activities, and identities. References to family members, family events, Jewish practice within the family, family relations, and the struggles to adapt
to and cope with family systems took up major portions of our interview
time. As in Gil's comments above, children are often the catalyst for Jewish
involvement, but their influence is equaled by that of parents, grandparents, and spouses—and not always in the direction of increased Jewish
activity.

This emphasis on the family is not at all surprising. Much like other ethnic and religious groups in the United States and elsewhere (Waters 1990),
Jews harbor a variety of powerful images of their families. Some see them
as centers of warmth and nurturing, placing particular emphasis on the
maturation and worldly success of the children. At times, so the popular
image goes, Jewish families may be *too* warm, too caring, and far too in-
trusive. However, even in their extreme versions, and whether substanti-
ated or not, images of intense Jewish families stand in contrast to allegedly

cold and loveless American WASP counterparts, images that likewise date back half a century and more (Clark 1949). Though Jews may differ as to their evaluation of their families, they generally concur as to their salience and centrality.

With respect to Jewish socialization, too, families are conventionally portrayed as the most critical, though not always the most effective, agents. This holds true for both the popular imagination and for the most authoritative scholarship—and accords with the view of family presented in many of the classical sources of Jewish tradition. Parents are almost always seen as positive role models of Jewish commitment for the children. They teach directly by way of their own behavior and comportment, and indirectly by attending to their children's Jewish schooling and bar/bat mitzvah ceremonies. The commandment to "love the Lord your God with all your heart" is immediately followed, in a passage from the Torah recited daily by observant Jews, with the commandment to "teach these words to your children." In fulfilling this function, the nuclear Jewish family has traditionally not worked alone, but as part of an extended family system in which grandparents, aunts, uncles, cousins, and relations that are even more distant provide a context that frames the nuclear family experience. Holidays, family life cycle celebrations (weddings, bar and bat mitzvahs), mourning, illness, and other forms of more regular contact all provide occasions for interaction filled with emotional and symbolic significance.

On the other hand, historians and social scientists (to say nothing of novelists and filmmakers) have often worked to qualify and in some cases to debunk these conventional images (Hyman 1991; Prell 1999). One line of research demonstrates that Jewish families have not always been as functional as the popular imagery suggests. Parents are not as loving and children are more tormented than many Jews would like to believe. Husbands are sometimes abusive, spouses often unfaithful. In particular, migration from traditional Europe to the modern West, and especially the United States, has been associated with all sorts of pathological behavior, readily visible in the press and other accessible documentation. Throughout the twentieth century, it turns out, Jewish men and women in America have held rather uncomplimentary stereotypes of the other gender. These images testify to a far more complicated and more qualified set of relations between husbands and wives, parents and children, than the idealizations and stereotypes would seem to suggest (Prell 1999).

Historians argue, moreover, that even if Jewish families have been central and powerful in recent times, they played far less dominant roles in the premodern past. Communal institutions, informal age-sex peer groups, and the community generally served as the agents of socialization and the loci of socializing, far more than they would in the post-Emancipation and post-Enlightenment era (Katz 1961b). The influential and emotionally central extended Jewish family portrayed in many classical sources, if it ever existed, did not exist then. Such images do not appear to be a fair characterization of the typical Jewish family in premodern Europe.

For our purposes, data on the modern period are of course far more relevant, and a considerable quantitative research literature over the last half century has pointed to the major influence of the family situation upon Jewish involvement of all sorts (Cohen 1983c, 1989a; Gans 1958; Sklare and Greenblum 1967). We know that, in broad terms, Jewish religious activity declines in the late teen years (as does religious activity among other groups). It begins to climb again with marriage, and jumps upward even more sharply with the arrival of children and, in particular, when the first child reaches elementary-school age. Affiliation of families with synagogues peaks immediately preceding bar or bat mitzvah, only to decline again in the years following this widely celebrated rite of passage. The departure of children from the home is associated with a further slight decline in religious activity, although its effect on communal affiliation and activity is ambiguous. Finally, the death, or divorce, of a spouse seems linked with further declines in Jewish activity in the home or community. Single adults appear to be less active in these spheres than are their married age peers.

Clearly, then, family status and family configurations influence all sorts of Jewish behavior, including ritual practice, synagogue attendance and affiliation, organizational membership and activity, and even friendship patterns and Jewish population density of one's residential neighborhood. (Parents of school-age children live in more Jewishly dense environments than, say, unmarried young adults.) These quantitative patterns point to qualitative relationships, suggesting the presence of complex and rich emotional linkages between family issues and expressions of Jewishness more generally. It is these linkages which we set out to explore in our research.

We were not disappointed. Our respondents attested to the Jewish importance of their families in a variety of ways, some of them quite surprising. They repeatedly raised family issues in sections of the interview bearing on quite disparate themes. Relations to (and feelings toward) parents and grandparents, spouses and children, we learned, are closely intertwined with both positive and negative feelings about being Jewish and enacting that identity. In the simplest of terms, affection for Jewishly active family members generally translated into affection for aspects of being Jewish associated with those family members. But we also found more complicated triangular relationships among respondents, their family members, and their feelings about being Jewish. A troubled relationship with a parent who represented strong Jewish involvement was sometimes at the root of an aversion to Jewishness. Parents who quarreled about Jewish matters left a legacy of Jewish discord in their adult children. Alternatively, family members may engage in a sort of "Jewish positioning."

may assume a stance toward Judaism that distinguishes them from
ⱼr family members, whether by being more involved, less involved, or
ⱼly involved in a different way from parents or siblings.

ₘily members are also repeatedly cited as the instigators of observance. Some years ago, Cohen questioned about a half dozen worshippers
of a Conservative congregation milling around the lobby of the synagogue
during High Holiday services. He wanted to know why the worshippers
had come to services. All the answers were of a similar sort: "My parents
expect me to be here." "My wife wanted me to come." "I came because of
my children—they should see their mother in synagogue on the High
Holidays." No one offered a totally inward motivation, such as seeking God
or spirituality, enjoying the cantor's chanting, or reflecting on the year
gone by and the one ahead, though these motives were indubitably present
as well, even if unstated. Instead, all those questioned referred to some
family relationship as their prime motivation for attending services. (Of
course, all were questioned while socializing *outside* of services rather than
seated and praying inside, which may have produced a peculiar sample.)

The family context itself has become an arena for the expression of
Jewishness that is second to none in its importance. Rises and falls of ritual
behavior in line with greater or lesser approximation of the conventional
family configuration (i.e., the presence in the home of two Jewish spouses
with school-age children) certainly suggest that, for many, ritual behaviors
are more meaningful in this conventional family context (Cohen 1983c,
1988, 1989a; Sklare and Greenblum 1967; Pinkenson 1987; Wall 1994).
Younger, unmarried adults, who are ritually inactive, frequently assert that
they *will* light Sabbath candles, or will keep kosher, or will attend services
once they are married (or married and the parents of small children)
(Nash and Berger 1962; Nash 1968). The statistical evidence lends cre-
dence to their claims; as we will report in chapter 4, our subjects repeatedly
linked both observance and its meaning to the presence or the memory of
close family members.

Our aim in this chapter is to elaborate on and further refine these
themes. We have organized the interview material around the four main
family characters mentioned most often in our interviews: grandparents,
parents, spouses, and children. That these four sorts of family members
occupied most of the family-related material in the interviews is in itself
worthy of note. Respondents made scarce mention of aunts, uncles, and
cousins, for example, recalling them only in the context of family celebrations of the major holidays, particularly the Passover seder. Friends, too,
were mentioned only rarely. Consistent with our imagery of the drawing in
of Jewish involvement, its concentration more and more in the intimate
spaces of the self and those closest to the self, the relevance of extended
family and friendship circles seems to have declined in importance over
time. The nuclear family or, more precisely, the "vertical family," stretch-

ing from grandparents to grandchildren, has assumed ever more significance. Those who are nearest exert the greatest influence upon Jewish
observance and supply its greatest meaning, serving as both stimulus and
audience to the enactment of convictions, which might otherwise have
remained deeply buried within the self. Not surprisingly, these highly
ambivalent relations to parents, spouses, and children also stamp Judaism
with profound ambivalence—making the role of grandparents, beloved
role models of authentic Judaism, all the more crucial. We begin, therefore, with them.

GRANDPARENTS: REPOSITORIES OF NOSTALGIA AND IDEALIZATION

Respondents recalled their grandparents with great affection. They easily recounted fond memories, vivid stories, and clear portraits of their
grandparents' personalities. Rebecca, for example, a Chicago woman in
her forties, spoke about her grandfather as "fun and funny, warm and
engaging." She remembered times "as a young child sitting on the porch
swing, talking with him about anything." Amy, a woman of about the same
age in Los Angeles, named her children after her grandfather and her
husband's two grandfathers, a clear sign of attachment, further attested by
the tears she shed at this point in our interview. Molly expressed similarly
powerful sentiments. "In my early childhood, my grandfather was probably the biggest influence in terms of what I wanted to be. The sweetest,
kindest person I have ever met. He was very insightful, but very nonjudgmental. . . . The way he interrelated with people . . . Being Jewish just
filled his life. . . . How he thought about everything. . . . I adored him."

As we shall see (and can easily imagine), respondents' descriptions of
their parents were, to put it mildly, more nuanced and less uniformly
positive than were those of their grandparents. Needless to say, we cannot
vouch for the accuracy of either set of reports, but only for the importance
of the fact that each generation of ancestors is recalled in the way that it is
recalled. Since one must presume that the grandparents' generation was
not objectively so much more sensitive and loving than the parents' generation, we need to explain the source of these strong, positive feelings
about grandparents in psychological terms. Clearly, the grandparent-
grandchild relationship is less filled with ambiguity and tension than that
between parent and child. Grandparents are generally free of the responsibility of disciplining their grandchildren. Their relatively greater physical and emotional remoteness from the grandchildren (as compared with
the ever-present parents) means that the grandchildren have less of a need
to differentiate themselves from their grandparents than from their parents. Therefore, years later, respondents can express feelings of unqualified love for and romanticized memories of their grandparents. Their
feelings—and statements—about parents are far more complicated.

Respondents often associated their grandparents with Jewish practice and piety. References to this link abounded, as the following examples document. Ann, a Detroit physician in her thirties, told us: "My grandparents on my father's side were Orthodox and on my mother's side Conservative. They were a strong presence, especially the Orthodox ones. I remember Shabbat dinner with them and the Shabbat candles. Saturday morning I went to my grandmother's house, which was strictly Orthodox. I went to an Orthodox shul with my grandfather and sat in the women's section."

Such sentimental memories of grandparents can be formed at a relatively young age. Ken, a young Los Angeles screenwriter, told us that "One of my earliest memories of being a Jew was going to shul with my grandfather.... He was a *macher* [Yiddish equivalent of a "big cheese"] there. It was great to be his grandchild. I have warm memories of singing *Sim Shalom* [a popular prayer] there. My grandfather promised to take me to Israel for my bar mitzvah, but he died when I was five and a half." Or consider this memory of Gil's: "My grandparents were Orthodox Jews, although they affiliated with a Conservative temple that leaned Orthodox. They were my mother's parents. My father's died when I was very young. They were Russian and fairly secular. My mother's parents were intensely observant. They spent a lot of time at their shul in downtown Philly. Every Saturday night they ate at a kosher dairy restaurant downtown."

The grandparents, then—or at least *these* grandparents—hold out powerful positive images of attractive Jewish role models. For the respondents who mentioned them (about a third did so), grandparents played a major role in anchoring their Jewish identity. Our sense is that they did so to an extent and in ways which have not adequately been recognized heretofore, be it by social scientists or by Jewish grandparents themselves.

In addition to generalized recollections of good times in Jewish contexts, some respondents recalled very specific and very moving Jewish encounters or conversations with their grandparents. Two are particularly striking.

Martha, a woman in her fifties, told us: "When I came home [from a Zionist camp], I remember sitting with my grandfather and I was talking about camp and singing songs. He was just sobbing that he had not succeeded in passing on a lot of his obvious love and concern for Judaism and Jewish music and Jewish history to his own children, but that I had it.... So that was a very passionate memory that I have. The singing and music was his passion in life. Actually, one of my daughters is named Shira [Hebrew for song]."

Lee, a New Haven businessman in his sixties, recounted an equally moving, poignant story: "Back when I was nine years old, my grandmother, my bubbe, was listening to a program called 'The Eternal Light' on a Sunday morning. It was a big Jewish program. She was listening to a melody on the radio and started crying, and I said, 'Bubbe, bubbe—why are you crying?' She said, 'Six million Jews went to their death singing this song.' [Respondent sheds tears here.] I said, 'Bubbe, what does it mean?' And she said, 'My God, my God, why hast thou forsaken me?' She didn't know the correct words, but basically that's what she said to me. That left a lasting impression on my life."

The fond memories of grandparents that we heard were frequently associated with food. In a national survey of American Jews conducted in 1989, 70 percent agreed with the statement, "Some of my best feelings about the major Jewish holidays are connected with certain foods" (Cohen 1991b, p. 60). Our interviewees testified that seders at the grandparents' homes played a particularly important role, combining family, food, and festival in a way which ensures especially stirring recollection decades later. Lee spoke "of everybody coming together at my grandmother's home for Passover. I remember my mother cleaning my grandmother's house prior to the holiday getting rid of the hametz [food that was ritually prohibited on Passover] and all that good stuff. They would give it away to Gentile neighbors and I was always impressed that they gave the food that near and dear to them." References to food and grandparents arose in other contexts as well. Several respondents mentioned the challah on Friday night and other aspects of the Sabbath meal. Others were more expansive, such as Liz, a New Haven woman in her fifties: "I have very fond memories of my grandmother. Just cooking and talking. I certainly don't have similar memories of my mother and me. My mother always hated to cook. My grandmother was very nurturing. She knew that my father loved rice pudding and she would always make it."

Apparently, the link connecting grandparents, food, and Jewishness continues into the present as well, as the following comment by Reuben, a New Yorker in his forties, aptly illustrates: "We started something called grandparents' school where my daughter will go over once a week to my mother's house for a couple of hours. They will be engaged in Jewish stuff which, to this point, has involved reading Bible stories, talking about the Jewish holidays, learning Hebrew around holiday cooking, and learning much about traditional foods." Holiday cooking and traditional foods constitute significant and noteworthy elements in the makeshift curriculum of this informal "grandparents' school." All three generations can be presumed to agree that learning the food-based folkways of the Jewish people is an important subject in its own right and one particularly suited for intergenerational transmission from grandmother to granddaughter. Along the same lines, Cohen recalls the names he used as a boy to distinguish his grandmothers: "bubbe [grandma] cake" and "bubbe cookie."

We are, of course, not the first to recognize the close connection between food and Judaism (see, most recently, Joselit 1994). A well-known religious studies scholar is said to have begun his course on comparative religion by announcing, "In this course, we are going to learn why Christians are hung up on sex and Jews are hung up on food." It is perhaps no coincidence that the Woman's Christian Temperance Union was started by Midwestern women of northern European Protestant extraction, and Weight Watchers was established by two Long Island Jewish housewives. Jewish comics have routinely made fun of the association of Jewish mothers and ethnic food. However, social scientists have often belittled the meaning of food, seeing it as part of a merely symbolic and largely superficial ethnicity. Apparently, our respondents take a brighter view of the linkage between Jewish food and Jewish grandmothers, lending it deeper meaning than many social scientists have recognized and making it a major causal factor in their adult Jewish development. Food patently and quite potently symbolizes deep family affection, especially maternal and grandmotherly love. The practice of grandmothers preparing those foods that were especially appealing to certain family members, referred to by Liz, underscores the use of food as a channel of affection.

Other factors are at work too. The survival of distinctive ethnic cuisines long after the disappearance of other markers of difference has made food a near-universal link to ethnic identity; its special prominence among Jews may have something to do with its particularly salient role in the Jewish religious calendar, as Reuben's comments remind us. Specific dietary practices are tied to almost every one of the holidays. Shabbat has its classic Friday night meal. Rosh Hashanah has its apples, honey, and circular challot. Yom Kippur centers around a solemn fast bracketed by two feasts. On Sukkot, celebrants eat their meals in makeshift huts erected outdoors. Hanukkah has its potato pancakes (latkes) and Purim the triangular hamantaschen symbolizing the tricornered hat of the holiday's villain, Haman. Passover, the holiday most widely celebrated among American Jews, is not coincidentally the holiday of the seder, a meal overflowing with numerous symbolic foods and the one best known for a distinctive diet item: matzo, which substitutes for the most basic item in the normal diet, bread. Shavuot is marked by the eating of dairy products. Beyond these holidays, more traditional Jews observe a number of other fast days. All this, of course, comes on top of the enormously complex and symbolically rich system of kashrut regulations that impinge upon daily life. Family affection, ethnic attachment, and religious meaning, then, are all associated with food, and their ties to each other are embodied in their connection with food.

The special fondness our subjects expressed for their grandparents, the potent connection with food, and a remembered context of organic Jewish commitment—the old neighborhood, the extended family, Yiddish, and the like—combine to produce a set of uniquely influential Jewish role models or images. Paul quite typically saw his grandfather as one of the most important figures in his development as a Jew. "He's still present in my mind as a Jewish model. [In contrast,] my father talked about Jewish identity as important, but he didn't model it." Martha was more expansive. "My grandfather . . . was a very big influence in my life and a very dear man. Perhaps the most clearly, of anyone in my extended family at the time, he communicated his Jewish identity and his concern for it to be passed on. My grandparents had a kosher home; the holidays were very full and enriching, some of the best memories I have of holiday observances as a child."

To be sure, not all grandparents fit the model of committed, involved Jews. We encountered a few stories similar to that recounted by Joy, a Manhattan fund-raiser: "My father was very assimilated. My grandfather went to Columbia University. So these were assimilated, educated Americans. . . . He was not at all religious. I mean, he would come to the seder and his lips wouldn't even move as the Hebrew was being spoken."

But Joy's was not the usual pattern. Quantitative research consistently demonstrates declines in conventional Jewish practice spanning at least three generations—immigrant, second generation, and third generation (Cohen 1983c; Goldstein and Goldscheider 1968)—followed by a leveling of this decline in the fourth and later generations (Cohen 1983c, 1988). Moreover, the process may take on different contours with families who arrived in the United States after the middle of the twentieth century. With this said, the generational decline model does seem generally applicable to the population we have been investigating. It obviously implies higher levels of observance, on average, among respondents' grandparents than among their parents. If that is the case, we would expect respondents to report that their parents broke with their grandparents' more observant lifestyles. They did, and their stories included accounts of tension between the parents and grandparents.

Martha remembers: "My mother never felt accepted by my father's family. So anything my father's family wanted to do was no good. There were a lot of arguments about going to holiday meals because it meant the gathering of the clan." The source of the problem may well have been unrelated to Jewish practice. Spouses can feel unaccepted by their in-laws for a whole host of reasons. But the issue quite typically gets focused around holiday gatherings for ritual meals—meaning that Judaism is stamped forevermore with those conflicts, and perhaps seen as their fulcrum.

Thus, memories of grandparents who were Jewishly committed in an authentic and compelling fashion can conceivably influence grandchildren (the respondents) in opposing ways. Susan Wall, in her qualitative study of the Jewish identity of "parents of pre-schoolers," draws this paradoxical implication: "Those who wish to emulate their parents can do so in one of two ways. They can accept the Judaism of their parents, which was a rejection of the grandparents' patterns of Jewish living. Or, they can follow in their parents' footsteps, by again rejecting the Judaism handed ɔwn from one generation to the next" (1994, p. 52). As role models, ɡrandparents may indeed serve to strengthen attachment to Jewish in- ɹolvement. However, grandparents may stand in sharp contrast with parents who, as a group, may be less Jewishly involved. Wall also points to the contrast in the perceived influence of parents versus grandparents. She too found that memories of grandparents were nearly uniformly warm, and understood by the respondents as lending support to conventional Jewish involvement. Parents brought a mélange of conflicting memories and images to their children's reflections on Jewish identity. More than tradition is passed on "from generation to generation." Conflict and ambivalence are transmitted as well.

PARENTS: COMPLEXITY AND AMBIGUITY

In a variety of ways, our respondents testified to Jewish upbringings that rabbis and Jewish educators would generally regard as deficient or, in the words of one well-known article, "culturally deprived" (Himmelfarb 1975). An extreme case is offered by David's description of his upbringing: "No Yom Kippur, never took a day off, never even knew about it, wouldn't have known what it was, zero. No emphasis on that from my parents. . . . No Hebrew school, no Sunday school. My parents lived four blocks from Temple Emanuel. I could see it from my front door, but they weren't members." All the stories we heard, of course, have idiosyncratic elements. One way or another, however, many families of origin arrived at stances fairly remote from conventional Jewish involvement. Steve, a Manhattan writer in his forties, told us, "I didn't have very much [Judaism in the home]. My father at a young age, he was thirteen, was thrown out of Hebrew school. He got into something with the rabbi. He hit the rabbi or yelled at him or something like that. So at a very young age, he was not subjected to religion. I would say my father was an atheist. My mother was the same." Brad, another New Yorker of about the same age, provides a somewhat more statistically normative account: "I would have to go to one service with my father on the High Holidays and that was it. We really didn't have a Passover seder. We had a family dinner which was called a Passover seder, but it wasn't really."

Few of our respondents could testify to a rich Jewish home environment, reinforcing the findings of an earlier qualitative study of parents of preschool children (Wall 1994, pp. 39–43). Those who did so tended to be older, and were reared in a time when Jews were more ethnically distinguished from the larger society. Some reported Jewishly weak homes of origin without comment. Others complained about their parents' limited interest in, or ability to articulate, the lessons and meanings of Judaism. Several told of prayers said by rote without any thought given to what they meant. Such comments reflect a wider criticism of the Judaism of mid-century adults voiced by many of their young adult children, who began to come of age in the counterculture of the 1960s and 1970s. Leaders of the Havurah movement of the period accused their elders, among other things, of failing to adopt a more learned, contemplative, reflective, and spiritual approach to being Jewish (Prell 1989; Reisman 1977; Weissler 1989). Eventually, these sentiments also came to characterize broader, less specialized, and less culturally sophisticated portions of American Jewry. Return to a Judaism perceived as more authentic—the Judaism of the ancestors, of the grandparents—could not but involve rebellion against the parents who had abandoned the tradition: a rebellion which in some cases made Judaism all the more attractive an option for personal fulfillment.

In large measure, these sorts of criticism derive from the cultural shift noted in chapter 1, and in particular from the move toward a greater emphasis on understanding the self as part of the quest for the self's fulfillment. They derive, too, from the spread and growth of higher education, and the professionalization of American Jewry's third generation—traits that sharply distinguish baby boomers from their parents.

However, our respondents not only differentiated their parents' lower levels of Jewish involvement from their grandparents' higher involvement and perceived Jewish authenticity. They were also capable of distinguishing between their mothers' and fathers' relative levels of Jewish interest and involvement. For the most part, by a ratio of approximately two to one, respondents who made such distinctions reported higher levels of involvement on the part of their mothers. The limited survey data directly related to this issue are inconclusive, however; respondents in a 1993 study recalled relatively equal levels of Jewish parental involvement (Cohen 1995). Our interviewees joined loving recall of their parents' personal characteristics with admiring, almost idealized views of the favored parent's Jewish identity—as they had done with their descriptions of their grandparents. Stuart, a Los Angeles filmmaker in his thirties, remarked, "My mother was a great influence because she's so in touch with God. She's cheery, happy, fun-loving, completely honest, sweetness and goodness [he gets a little teary]. She's more comfortable with who she is than anyone I ever met." Martha offered a more detailed description of her mother's Jewish identity: "Through the year, my mother made it clear that she had more concern about things Jewish [than my father]. In fact, she got on my brother about some Hebrew school which was short-lived, and then he got into some sort of tutoring to prepare for his bar mitzvah. It seemed to be her push, and my father was always pushing the other way. Though a clear leader, he provided no stability in the family in terms of any Jewish observance."

Suzanne, a Bay Area therapist in her fifties, echoed these themes and detailed the elements of Jewish identity for which her mother was responsible. "My mother came from a very religious family—very Orthodox, so we kept kosher and did all of the holidays and we had all of the stuff at home and we went to temple and I was bat mitzvah. My father was very much on the periphery until we were just about grown up and he got involved in the temple." The stronger impact and involvement of women may even extend to mothers-in-law. Joy recounted, "I have probably developed a bit more of a Jewish identity through my husband and his family. His mother . . . has made me feel more Jewish than anything else in my life."

We suspect that the more frequent reports of a stronger impact of women on their families' Jewish identities derive from two patterns—both of which, as we will see, are still evident in the current generation. First, as some scattered quantitative evidence suggests, women may simply be more active and Jewishly identified than men (Cohen 1989a), consistent with patterns of gender-based variation in American religious life (see, for instance, Roof 1993).

Second, and more critically, we think, women have been more involved in the intimate aspects of their families than men. This too is in keeping with a general American pattern that goes back at least half a century and probably longer. Cultural transmission, one historian of the interwar years observes, was very much a "maternal matter in which fathers played a secondary and largely ceremonial role." This division of responsibilities led some rabbis to blame the disaffection of Jewish young people on the notable inattentiveness of their fathers. If ritual matters were left entirely in female hands, one rabbi complained, boys would be tempted to conclude that "religion in general and Judaism in particular are feminine accomplishments and Jewish life a feminine indulgence" (Joselit 1994, pp. 86–87). Our respondents did not portray the matter quite that starkly, but they did report, in most cases, that responsibility for Jewish observance in their homes of origin rested primarily with their mothers.

Scott, a man in his twenties who was studying in Jerusalem when interviewed, attested to a multigenerational dominance of women in shaping his own family's Jewish identities: "Being Jewish was important to my mother. My father grew up in a house where his parents were told to deny their Jewishness. That first generation, like my great-grandfather, came over to America, and so they grew up in a place where being Jewish was a liability. So my grandmother was the entire religion; my grandfather was kind of indifferent. He changed his name. He grew up with Christmas trees in the house. He read the Torah at his bar mitzvah, but he had no idea of what he was saying. It was never important to him."

Suzanne described her father's late-blooming, Jewishly active period as primarily a social commitment that emerged in later life and that revolved around the synagogue's Men's Club. "He joined the Men's Club . . . and got very involved in getting people to come to the temple. . . . It wasn't so much as if he got religious, but he got involved with the community. He was a very social guy and liked the social aspect." At the same time, the limits of his commitment to traditional Jewish norms could also be seen in his mild reaction to his son's marriage to a non-Jew, unusual at that time. "My father never said anything about it. He didn't show a lot of active distress about it."

Women are more invested in the conduct of home life, by way of their greater responsibility for orchestrating the social calendar and the preparation of food. Since much Jewish life and children's Jewish socialization occurs within the home, mothers also seem to their children—or are remembered years later—as more invested in the children's Jewish upbringing. When asked to identify the important experiences or people influencing her Jewish development Rebecca immediately remarked, "My mother." She then proceeded to link her mother with "making Shabbat, together as a family for Shabbat, even though we weren't completely observant." Sonya, a woman in her thirties interviewed while studying in Jerusalem, reported: "It [being Jewish] was important more to my mom. We definitely were required to be home for Shabbat dinner. My dad worked retail, though, and it was actually the only night of the week that we ate together as a family. . . . I could go out only if it was BBYO [B'nai B'rith Youth Organization] or USY [United Synagogue Youth] activity Friday night, and even then, if it was something other than services or a program that was just going out for pizza, my mom would throw a fit."

There are exceptions to this pattern. Several fathers were singled out as the Jewishly stronger parent. However, when this happened, the associations with fathers were very different from those with mothers. In response to the question on "who had a decisive influence on the type of Jew that you are today," Reuben immediately cited his father. Then he used words that clearly seem more appropriate to men of the era than women: "He had a very traditional Jewish upbringing and very strongly followed the Jewish tradition and customs." Dave, another New Haven man, likewise in his forties, spoke highly of his father as steeped in "Jewish values and ethics." He recalled proudly that his father worked closely with the rabbi on the synagogue's education committee, that he "knew more [Judaica than most people], he really did," and that he was "a very political person." We heard similar images from Brad, who told us proudly, "To my father, being Jewish was quite important, he was quite religious. He had come from a small town in upstate New York where there had been no synagogue and his father had started this little community something or other. He observed the holidays. My mother was not religious at all. In fact she was quite anti-religious, although she could identify with being Jewish."

Jewishly committed fathers, in contrast with Jewishly committed mothers, emerge as principled, learned, educationally oriented, and involved in synagogue life. Mothers are remembered for their immediate relationship with the children and other family members, for their greater responsibility for the home, holidays, and kashrut (or, to use the alliterative phrase coined earlier: family, food, and festivals). We believe these gender-based distinctions are closely aligned with sex-role differentiation. The mothers of baby boom children, which the majority of our respondents were, took on the major share of child-rearing, and near-total management of the home. As such, they played roles that were more prominent in shaping their children's Jewish identities.

Insofar as sex-role differentiation has diminished since then, we would expect to see diminished discrepancies between the sexes in taking leadership in shaping the home's Jewish involvement. As we shall see, that has not occurred. Jewish women, at least those in moderately affiliated households, continue to play far more significant roles in shaping the Jewish character of their homes than do the men. Their adult children a generation hence will almost certainly recall them, rather than their spouses, as the leading Jewish actors and influences.

Despite positive memories of one or another parent, however, the prevailing view presented by our respondents was the one we described earlier. Parents, as they recalled them, had generally failed to evince an intense commitment to Judaism, and/or were not particularly reflective about the observances they did perform or demand. To the parents, being Jewish was taken as a matter of family loyalty and affection far more than a principled or rational adherence. They apparently assumed that its intertwining with family, love, food, and the interpersonal tensions these generated would and should prove sufficiently powerful to guarantee their children's continued commitment to Judaism. Our subjects recall themselves as wanting more (or less)—and, given the chance to act on these desires as adults, they have done so.

Only one clear exception was reported to this generalized memory of parental laxity when it came to matters Jewish. Even respondents with relatively uninvolved parents reported strong objections to their dating non-Jews. Liz at one point described her childhood Jewish home as "nearly Methodist," but had this to say on the topic of her dating partners: "I knew that I was Jewish and I knew that my parents wanted me to marry someone who was Jewish. Clearly, I knew they wanted me to date Jewish. I never went out with anyone who wasn't Jewish." Suzanne, too, noted that her dating non-Jews caused her mother some anguish: "I knew it was very hard on my mother and it was always a source of some conflict. Since that time there have been a number of things that I felt are disloyal about relating to that because of my mother and her feelings about being Jewish."

Molly's story of her marriage to a non-Jew, reported in chapter 1, highlights the extent to which marital issues intimately involved with Jewishness are played out in a larger context in which parents play a major role. She "could not ask [her fiancé] to convert," Molly told us, because "that

was important to her parents," but not to her. Molly's parents "went crazy
. . . they went off the deep end." Asking her husband to convert would have
signified capitulation to her parents' wishes, and a submersion of her own
individuality. Going through with the wedding helped establish her independence. The story, however, is more complicated. Molly reports both
parental involvement and parental alienation. Her mother found the Reform rabbi who performed the intermarriage, but even so it "took five
years for my parents to accept him [her husband]." When her husband,
about sixteen years into the marriage, decided to convert, Molly's parents
again took on a central role—both in her life and in her narrative.

> My parents went crazy in the other direction. He did a Reform conver-
> sion and I thought they would say it wasn't good enough. I miscalculated.
> They were thrilled beyond belief. My father gave him the tallit [prayer
> shawl] given him when he married almost sixty years ago. I have mixed
> feelings about this part too. It's nice, but he [her husband] is not a dif-
> ferent person than the day before.

The account is striking: a mature woman, someone we found extremely
thoughtful, is struggling with issues of parental acceptance—both accepting them and being accepted by them—as she and her husband move
through complicated patterns of accepting and not accepting Judaism.
The couple's developing relationship to Judaism is still being played out
around their relationship with Molly's parents, just as it was when they
courted.

Running throughout Molly's remarks is a rejection of her parents' tribalism. She rejects their sense that one qualifies as a member of the family
not merely through personal characteristics, but through a simple condition of belonging to the Jewish people. In fact, as we shall see in chapter 5,
virtually none of our respondents articulated an unambiguous commitment to endogamy. That had been their parents' Jewish way, one which
they have decisively rejected. Our respondents' range of views regarding
intermarriage stands in contrast with their parents' largely unequivocal
opposition to dating and marrying non-Jews—although, as we shall see,
for this generation as well, romantic relations with non-Jews occasion profound questioning and reflection about their own Jewish identities, and
for several proved the single most decisive stimulus to heightened Jewish
involvement. Non-Jewish partners, we discovered, not only served as the
lightning rod for conflicts with parents; they also exposed conflicts inside
Jewish selves.

In sharp contrast with the divisive question of intermarriage, the crisis of
dealing with ill or dying parents seems to bring about some reconciliation
both with parents and with the Jewish way of life they have represented.
Indirect evidence of this was provided by Linda, a woman in her thirties
who lives in suburban Boston. Linda recalled at one point in the interview

that her mother had died of breast cancer about ten years earlier. In the very next sentence, she observed that she had then "started going to shul regularly." More directly, we learned from Paul that the "death of my mother when I was in college had an immense effect on me." He returned to her death repeatedly in the interview. The passing of parents of course stimulates lasting memories and feelings of connection. Referring to her "usual attitude, just to pick something [from Judaism] that means something to me," Suzanne remarked, "You know, on the anniversary of his [her father's] death I light the Yahrtzeit candle."

The interplay of affection and distancing (two features of intense relationships) threads through all these stories told by adult Jewish children about their Jewish parents. The latter are models of Jewish commitment and non-commitment. Jewish autobiographies are routinely punctuated by discrete and sharp memories of special events in which parents figured as a matter of course. Our respondents' Jewish involvement almost always developed in a family context, but not as a matter of developing certain principles or beliefs or of acquiring familiarity with ancient Jewish texts and traditional customs. Rather, the family of origin, with all of its manifold tensions and interactions, shaped the respondents' current attitudes toward things Jewish—attitudes, we note, often not formed in childhood under direct parental influence, but decades later, when the adult children had departed their parents' homes and formed homes of their own. In those homes, and in like fashion, relationships with the closest members of *current* families (husbands, wives, and children) continue to dramatically influence when, where, and how Jewish identities take shape.

HUSBANDS AND WIVES: COMPLEX INTERACTIONS

The limited survey research available that traces the impact of spouses upon Jewish identity strongly documents the unquestionable influence of husbands and wives upon each other's Jewish psychic commitment and behavioral involvement. In the most general of terms, one study using quantitative modeling (Bock 1976; see also Dashefsky and Shapiro 1974 and Himmelfarb 1974) demonstrates that spouses have more influence on Jewish practice than any other individual. Relevant to these concerns is the considerable body of research on mixed married couples (Cohen 1997c; Medding et al. 1992; Phillips 1997; Winer et al. 1987). That literature convincingly links marrying a non-Jew with lower levels of ritual involvement, community affiliation, in-group friendship networks, and other important indicators of Jewish involvement. Assertions of causality are complicated, and contrary cases abound. Nevertheless, marriage to a non-Jew does seem to repress conventional Jewish activity. In some cases, we discovered, marriage to another Jew does so as well.

Generally, marriages between Jews do not present as wide a gap in approaches to religious life as do marriages of Jews with non-Jews. Nevertheless, in-married Jewish spouses bring different understandings and commitments to the marriage, at least initially, thereby raising the necessity of some sort of harmonization and the likelihood of some sort of mutual influence—or contention. Our interviews clearly substantiate the intuitive inference of a close connection between a spouse's Jewish identity and one's own, and they lend some depth and color to that understanding. However, they also testify further to the extent to which Jewish identity is rooted in the most intimate of family relations. As we shall see, the respondent-spouse relationship, both in general terms and with respect to the Jewish dimension, touches and is touched by relations with parents and relations with children. The bilateral relationships (both those of immediate Jewish relevance and others) sit in a setting in which parents and children, if not others, exercise influence and lend meaning.

We shall postpone until chapter 5 detailed consideration of our respondents' recollections of how they met their spouses and, more specifically, the extent to which, and the ways in which, their prospective spouses' Jewish identities were important to them. This material will be reported on there because relations with non-Jews quite naturally served our subjects as a reminder of, or became a major element in, their own commitment to Jewish ethnic distinctiveness. Suffice it to say at this point that the Jews we interviewed represented a broad spectrum with respect to the importance they attached to their spouses being Jewish (though, because we intentionally limited our sample almost entirely to moderately affiliated Jews, the spectrum of views on this matter is somewhat narrower than we would observe in a study of American Jewry as a whole). Our focus here is on the dynamics within couples in cases where both partners are Jews—and we found across the board that the different approaches toward being Jewish that the spouses brought to the marriage demanded some sort of harmonization. Unlike religious systems that emphasize faith, belief, personal prayer, meditation, and other highly privatized forms of religious involvement, Judaism encompasses a variety of practices that enjoin familial and communal participation. These have to be negotiated—sometimes even before children of school age make the need for agreement inescapable.

Kashrut, for example, emerged in some of our conversations as an important focus for interspousal decision making, a practice that for obvious reasons demands family cooperation on many levels. To observe kashrut, the family needs to decide what foods to eat, with what utensils, and in which locations they are to be stored. The rules on separating utensils for meat and dairy products not only demand a significant financial investment at the outset; they also require an ongoing commitment on the part of all family members to maintain the physical separation of dishes, pots, pans, silverware, and even, in some homes, soaps, sinks, washcloths, dishwasher racks, and tablecloths. The numerous customs and practices associated with kashrut have spawned a diversity of regimens among American Jews. In our quantitative survey just 18 percent of respondents reported that they maintained separate dishes for meat and dairy products. Among members of Conservative synagogues the figure is higher (28 percent), while among Reform Jews it is lower (10 percent). But the possible ways of observing some, but not all, traditional kashrut requirements are more varied than this. Jews may observe the dietary laws (or some version of them) at home, but not in restaurants. They may avoid foods that have taken on the symbolism of being classically non-kosher (pork and shellfish), while eating meat from animals not slaughtered in a kosher fashion. At home, Jews might observe selected dietary restrictions without actually maintaining separate meat and dairy utensils. The predominant configurations are not endless, but they are numerous, and they are especially numerous in the moderately affiliated population that lies at the heart of this study.

Ken discussed "questions of kashrut, shul, etc." with his fiancée and "she was open to it. So when we registered for dishes, we did it for two sets." At the same time, the man who pushed his future wife to keep kosher at home reported their rather unorthodox culinary habits before marriage. "I loved bacon, lettuce, and tomato sandwiches. I had it for lunch each Shabbat. She had had beef fry [a kosher substitute for bacon] in her home, to which she introduced me." In line with their new sets of dishes, Ken and his wife appear to have assumed at least some of the requirements of kashrut in their dietary choices. The selectivity is typical of our respondents; it makes negotiations all the more necessary, and all the more complicated. Resolving differences over kashrut took center stage in our conversations with several respondents on the matter of how, in general, they dealt with different approaches to Judaism with their spouses. Their stories are filled with clear references to both affection and conflict.

Saul thought back to his courtship of his future wife, E, when he apparently was more observant of kashrut than she:

> After our first couple of dates, E decided that at least on our dates, she would order only things that we could share. Through our discussing of who we were and what was important to us, there was never any question from the beginning that these things were important to me; and there was never any doubt that this was the way I was going to continue. She didn't have anything against keeping kosher. It just never had been an issue for her before, so I don't think it was really difficult for her to make a decision that that was something she was going to do.

The importance which Saul attaches to the subject should not be overlooked. Kashrut is mentioned in the context of "who we were" (fundamental identity) and "what was important to us" (ultimate values). It is no trivial matter—any more than food is a trivial matter, or peripheral to Jewish identity, in the family of origin. The question of what to eat demanded resolution before the marriage, as E clearly sensed in her effort to accommodate her future husband's more observant dietary practices. Her husband continues:

> I don't think it [the marriage] would have worked out if she didn't [keep kosher]. I wasn't going to not keep kosher and I think it's very difficult to live in a house where you have a major source of conflict to start out with. She doesn't have to attach the same importance to keeping kosher that I do. But at least one needs to agree that this is what we're going to do, and we're going to teach our children a consistent message, which they may or may not follow through with when they get older. We do have some compromises. For example, on Saturday I don't do commercial things and E does sometimes go to stores in the afternoons.

Kashrut takes on such significance that failure to harmonize the two approaches could have led in this case to severe marital problems. It takes on added significance in the context of children and parenting, where the issue is not merely a particular practice, or the identity it maintains and signals, but transmission of that identity to the next generation.

Shabbat is another area of practice that requires attention and resolution. Our survey found that Sabbath candles are lit in about 28 percent of American Jewish homes, while about 26 percent of respondents reported attending synagogue services on the Sabbath at least once a month. Thus about one-fourth of American Jewish adults claim to observe the Sabbath in a clearly recognizable fashion. Unlike dietary laws, however, Shabbat presents the option of *divergent* practice, with one spouse observing the day in a manner different from the other (and this does not even take account of variations in the practice of the children).

Uniformity of observance is often the result of negotiation. We heard reports from families in which the more observant partner "won out," i.e., where the household adopted the higher standard of observance. However, spouses can also work to limit Jewish practice in the home. Amy reported that her husband "had a fabulous Jewish education. Mine was poor until I got to study with a rabbi. I wanted to keep kosher, but my husband is against it. He's knowledgeable and interested, but not in raising the level of observance." Many factors may explain Amy's concession to her husband's limit on kashrut in the home, but one that may be surprising is his greater Jewish education. By virtue of his having spent more years learning, he apparently earned the right, at least in his wife's mind, to exercise more influence on the home's Jewish character, even if that influence worked against the demands of Jewish tradition.

Joy provides further evidence of the complex negotiation between husband and wife. Her case too is influenced in part by her husband's stronger Jewish background and his consequent credibility in the marital give-and-take about Judaism:

> I want to raise my kids more Jewish than I was raised. My husband, who was raised in a house where they kept kosher and went to synagogue every Saturday morning, refuses to allow us to be affiliated with the temple. He hated it so much that he doesn't want to have anything to do with it. He says he married me because I was the closest thing to a WASP that he could find.

As is apparent in all these cases, decisions on jointly practiced home observance are arrived at in the context of the power struggle between husband and wife, and cannot but become a feature of that struggle. We can well imagine (but, unfortunately, did not elicit much direct evidence of) these issues being negotiated in the context of the wide-ranging and ongoing negotiation of the multiple issues that arise over the course of a marriage. Moreover, as Joy's comment illustrates, other family members are metaphorically present in the room when Jewish issues are negotiated, as they are when other issues arise. Joy ties her own Jewish aspirations to the upbringing of her children, and sees some of her husband's opposition to increased involvement as stemming from his own upbringing—in turn implicating his parents.

Although spouses can block or veto increased Jewish involvement in the home, we found that they more often bridged their disparities in Jewish involvement by moving closer to the wishes of the more Jewishly involved spouse. One partner—usually the woman—needs to take interest and lead the family in a particular area of observance, and the other spouse accommodates accordingly. Suzanne made these pertinent remarks:

> Ritual didn't really have any meaning to me when I was young. . . . If it weren't for H, I might not have celebrated anything between then and now. He was always pushing. . . . I would want to have a seder, but I would just want to have our family . . . and not have to deal with other people's ideas about what kind of ritual they want. . . . Basically I started to think I went along somewhat passively with all of the holidays till now when I'm having this whole experience of deciding I will find some way to have ritual.

We found several instances, some noted above and some noted below, in which the more observant spouse was able, or at least had the potential, to elevate the observance in the home. We suspect, but cannot prove, that a quantitative analysis, were it possible, would establish that the mean level of observance is higher than the simple average of the spouses' independent preferences would have "mathematically predicted."

Brad provided an example of the unrealized potential for this process to unfold: "To tell you the truth, if my wife took the trouble to celebrate the

Sabbath, and carried on with most of the work with it, I would go along with it. The fact that she doesn't and I don't, that is fine also." Others reported how they took initiative, with their spouses' acquiescence, to introduce more ritual in the home. Rebecca told us that "each year our level of observance has grown, [mostly because of] my influence. . . . [Her husband] has let me make decisions about our children's Jewish education, and he wasn't too particular about which synagogue we joined. It's basically me making the choices." These comments testify to the greater influence of wives on the Jewish character of the home, a point on which we shall elaborate when we turn in the next chapter to our subjects' ritual practice.

As always, there are exceptions. Rivka, a New Yorker in her sixties, provided an example of a woman who stood at the receiving end of spousal encouragement for ritual observance. She reported that her ritual practice "evolved. For instance, when I was in college, there was a big lobster place and my mother and I would have lobster. My mother adored shrimp cocktail. When I first married, I had lobster in restaurants. Then there became a point, I think it was after the children, that my husband didn't want me to have lobster, so I didn't."

Note that in this one brief comment Rivka brings in almost all the essential characters in her evolving patterns of ritual practice. Her *mother,* with whom she was quite close, held out one non-traditional model of dietary observance. Her *husband,* motivated apparently by concern for his *children*'s Jewish identities, prevails upon Rivka to forgo the food that has powerful positive associations for her. Certain foods bound her to affectionate memories of her mother; but for a Jew with traditionalist sensibilities such as her husband, the same foods symbolized a clear rejection of kashrut. Once again we see how the vertical family of three generations, spousal relations, memories of the past, hopes for the future, love, food, and ritual all interact to shape the Jewish lives of our respondents. We will now consider in more detail the impact that children exert upon their parents' Jewish identity.

ALL FOR THE CHILDREN

As noted earlier, one thing we know about the presence of children in Jewish homes is that they elevate Jewish practice of all sorts. Parents with school-age children, in contrast to married couples without children, more often belong to synagogues, attend services, perform rituals at home, belong to Jewish organizations, and live in areas with more Jewish neighbors. In these patterns, Jews are not much different from other Americans, whose church involvement is often clearly provoked by the presence of children. The boom of church construction and attendance in the 1950s was explained by Nash, in a social-scientific article entitled "A Little Child

all Lead Them" (Nash 1968), as a direct consequence of the baby boom
:e also Nash and Berger 1962). What underlies the seemingly straight-
..rward quantitative observations that link children with Jewish involvement?

One factor—our subject in the chapter which follows—is that children make holiday observance far more meaningful for adults. Examples
abound, even if we limit ourselves to "official" liturgies and customs of
American Jewish celebration and do not consider the significance which
observers of the holidays add to or substitute for those liturgies and
customs. Hanukkah has evolved into one of the most child-oriented holidays on the calendar. Children often play the lead and central role, in
lighting the candles, singing the songs, or, in some cases, receiving the gifts
that undoubtedly reflect the influence of the Christmas season at the same
time of year. Purim is celebrated by somewhat raucous synagogue services
in which children (and even some adults) appear in costume. The building and decorating of sukkot (booths) on the fall holiday of the same
name lends itself to joint parent-child activity. It also serves another function: allowing for a rare male-oriented role (construction with wood, tools,
and nails) that affords the father a leading part in Jewish ritual observance.
(Conducting the Passover seder is the other male role played by our informants or their spouses.) Simchat Torah is marked by young children
leading parades through the synagogue services. For many families, the
highlight of Passover is the asking of the Four Questions by the youngest
child capable of doing so (assisted by other children keen on displaying
their ritual competence to the admiration of parents, grandparents, aunts,
uncles, cousins, and dear friends).

The seder also highlights another critical consequence of the presence
of children in the household: it makes parents assume actual responsibility for teaching their children to function as Jews. This, in turn, has two
consequences. One is that parents begin to see themselves as role models.
The other is that they turn to synagogues and schools to educate their
youngsters, most often with the intention of preparing them for bar/bat
mitzvah.

As role models, parents undertake religious activities more often than
they would otherwise, both within the house and at the synagogue. Moreover, the activities they undertake tend to be more joyful when small children are at home, endowed with greater significance and seriousness (and
the benefits of greater preparation!), given that the point of the observance is to influence the children and so assure the family's Jewish continuity (Pinkenson 1987; Wall 1994). By joining synagogues and enrolling
their children in Jewish schools, parents encounter other Jews of similar
age, family circumstance, and interests. They connect with the informal
networks of Jews that inhabit and surround those institutions. Like other

Americans, they make friends with the parents of their children's friends, and—owing to the synagogue or school context—these new friends are not just other Jews, but other Jewish *parents,* likely possessing similar commitments and facing similar choices. Children can affect Jewish home observance in yet another way. In part because of their Jewish education, they may express an interest in adopting more punctilious ritual observance in the home, or attending synagogue services more frequently, possibly to the consternation of their parents.

These are only the major ways in which the presence of children makes Jewish life more meaningful for parents and tends to bring about elevated levels of Jewish activities. In the interview materials, we learned more of the details and complexities that surround the presence of children in Jewish homes. Lynne, a New Haven woman whose Jewish involvement puts her near the top of the Jewish identity spectrum in this study, related how her seven-year-old son provoked a variety of Jewish practices in her home:

> He is getting a very strong Jewish education. I wanted to support that at home. We [Lynne and her husband] both did. We both definitely wanted to support that, so when he started really learning Torah, my husband started doing the *parsha* [the weekly Torah portion] with him when he came home once or twice a week. We make Shabbat on Friday nights. I can't remember a time when we didn't, which is something else that somebody once said to me—your children should never remember a time when your ritual practices were different than they are today. It is easier to start when they are born than to start when they are thirteen and you decide that they can't go out on dates on Shabbat.

For Paul, the connection between role-model responsibilities as a parent and many forms of Jewish involvement is clear and explicit:

> We come to shul every Shabbat. On Friday night we light candles. So, we are modeling. Parents must be teachers. My son's favorite game is to play Torah. He loves the video of the Torah service. He'll go to the JCC preschool and then to day school. I want him to have fluency with texts that I don't have, to have a different Hebrew school experience, not like the one I had.

Of course, few respondents were as traditionally oriented as Lynne, or even Paul. For such Jews, less motivated to observance themselves, the effects of children are felt more keenly—usually around activities in which children play a prominent role. The Passover seder, remembered by our subjects as a special moment in their childhoods, takes on equally special significance for them in the role of parents to their own children. Saul told us that his family "had one of the best Passover seders we have ever had because my younger one, in the first grade, was able to read Hebrew, including the Four Questions, for the first time." His older daughter, then in third grade, had not shown much interest before, but, said Saul, "Of course, she wasn't going to be shown up by her younger sister and if her younger sister was going to say something, then she was going to show off all her stuff." Children not only provoke parents to undertake more activities, or to derive more joy and meaning from them. They also induce a greater degree of seriousness in ritual performance, and, in some cases, elicit more advanced study and preparation.

"Did having kids affect your involvement in rituals?" Dave responded, "Yes it did. I believe that the first year that we threw our own seder was a year after S was born. It was a very interesting type of thing in terms of throwing one. I didn't want to do what my father had done, which was having it and then making a little fun of it. I mean, he would do it and could read the Hebrew fine, and he felt that as long as he was reading the Hebrew fine he was doing it. But there was still a little feeling that we were scoffing at this a little bit. So, I wanted to bring a little bit of intellectual color into this thing." It is especially remarkable that this seder took on a more serious character even though the child in question was but one year old. Obviously, Dave is not simply caring for his toddler's cognitive development as a Jew. Rather, the presence of his firstborn recasts the symbolic significance of the seder. The youngster put Dave, for the first time, in the role of Jewish father. As seder leader, he now bore the ancestral responsibility for assuring an appropriate Passover experience for his immediate family.

Sometimes (although, in truth, not all that often), we heard of instances where children actually asked for increased ritual observance in the home. Dave provided an example of this as well. "About a summer ago, G [Dave's wife] would ask me if I minded lighting candles on Friday night. I said it was okay to light candles, even though I didn't think it was. But what I had to deal with was when S, after we came back last summer, said, 'Can we keep lighting candles on Friday?' So, . . . we do light candles. . . . I think it's S's reminder that she is Jewish." We sense that youngsters who attend intensive Jewish educational programs (such as day schools) are the most likely to push the parents to higher levels of observance. The discrepancy between the practice of the parents and the teaching of the schools is especially pronounced for families with less traditional or weaker Jewish involvement, as the following remarks by Amy demonstrate:

> When it was time to start looking at schools, I told my husband I wanted a day school because I had never had the option of a good Jewish education. My husband was opposed. . . . We weren't happy with the public school our daughter got into, so we chose the private day school. We found that our level of observance increased because our daughter saw a higher level at school than in our home. She wanted all the prayers, all of the Grace after Meals.

We learned later in our interview with Amy that her daughter wants even more observance in the home. As noted in the analysis of spousal give-and-take on matters Jewish, the issue is joined over kashrut.

> Six months ago our daughter said she wanted a kosher house. She asked why her parents chose not to. My husband said, "It involves buying dishes and other things. Why should we do it on a whim?" Then he agreed to try it on a six-month trial basis without new dishes. We inherited enough dishes to keep separate sets, so we did it . . . and found it a minimal change. Even my husband is into it!

Children serve to entangle their parents in both Jewish practice and the organized Jewish community. For a single adult, certain holiday celebrations are optional, or at least there is little sense of urgency; the same holidays will invariably come around next year. But for the parent, the children's childhoods are fleeting. Parents have only a small window of opportunity to celebrate a limited number of annual holidays with their children. They have only a few years to capably discharge their responsibility as their children's home Jewish educators. Similarly, parents encounter a limited period, when the child is between the age of about six and eight or nine years old, when they must enroll their child in some form of Jewish schooling, if they are to do so at all. These constraints, at least in the population we have been examining, encourage Jewish involvement in the home, the school, and the synagogue.

Suzanne's narrative is quite typical:

> I started to sort of celebrate the holidays when my daughter was little. I don't know if it was for her or for me. Probably for me. We went through this thing of should we join a temple or shouldn't we. H [her husband] really didn't want to, and basically, I didn't want to for myself. It seemed hypocritical to just send the kids, so we didn't; but I tried going. I took her to one of these Sunday schools in Palo Alto for a year. And she went to JCC camps.

Gil, whose remarks about the impact of his daughter upon his synagogue involvement opened this chapter, expanded on how her bat mitzvah provided yet one more occasion for increased involvement in the synagogue and its networks:

> Kids are encouraged, a year or two before their bar or bat mitzvah, to become a member of the main sanctuary, to learn the choreography. So, we were ready for the transition. We met and became friendly with another couple at services. He is Mr. [Temple X]. Any time unknown faces show up, he introduces himself and finds out who they are. He took B [Gil's daughter] and her close friends under his wing and we grew to be friends with him.

We asked respondents to describe the types of Jews they hoped their children would become, as well as the sorts of outcome they would want from their children's Jewish education. Answers to these speculative questions provide, in an almost pure form, a clear articulation of those aspects of being Jewish that are most important to the respondents. As one would imagine, we are not the first researchers to try to ask such questions in the attempt to understand American Jews' conceptions of Judaism and Jewishness. Sklare and Greenblum (1967) asked their respondents to describe their notions of the "good Jew." On a list of several characteristics, "lead an ethical and moral life" ranked highest, with 93 percent regarding it as essential (p. 322).

Two decades later, Charles Liebman observed (1990) that conceptions of Judaism may be arrayed on a continuum ranging from a pole that combines *universalism and moralism* to one that combines *particularism with ritualism*. In this context, universalism refers to the tendency to see Judaism as advocating lessons shared by the larger society and rejecting any notions of giving special preference to fellow Jews in any manner. Particularism refers to the opposite of these notions. The lesser known distinction between moralism and ritualism refers to the degree of emphasis in religious life and practice placed upon the ethical values (generally shared by all religions) as against the customs and ceremonies that are peculiar to the religious system, in this case Judaism. Liebman understands traditional Judaism as inclined to the particularism-ritualism pole, as against the stance of most American Jews, which is far more universalist and moralist. Our own findings support Liebman's observation, although we clearly uncovered a range of views on the matter—and, as we shall see in the following chapter, a premium on family in and of itself as giving a motive and meaning to observance.

Joy, who stands on the lower end of the spectrum regarding ritual practice, clearly emphasized morality and ethics in thinking about what she wanted for her children: "I do think that certainly the basic morals and ethics of the religion are sound. I think the kids are going to get that at home anyway. The Ten Commandments really do make sense. If you think about child-rearing, that stuff is very important. So, it would be wise for us to have that as part of their education." Rebecca offered a response with a slightly more activist bent, but she too placed almost exclusive emphasis on her children being "good people": "At this point in life, maybe it's just making kids socially aware. Part of your responsibility to your family is . . . you want them to be good people, to have an inner core of what's truly important in life. They will have to decide as adults, but you help by showing what's important to you."

The emphasis on social action in these comments is consistent with the teachings of Reform Judaism, as well as with a more general understanding among many American Jews that views involvement in progressive causes as the embodiment of the Jewish value of leading an ethical and moral life. Half the respondents in our survey thought it desirable or essential for "a good Jew to work for social justice causes," as did 64 percent in a 1989 survey (Cohen 1991b). Both the interviewees just cited have Reform affiliations or attachments. The other noteworthy aspect of Rebecca's comments is the respect it signals for individual autonomy. We heard the themes of social action and autonomy from other people as well, for example in these comments by Gil, one of the more involved Jews in our sample: "I want [my children] to grow up to be happy, caring, and socially aware and active. I come from a tradition where lots of things— ecology, social justice, etc.—are at the forefront of religion. I hope they will marry if that's what they wish. I want them to have what they wish for, values to carry with them." Note that Gil is careful ("if that's what they wish") to allow his children the option of not marrying.

The moralist emphasis on values was quite widespread in our interviews. In accord with Liebman's observations, Saul clearly distinguished ethical and moral values, which are essential in his view, from Jewish ritual practice and observance, which, for him, are merely desirable. He too made mention of children's autonomy, though more as an objective fact than an inherent value:

> I would continue to love them as my children and hope they would lead good, moral, and ethical lives even if they didn't follow Jewish observance and custom. I would be disappointed but one can't control someone else's activity. You can push them in the right direction but you can't guarantee.

Stuart succinctly echoed the same theme: "What's my hope for my kids? That they'll be kind, sensitive, honest, giving. That they'll get lots out of life, lots of joy." Except for their failure to include specifically Christian theological beliefs, these responses can hardly be distinguished from those one would expect from well-educated, liberal American Protestants. Indeed, the extent to which the answers do, in fact, shade over to a thoroughly universalist-moralist stance uncomfortable with Jewish distinctiveness can be seen in Joy's openness to private non-Jewish contexts for her daughter's schooling:

> Ethical Culture is interesting to us. I would be perfectly happy to send my daughter to St. Hilda & Hughes or Trinity as long as we are affiliated with a temple and she is getting some kind of religious education outside of school. I would think of her five-day school as the academic side and I would try to get some kind of religious education for her on weekends, in a Hebrew school. . . . We will have to see [about religious schooling], but at the moment we are not looking.

The "Ethical Culture" that Joy refers to is a non-theistic, humanist movement whose New York branch was pioneered by Reform Jews in the late nineteenth century. Its schools in New York City enjoy an excellent reputation.

Such highly universalist-moralist responses may be contrasted with others we heard that did emphasize peculiarly Jewish elements. But even there we found a distinction between those responses emphasizing inward feelings and beliefs and those that emphasized specifically Jewish practice. Among the former is one by Molly which weaves in her own experience as a changing and developing Jew:

> What I'd like [for my children] intellectually and what my emotions tell me are different. Intellectually, I'd like them to carry this feeling that being Jewish is something that affects how you do everything, and what we can learn from Torah affects (or should) how you relate to people, view education, choose a career. . . . I confess I have felt uncomfortable with being a doctor—people feel doctors do it for financial reasons. The rabbi said Jews have always chosen service. This made me feel better . . . good about what I do. I work in a suburban, middle-class practice where everybody has enough. . . . But the rabbi made me feel better, that there's something about this choice that's grounded in where I come from. I'd like my kids to feel that on an everyday basis, to feel connected to the Jewish community.

Contrast this response with that of Saul, though even his comments betray some qualification of the imperative to Jewish particularity:

> I hope that they become practicing Jews and believing Jews. In other words that there is a consistency there, that they are not just practicing. It's because they actually believe the prayers and it's important. And somehow I would approach that question by saying that all these other qualities that I want for them are the things that instigate whatever their Jewish practice is. I don't particularly care if they want to join an Orthodox congregation; that doesn't bother me. If they become Jews in such a way that it excludes me or any other members of their family, that's a different story.

Saul's answer, far different from Molly's, also clearly contrasts with a more traditionalist stance that would endorse obeying Jewish law and performing Jewish ritual practice as a matter of absolute divinely ordained obligation. We find in his words a strong emphasis on sincere belief. Moreover, despite seeming openness to his children adopting a very traditional lifestyle, he fears their adoption of a strict Orthodoxy that would necessitate a rupture in his relations with them.

The aspiration to remain close to one's children, and to avoid such a rupture, also arose in the context of questions on the possible intermarriage of the respondents' children. We shall once again postpone consideration of this issue until chapter 5, where respondents' thoughts concerning both their own marriages and those of their children will loom large in their thinking about Jewish distinctiveness in a Gentile world. Some people whom we interviewed (Joy, for example) seemed unconcerned about the possibility that their children might marry non-Jews; others, like Gil, expressed a strong preference for Jewish marriage partners for their children, but indicated they could learn to live with a Gentile son- or daughter-in-law without too much difficulty; still others betrayed deep angst about the matter.

Our respondents of course may have been influenced in this matter by the recognition—which dawns on all parents in contemporary America sooner or later, and usually sooner rather than later—that at the end of the day they will exercise precious little influence, and absolutely no control, over what their children will make of the guidance that their parents have sought to provide. Those of our respondents whose children had reached the teen years reported that their children were often strikingly different in terms of their attraction to Judaism. One sibling could be utterly enthused and another utterly indifferent; one could be attracted to ritual X and another to observance Y—mirroring their parents' selectivity and offering a cautionary warning about the uncertainty of outcomes when one seeks to transmit a particular tradition in an open society. Allegra Goodman has brilliantly captured this variation among children raised in the same home by the same parents in a short story, "The Four Questions," describing a Passover seder for which the four children have returned home to be with their parents and grandparents. One daughter, newly Orthodox, is dismayed by the non-traditional character of the observance, thereby dismaying her parents, who feel rejected. Her brother arrives at the seder with his Gentile girlfriend, arousing consternation in his grandmother that is followed by eventual acceptance. Their younger siblings don't seem to care about the meal at all—perhaps because their parents (and older siblings) seem to care so much. The grandparents seem to care only that the family is together.

The issue of intermarriage is only one further example—albeit one of the most dramatic—which testifies to the multiplicity of ways in which children entangle their parents, as well as their siblings and grandparents, in Jewish matters. They can propel parents into the unavoidable (and, to some, uncomfortable) position of serving as Jewish role models. They can make the acting out of Jewish life more significant and more meaningful, or simply more likely. They can impel critical decisions regarding Jewish schooling, synagogue affiliation, and membership in the informal communities that surround schools and synagogues. Not least, they can serve as the cause of and focus for reflection on the meaning of being Jewish, and on the meaning of being a Jewish parent.

In all these ways, children interact with the other personally and Jewishly meaningful family relationships that we have reviewed. They elicit from grandparents—without much coaxing—the Jewish activities later recalled with great affection. They provoke the spouses who are their parents to consider and refine their differing approaches to establishing a Jewish home and raising Jewish children. They offer parents, separately and together, the opportunity to put into action the lessons they have learned about Judaism and to play out the emotions they bring with them to their Jewish home, as a result of the impact of their *own* parents and grandparents. In sum, children powerfully exemplify the confluence of affection, reflection, conflict, and meaning-creation that are at the heart of the family relation, making family the principal arena for the expression of contemporary American Jewish identity.

We now turn to the activities and occasions in which family dynamics and Jewish commitments are most vividly joined and displayed: the celebration of Jewish holidays.

RITUAL OPTIONS

Pesach means the most to us. When I was growing up, my grandfather
did everything . . . [now] we have two big seders, eighteen to twenty
people both nights, most not Jewish. Most of our friends are not Jewish
. . . Shavuos we don't really do anything. Often I'll go to services and
read Torah. This year I'll go to work, maybe services at night. . . . I have
tremendous difficulty with High Holiday services. Sometimes I go to
hear Kol Nidre. This year I didn't. My wife and son went. My wife said,
"Aren't you going?" I said: I can't do it.

—Tony

Ritual observance is without doubt the single most important way in
which moderately affiliated Jews express their Jewish commitments. It is
the principal means through which "the Jew within" steps outside the self,
in the company of family, into times and spaces hallowed by centuries of
tradition. It is around Jewish holidays that contemporary American Jews
of whatever denomination or commitment most often discover, construct,
and insert Jewish meaning into the stream of everyday life. And that is all
the more true for moderately affiliated Jews: individuals for whom observance is neither imperative nor routine. As a result, the approach of the
holidays impels them to reflect again and again on whether and how the
Jewish calendar should impinge upon and shape them.

The present moment is especially propitious for the study of ritual
observance among American Jews. One reason is that in some selected
quarters, there is more of it to study. "Symbols of a Desert Exile Bloom in
Jews' Backyards," proclaimed a 1995 *New York Times* article chronicling the
resurgence of interest in sukkah building. The leadership of the Reform
movement, once known for its opposition to ritual regarded as outdated

and irrational, has of late been furthering a "return to tradition" of major proportions, as embodied in its latest platform, adopted in 1999. At the other end of the spectrum, Orthodoxy, in both its "modern" and "traditionalist" varieties, continues to prosper. It does so in significant measure, we believe, because it offers Jews a tightly bound community and a set of ritual practices which together structure and sanctify everyday life (Heilman and Cohen 1989). Among congregationally affiliated Conservative Jews, the youngest cohort of adults is the most observant, and the first generation to outpace its parents substantially in level of practice (Cohen, forthcoming [a]). Ritual has renewed appeal to many American Jews of diverse backgrounds at the present moment, though, as we shall see, observance remains extremely selective.

Recent theoretical approaches to the study of ritual practice can be of great assistance in making sense of this development. Scholars such as Mary Douglas and Clifford Geertz, Peter Berger, and Victor Turner collectively represent a decisive turn away from once-dominant Marxist, Durkheimian, and Freudian explanations of ritual observance. These classical theorists often explained ritual by explaining it away—reducing it to an effect or "epiphenomenon" of economic, sociological, or psychological forces. In contrast, more recent theorists insist that we pay careful attention both to "external forces" such as those just mentioned and to the significance attributed to a given ritual by those who are performing it. Scholars now assume there are multiple causes of any given observance, and multiple meanings ascribed to it. No less important, ritual is viewed as more than the mere "reflection" or "enactment" of beliefs which allegedly exist prior to the practice and independent of it. Increasingly, practice is seen as a potent source of meaning in its own right, one which may stimulate the quest for reasons which make sense of it. It is rare today in the academy to find ritual dismissed as rote, mechanical behavior lacking in meaning. Douglas in particular has taken pains to attack the Protestant and Enlightenment prejudice *against* ritual that in her view resulted in common "use [of] the term ritualist for one who performs external gestures without inner commitment to the ideas and values being expressed" (Douglas 1982, pp. 1–2). We will draw upon these new approaches in order to make sense of the new ritual patterns among American Jews, and the new meanings those practices carry.

Most of the themes which will preoccupy us in this chapter are evident in the brief quotation from Tony with which the chapter begins. Tony is an engineer in his early fifties who has recently become more active in his suburban Boston congregation.

First, and most important, there is *family*. Passover in Tony's account means what it means to "us"—Tony's wife and children are included—and this meaning is immediately connected as well to Tony's childhood experiences with his grandfather. Family provides a crucial part of the meaning to ritual observance for moderately affiliated Jews. It is the major locus of such observance: the context in which ritual activity takes place, and without which such practice probably would *not* take place. In an earlier survey of American Jews, 91 percent agreed that "for me, Jewish holidays are a time to be with my family" (Cohen 1991b). Surveys also point to the rise and fall of ritual observance in line with changing family circumstances; spouses and children, as we saw in chapter 3, exercise a major influence upon the nature and the amount of practice that takes place in the home. Family is the context in which Jews most often seek and find Jewish meaning—perhaps because it is for many the single most important source of meaning in life as a whole. It is no surprise, then, that the meaning ascribed to ritual by moderately affiliated Jews is almost always connected to the people who are the sources both of family and of Jewish family traditions: parents and grandparents.

Note too that Tony reflects upon and chooses from among a menu of possible ritual observances, a menu which consists almost entirely of the annual cycle of Sabbaths and festivals. Moderately affiliated Jews report infrequent observance of dietary laws. No one whom we interviewed used the mikva (ritual bath). None spoke of a discernible influence of Jewish law upon daily matters of business, dress, sexual relations, and the like. For these Jews, ritual means major holidays. Each holiday must, as it were, make the case for its own observance by people who have in large part forsworn or forgotten Jewish ritual practice. The persuasive power of a holiday—the arguments it offers for and against its own observance—is thus more important than ever before. That power lies in the range of meanings attached to the holiday by the individual Jews who must choose whether to embrace or reject it. We will probe these meanings, cognitive as well as emotional, in order to make sense of the decisions made by the Jews in our sample for and against observance. We want to understand the "yeses" Tony utters as well as the "nos." We also want to understand why some holidays figure in his decision making while others are not even considered.

This points to the final theme to be considered here: the unprecedented *exercise of autonomy* among the current generation of Jews when it comes to ritual observance. For today's Jews, Jewish practice is not an all-or-nothing matter. Three-quarters of the Jews who participated in our national survey agreed that "I have the right to reject those Jewish observances that I don't find meaningful." Moderately affiliated Jews are not committed to a package of detailed behaviors that is set out in a code and sustained by communal pressures. Nor are they committed to the wholesale rejection of observance on grounds that it is premodern superstition or that they lack the sort of faith that the practice requires. Even a fairly observant Jew such as Tony, enough of an insider to call Passover "Pesach" and Shavuot "Shavuos," picks and chooses. Tony is typical of moderately affiliated Jews in that he selects from among an array of possible practices, often for quite personal reasons, and takes the fact of this choosing utterly for granted. He is typical, too, in that he alters his practice from year to year, discovering or discarding meanings as he goes. He probably believes, as do 86 percent of our national sample, that "a Jew can be religious even if he or she isn't particularly observant."

AT HOME WITH JUDAISM

The many and inseverable connections linking family to observance are evident in every single account of ritual practice that we encountered.

Let us begin with the family which actually participates in that practice. For most of our sample, concentrated in the age range between thirty and fifty, that means spouses along with children who are still in the home or who have just left it for college. Linda, a professional fund-raiser who is currently not working outside the home because she is bringing up two children ages eight and ten, ticked off her family's ritual calendar in a way that highlighted the decisive role played in it by considerations of family. On Rosh Hashanah the family goes to her father's house on the first night, then to their own congregation for the second. "Yom Kippur we are here." Sukkot observance began for them three years ago with a family education program at their Conservative synagogue that included help with the building of the sukkah and the making of the lulav (palm, myrtle, and willow branches bound together and waved ceremonially at certain points in the service). Linda and her husband keep the children home from school on the first day and are conflicted about whether to send them on the second. They always attend services on Simchat Torah. "The kids love it." At Hanukkah they light candles and have a party. At Purim they all attend the reading of the megillah (Scroll of Esther) in synagogue and send gifts to their friends in accordance with the custom of *mishloah manot*. This practice, too, is organized by the synagogue through its Hebrew school. "The seder is always a big deal. We don't clean out the house, it's not a kosher home, we just don't eat hametz [leavened bread or related food products]. We don't go to services." Shavuot is meaningful because their son was born that day. They attend the earlier study session (tikkun) of the two held at their synagogue on the evening of the holiday; the one that continues throughout the night is ruled out by work and the children. On Yom Hashoah (Holocaust Remembrance Day) Linda sings in her synagogue's choir. On Yom Ha'atzma'ut (Israeli Independence Day) her family attends a family education program at the synagogue. They observe Shabbat almost every Friday night—"candles, challah, a nice dinner, chicken."

The calendar of observance is extensive, despite (or because of!) Linda's freedom to accept or reject the individual items that make it up. We offered no prompts about particular holidays during the interview, but simply asked our subjects to take us through the annual cycle of holidays, Jewish and non-Jewish, so as to see what was included and omitted. Linda's calendar resembles that of most observant Conservative Jews, and is like theirs, too, in its omission of Tisha B'av, a major fast day that is normative for Orthodox Jews (along with a series of "minor fasts" that for most non-Orthodox Jews are not only not practiced but not known). Note that Linda did not provide any explicit reasons for observance in terms of a holiday's particular content: a message or symbol that is especially salient or meaningful. Others in our sample did provide such reasons for observance, but for them, as for Linda, family either is *the* principal reason for observance, or is bound up with that reason, because it is the most palpable meaning which the holiday bears.

Molly presented her holiday cycle to us in far greater detail but with the same emphasis upon family. Take for example the High Holidays. On Rosh Hashanah, "We usually try to round up company to come here for meals. We go to shul both days." She and her husband have not been going to Kol Nidre, "because it requires getting a sitter, often on a difficult night, and it is hard after work to rush home and run out on the kids, so it's better not to do that." Their synagogue staggers its services during the day of Yom Kippur, and Molly preferred the afternoon service she attended when her children were younger to the one they go to now. Her family has for the last several years built a sukkah. They begin construction immediately after breaking the Yom Kippur fast, in keeping with Jewish custom. They eat in the sukkah every night of the holiday except during pouring rain. "It was a great experience." Molly has not yet found a satisfactory Simchat Torah experience for her children—"at our shul it's really chaotic." She complains that while in general her synagogue does wonderful programming at holidays for younger children, as they get older the quality declines. This is especially true of Hanukkah and Purim.

Other meanings to Molly's observance appear when she comes to, and lingers at, Passover. "Pesach is my favorite holiday. I look forward to it for ages." Her husband has accumulated many different haggadot, and every year they construct a service drawn from several of them, mixing Hebrew with English and old passages with new. This year he assigned each person at the seder a topic on which to write a midrash. "Children wrote stories, and we read them. Adults did it . . . It was really fun." Molly tells us proudly that there are now people who depend upon her and her husband to make the seder. She then reports that last year her baby-sitter took the kids to McDonald's on the first or second day of the holiday. "I was beside myself. She just didn't get it. She knew it was Passover but the idea of a holiday that lasts for eight days was out of her experience." The sitter was apologetic, and then two days later took the kids to Dunkin' Donuts. When the children were reminded by their mother that it was Passover, they said, "Oh no!"

Molly does not mention the universalist themes of freedom and oppression that, we learned elsewhere in the interview, captured her husband's interest long before he converted to Judaism and thus enabled the family to celebrate all of the holidays as a family, without tension. We suspect these themes constitute an important meaning to her family's observance. But Molly provided another when she answered the question "What do you like about being Jewish?" by referring to the pleasure of "feeling part of a community that was both recognizable but also never felt very mainstream." She has always "liked the feeling that I am part of this group." As she has studied more about Judaism, she has come to appreciate "this continuity over thousands of years, to develop a relationship with writings people have studied for thousands of years and I can read them and think about them as well." This connection to the Jewish past has deep resonance for American Jews. As many as 91 percent of the respondents in a recent survey agreed that "the major holidays make me feel connected to my Jewish heritage and traditions" (Cohen 1991b).

Molly enjoys the fact that she can and does eat at McDonald's and Dunkin' Donuts throughout the year, but chooses not to do so at Passover. The holiday reminds her and her children of the degree to which they belong to America but stand apart as part of a people that has existed for a very long time in many different societies and cultures. For her the holiday is about freedom and identity—two of its traditional themes—in a personal way that is very much part of her immediate experience. She also likes the way "my holidays set my year. . . . There is a progression, always something to prepare for and look forward to and think about. There is a neat sense of history and purpose to these holidays that's not secular." This too seems part of the appeal of Passover, which she "look[s] forward to for ages" in part because Jews have "for ages" looked forward to the holiday and prepared for it in a similar fashion. She and her family are part of a larger group, one to which—as her celebration of Passover each year demonstrates—she and her family fully belong.

"My holidays," Molly called them happily. They structure "my year." First-person possessive in relation to a tradition "thousands of years old" is a potent source of meaning indeed. Content offensive to Molly's sensibilities might have gotten in the way of her celebration of the holiday. But, the content safely assured, the primary meaning of the observance seems to be the way it draws Molly's family closer together as a family at the same time as it draws the family into an age-old people, history, and tradition.

Men as well as women emphasized the role that family plays in their observance. Recall Saul's pride in the participation of his two young daughters in the family's seder. Ken, a filmmaker in his thirties, married and the father of two, described a very full ritual calendar and a high level of observance. He blows the shofar in his synagogue on Rosh Hashanah, wears white clothes and canvas shoes on Yom Kippur, builds a sukkah every year, conducts two seders at his home, and goes to synagogue on every holiday. Ken said he likes being a Jew who cares about being home for Shabbat. He appreciates the gift that effort gives him: "Home and family are where my life really is."

That said, it is clear from the comments made by both men and women in our sample that women are expected to take the initiative where ritual is concerned. Even if they work outside the home, women bear primary responsibility for what goes on there, all the more when that activity involves food. What is more, women continue to bear primary responsibility for raising the children. Ritual thus falls doubly in their domain. Several of our subjects put the matter bluntly. Matthew, a New Haven executive, called his wife "the keeper of the tradition." Ann, a Detroit physician whose second husband is a Jewish atheist who wants nothing to do with Judaism, said she will be trying over the next couple of years to "find a comfort level, where [Judaism] will fit in my life" and the life of her little boy. She would do so "irrespective of my husband's feelings—with or without him." (She explains his antipathy to Judaism by his having been orphaned as a child and hence deprived of the association between family and tradition that is so important to her.) Nina's husband is more agreeable to their family's observance, which is likewise child-centered. But she confessed that she "does not enjoy many holidays tremendously because they are a lot of work," and she therefore sees them as an imposition. No one helps. "My husband is not really into it. He says, 'You don't have to do it'—but it's his family!"

Implicitly or explicitly, we got the message that this is by and large the case for the vast majority of moderately affiliated families. Men are accomplices or impediments to observance. They are rarely its driving force.

❧

The family members with whom American Jews actually celebrate Jewish holidays are, of course, not the only ones who are important to those observances. Parents and grandparents loom large in the meaning of the holiday as well. Sometimes they are present in the flesh on these occasions, serving as a physical link to past celebrations. In many cases, however, they constitute a far more powerful source of meaning precisely because they are *not* present. The holiday conjures up precious memories accessible at no other time, and thus elicits powerful emotions. We have already discussed the overwhelming significance of families of origin for the Jewish beliefs and behaviors of the generation now raising its own children. Nowhere is that significance more evident than at holidays. It came through in our interviews in a variety of ways.

First, individuals who were raised as Jews almost invariably recalled the holiday celebrations of their childhoods when describing their observance of the same festivals today. This is in keeping with an earlier national survey, in which 85 percent of American Jews agreed that "certain Jewish holidays evoke in me some very fond childhood memories" (Cohen 1991b). We heard repeatedly about people and times that had been lost but which are recovered in the smells of a Sabbath kitchen or the tastes of a Passover seder. This is an inherent feature of ritual observance, of course: the forms and repetitions of the performance seem to create a "time out of time" that transports one from the present moment to a past that is thereby made present. The emotion experienced at these moments in turn becomes an indelible part of the holiday itself, expected and experienced at future celebrations.

"Passover was probably the most important holiday," Lee, the New Haven businessman, told us, "primarily because my grandmother, before she lived with us, lived a block away. My aunts and uncles . . . lived in the same house with my grandmother on two different levels." Passover was a time of "everybody coming together at my grandmother's home. I remember my mother cleaning my grandmother's house prior to the holiday, getting rid of the hametz. . . ." Lee is in his early sixties, and his memories of grandparents are therefore redolent of the immigration around the beginning of the twentieth century, a period which plays a crucial part in the collective American Jewish imagination. However, others whom we interviewed provided memories of their own childhoods in more recent periods. These tales were no less evocative or significant. It seems to make no difference whether grandparents are called bubbe and zeide or grandmom and grandpa, no difference that the ancestors spoke English rather than Yiddish or lived in the suburbs rather than "the old neighborhood." Nor does it seems to matter overmuch whether the remembered observance was highly traditional. The point is that such observance, *if it took place* (or *is remembered as having taken place*—we have no way of getting at the facts of the matter), offers both meaning and motive to present-day practice.

Parents and grandparents can also offer legitimization for changes instituted in current observance. Molly, describing the original midrashim that her family told at its Passover seder, added at once, "My grandfather always said, you do what you can." His blessing, conferred on the holiday more generally, made changes in the format of the practice all right in her eyes.

Suzanne described still more dramatically the linkage effected between the generations by ritual observance. She and her husband have never joined a congregation, despite his abiding interest in theological matters and her extensive childhood experience with synagogue, Hebrew school, and Camp Ramah, a camp affiliated with the Conservative movement.

Their home observance has been limited to Hanukkah celebrations (lighting candles and telling the story of the Maccabees) and Passover seders (which, when the kids were little, featured the telling of the story via puppet shows). Suzanne is clear about the attraction these rituals exercise for her. "I always have some sort of seder and tell the story because that was a part of my childhood that I really loved, it felt good. It's more the community observances I think that are sort of skewed" (i.e., unattractive). It is important to Suzanne—a reason for her alienation from Jewish organizations, religious or secular—that she not simply go through the motions. She feels this about non-Jewish as well as Jewish holidays. "I have to feel like it's coming from inside out, and isn't just somebody else's idea of a ritual."

Then Suzanne told us the remarkable story of how she began lighting Sabbath candles every Friday night.

> I recently went to visit my mother and she was saying how sad she felt that there would be nobody to light the candles after she died and that these beautiful silver candlesticks that her mother gave her would not be used. Whereas in the past I might have felt guilty, this time I sort of reacted with more sympathy about her feelings and her sense of self. This was important to her, and she wanted this part of her carried on. So I said, "I'll light them."

Her husband was incredulous. Did she really want to do this? Would she do it? Suzanne was sure that she did, and would.

> My feeling was that she and I have made a connection about a ritual that would have meaning because it was about our relationship and it was even more wonderful because it was about my grandmother and because it was about the culture and being Jewish. But mostly it was about some connection between us and a way to be connected to her even after she died. So, I think that I am sort of struggling tremendously with this whole thing about having some kind of ritual that has meaning, and I certainly have no idea where that is going to go, but I basically have spent most of my adult life having very little ritual.

The motive for observance in this case is identical to the source of its obligation—and to its meaning. Suzanne has elected to observe this one part of Sabbath ritual because it tangibly connects her to her mother, and her mother's mother. The inherent connection between mothers and tradition of course needs no explanation. It is perhaps all the stronger in Suzanne's case because, as she reported, the religious aspect of Judaism was an important part of her mother's identity, but not her father's. Judaism was transmitted to Suzanne by her mother—the source of the candlesticks which she would now light as her only regular observance of Judaism. The ritual is meaningful, then, because of the reason that led Suzanne to choose it—and because she *did* choose it, voluntarily, against a background of non-observance that makes this one practice stand out all the more. No other element of Sabbath observance was even considered. Kiddush had not been performed by her father growing up, and would not be performed now by her husband (or herself!). Synagogue attendance has always been out of the question.

Increasingly, we believe, American Jews are exhibiting both of the patterns examined thus far: ritual inheritance directly carried on from parents and/or grandparents, with or without changes in the form of observance; and practice adopted after a number of years of non-observance and then valued retroactively as a parental inheritance. We are also seeing a third and much newer pattern: the practice of rituals that were *not* part of home observance growing up; or the carrying on of practices which informants recall having initiated in their parents' homes, with the parents supportive or indifferent but not actively involved; or the radical alteration of observances first learned at home—in some cases simply by performing them seriously.

Jewish identity inevitably carries multiple associations with parents and grandparents, alive or departed. It is freighted with all the love, complexity, and ambivalence of those relationships. The personal decision to observe a particular holiday invests that practice with a host of personal meanings superimposed upon the ones handed down from parents or inscribed in the tradition.

"MY HOLIDAYS," "MY YEAR"

The ritual calendar among moderately affiliated Jews typically contains four elements, listed and described here in decreasing order of importance: (1) a *Passover* seder, at times accompanied by other aspects of the holiday such as eating matzo or going to synagogue; (2) some practice or set of practices, usually performed on Friday evening, which sets the *Sabbath* apart from the rest of the week; (3) candle lighting, singing, and gift giving at *Hanukkah,* particularly when children are at home; and (4) attendance at *High Holiday* services. The more active Jews in our sample add other festivals to the list (most notably *Sukkot* and *Shavuot*) and observe whatever holidays they observe with greater frequency and/or intensity than those who are less active. *Purim* and *Simchat Torah* generally figure in the calendars reported to us only so long as the family includes small children. Tisha B'av was almost never mentioned by our sample, let alone observed. Of the non-Jewish holidays on the American calendar, only *Thanksgiving* seems to be practiced universally and regarded as existentially meaningful. *New Year's Day* and *July Fourth* are occasions for parties, if that. More importantly, *Christmas*—observed at home by a notable minority of American Jews a generation ago—is now celebrated only rarely among the members of our sample, and almost exclusively among couples who are intermarried, when it often becomes a major source of contention. Let us consider each of the major holidays in turn.

According to a recent survey, American Jews in general are more enamored of Passover than of any other holiday and have been for some time (Cohen 1991b, p. 62). The reason is perhaps that Jewish *memories* seem to revolve around Passover more than any other single observance. Indeed, it was striking to us that few individuals, when asked about their Passover observance, responded primarily in terms of the themes of the haggadah, universalist or particularist: liberation, plagues, redemption, and the like (all of which loom large in recent retellings of the Passover story). They seemed, rather, to take these themes for granted—as if they knew about them, and knew that *we* knew they knew about them—and were eager to describe the more *personal meanings* that they found in the holiday. These meanings were almost invariably connected to family.

Rebecca, for example, remembered childhood seders at an aunt's house, her grandmother cooking in the kitchen. She told us that she and her husband now celebrate the holiday each year with the large extended family that he has in the Chicago area, where they live. This makes the seder an occasion of tension as well as celebration. The problem is that many of her husband's cousins are married to non-Jews, some perform no other Jewish activity over the course of the year, and their children receive no religious education. What then could the holiday mean to them? How could the seder hold their attention? How could it not alienate them? Someone in the family had addressed the situation a few years ago by writing a haggadah with which Rebecca was most uncomfortable. It told an almost completely universalist story of human bondage and liberation, one nearly stripped of content relating to the particular slavery and redemption of the children of Israel. Rebecca did not like the text at all. She and her husband rewrote it for use in their home.

Note that the holiday's themes, when cast in purely universal terms, are in this case a disincentive to observance. Rebecca wants more Jewish content to her seder—though not so much that she and her husband adopt a traditional haggadah for their own use. Until she gets the proper balance, we infer, the real meaning of the day for her—at least the story she tells about the seder—will lie to a significant degree in the family struggle *about* that meaning. A partial contrast is Sarah—single, in her late twenties, and the fairly unobservant daughter of a Reform rabbi—for whom the most particularistic sections in the haggadah are a source of distress. Traditional texts "have this terrible passage about smiting the non-Jews, I don't recall exactly what it is . . . sometimes I've been off in the kitchen or something and then I noticed that everybody's kind of going, 'What's this about?'" For her too, the highlight of Passover observance seems to be making the seder for her friends and for her parents, who come from a great distance to be present. She likes putting together her own text so that "I could get the haggadah that I wanted to use."

Saul, whose pride at his daughters' participation in a recent seder we quoted earlier, fondly remembered his father's seder as being very participatory, with everyone sharing in the reading and lots of discussion. Over the years, he continued, his family has accumulated its own distinctive seder customs. There is, for example, the cousin who had long wanted to go to B'nai Brak in Israel because the place is mentioned in a story in the haggadah, and one year he finally got to go. At every seder since then he has told about his trip at the appropriate point in the service. Another cousin tells the same funny story each year about a suit made by his father, who had been a tailor in Europe—the point here has nothing whatever to do with the holiday, except of course that it concerns a father delivered to America from a land of persecution. The story is a long-established part of family seder routine. "So we sort of have all these stories that we hear over and over again." Every seder in Saul's family ends with that same cousin telling the same joke at the singing of "Had Gadya." Stuart, still more poignantly, said that he remembers his childhood seders with special fondness because they were the only times when he remembers seeing his father totally happy.

We heard many such accounts. Our subjects, like Saul, seem to associate the holiday with family members present at the seder or absent from it as much as, or more than, they remember the recital of the haggadah text. Those seated around the table, partaking of the meal, as it were, occupy the foreground of both observance and remembrance. The reading, the dipping of the parsley, even the eating of matzo and horseradish, are in the background. They constitute the general framework, the ritual script, through which the meaning which matters most—particular, unique to each family—is transmitted. The script rarely *constitutes* that meaning.

We also interviewed Jews who, like Rebecca and Martha, remember or experience the seders as "toxic" rather than happy events because of the family dynamics on display around the table. Both women have found their way to observance of the holiday nonetheless, positive associations canceling out negative. But one wonders how many observances of Judaism do *not* take place in America because of such memories—a casualty of the inevitable linkage between family observances and family, with all the attendant ambivalence.

One final example is illuminating in this regard. Nancy, an active member of a Los Angeles Reform congregation, said that "we do Passover in my house a lot." (Indeed, her holiday observance as a whole is extensive.) She aspires to having two sets of dishes for Passover, and tries not only to "eat just matzo but to eat vegetarian that week, [which] gives me a way to sanctify and have holiness...." On the first night of the holiday Nancy generally joins in an all-women's seder. She is a lesbian, and women's issues loom large in all of her observance. On the second night she usually goes to other people's homes or to a seder at the synagogue. Her own seders have in some years featured music, and in others poetry or personal sharings. The holiday "is significant, really inclusive for non-Jews . . . a wonderful holiday."

Nancy's partner is not Jewish, and so we can infer that a celebration less universal in its import than Passover, as she interprets it, would not be acceptable—or would have to be radically re-interpreted in a way that conformed to her commitments. For example, Nancy prefers to celebrate Purim—notorious for the fight to the death between the evil Gentile Haman and the righteous Jews, Esther and Mordecai—not at her own temple but at a nearby gay synagogue, where other themes of the holiday important to her, such as costumes, masks, and the role played by the queen, are more appreciated. Almost all of Nancy's holiday observance is endowed with personal meanings that reflect her commitments to lesbian and progressive causes—meanings analogous to the family associations with which observance is laden for our "straight" subjects. Jews who are single, lack partners or children, and live far from families of origin have an especially difficult time with holiday observance—a subject to which we shall return.

⚜

The *Sabbath* is likewise intimately involved with family. For Jews such as Rebecca who have small children at home, the day's practices include Friday night dinner with spouse and children, the family lighting candles together, saying kiddush (the blessing over wine), and reciting the *motzi* (blessing over bread). They sometimes go to an early family service. For those without small children at home, Sabbath observance means primarily synagogue attendance either Friday night (Reform) or Saturday morning (Conservative). The meaning of the day for these Jews is therefore bound up in the meaning that they do (or do not) find in synagogue. Many view services as a time for personal reflection, a moment of peace in an otherwise hectic week. They do not focus on the content of the liturgy as such, and when asked about the meaning of the Sabbath rarely respond in terms of traditional themes such as creation or redemption. The day is holy because it is set apart from the other six days as a time for attention to what matters most in life, family first of all.

In Molly's home, each Sabbath the family reads prayers that have been written by her husband or their seven-year-old son. She tries to make Friday evening have a different feel, "not running out or worrying about getting the kids to bed or getting lunches made for the next day." Molly and her husband purposely do not go to services, because, she says, they feel the need to have a peaceable evening at home. She generally goes to synagogue alone on Saturday mornings. Their seven-year-old now "has *tefillah* [prayers]" three times a week at Hebrew school, so "it matters less" and he has stopped going with her. Her husband is not interested.

One woman told us that she had recently begun to light candles and recite the blessing over wine with her family by doing the appropriate actions to the accompaniment of a tape prepared by the cantor of her synagogue. Nancy said she observes Shabbat regularly: usually by lighting candles at home (except if she is running off to synagogue), and by not entertaining or spending money on Friday night—"It's a little much for me to do that on Saturday"—and, in general, by making a separation in some form. She tries not to work at her job on Saturdays if she can avoid it, and, if she has Friday off, spends much of it preparing for the Sabbath. Nancy regards observance as connected to the performance of good deeds, and the latter supersedes going to services. For example, she stayed away from synagogue one week and gathered donations for a friend going on a fund-raising ride for AIDS.

The specifics in these cases, as in others, are idiosyncratic. That itself is a major feature of observance among moderately affiliated American Jews today. But the pattern of selective observance—the individual practices chosen according to personal preference, within constraints given by the environment (e.g., the need to work late on Friday or on Saturday), and endowed with personal meaning—is nearly universal. The more active Jews in our sample do more of the prescribed rituals, and do them with greater regularity. For them too, however, the meaning given Sabbath observance is almost always personal rather than prescribed. It is a time to pause, a moment for quality time with family. Less observant Jews seem more content to have the day pass without any marking whatever. Our survey sample split almost evenly on the statement, "Even if I don't observe every aspect of the Sabbath, I do try to make it a special day": 47 percent agreed; 49 percent did not. This pattern is long-standing. Many American Jews at mid-century, Joselit summarizes, did not want to jettison the Sabbath entirely, but preferred to experience it on their own spatial and temporal terms (1994, pp. 252–259).

In all our interviews, we heard exactly one disparaging remark about Sabbath observance: the charge that it is outdated, because "in today's society we don't need a special day to rest and not do anything but stay at home and stare at the walls." The comment came from Sam, a teacher in Queens who is in his fifties, who also believes that dietary laws are unnecessary now that "there are strict health laws." His observations are notable because a generation ago such rejection of ritual practice, on grounds that it affirms or requires beliefs that are no longer relevant, was far more common. Our respondents seem to like observance, and to value it—in part because the meanings it carries are meanings that they themselves have supplied, and because they feel utterly free to pick and choose among ritual possibilities, without guilt or even self-consciousness.

✼

Hanukkah is apparently observed with greater regularity among moderately affiliated Jews than the Sabbath, at least when small children are in the home. The holiday comes only once a year rather than weekly. But it apparently carries no significant meanings and elicits no strong emotions. The festival appeared on virtually every list of observance supplied by our subjects (94 percent of the respondents in Cohen's 1991 survey claimed that they observe the festival at least "sometimes"), yet it occasioned virtually no comments by them. Joy described her observance of Hanukkah as "only social, just to have something to do at Christmas time." Asked to explain herself, she added, "It's not really a holiday, not a meaningful holiday. The meaningful holidays are the ones where there is something to think about or some kind of lesson to learn." Suzanne, we recall, observed only Passover and Hanukkah before beginning to use the candlesticks passed on by her mother, the reasons being that both holidays are child-centered, carry (in her view) a universal message of human freedom rather than a message that is particularist or religious, are observed by her at home rather than in synagogue, and have become part of Jewish culture rather than belonging exclusively (as would, say, Yom Kippur) to Judaism as a religion. We suspect that these sentiments are widespread, and that our respondents make a distinction between rituals performed only or largely for children, and those they themselves weight with meaning. It is also probably the case that Hanukkah's theme of religious freedom, which resonated so dramatically with American Jews of earlier generations, is less compelling to this generation, which takes its ability to practice (and not practice) Judaism for granted, and is looking for other meanings when it does so.

The *High Holidays*—Rosh Hashanah and Yom Kippur—present exactly the opposite dilemma. Their observance, while involving immediate family (e.g., children's services at the synagogue, eating apples with honey at home) as well as extended family (with whom meals or the break-fast are celebrated), is centered on a message that is adult—sin, atonement, forgiveness, mortality—and on activities that take place in the synagogue. These factors, as we have seen from Tony's comments at the start of the chapter, make the holidays difficult for many moderately affiliated Jews to observe. They believe they should be participating (and the vast majority of American Jews report doing so at least some of the time: see Cohen 1991b, p. 62), but they don't quite know how to endow Rosh Hashanah and Yom Kippur with personal significance.

Observance of the High Holidays also differs markedly depending on one's relation to Jewish life and Jewish tradition as a whole. Those who find themselves alienated from the community and are only marginally observant tend to have the most trouble with the High Holidays. Sarah, squarely in the latter category, reported that she "had a big Rosh Hashanah dinner" this year, has done something similar for the last several years, but "I don't think I even took the day off of work . . . it was really just the dinner thing." This year Sarah went to the Kol Nidre service and returned to synagogue for the morning prayers, staying until noon, "and then I decided not to go back so I went off to a park and wrote in my journal. So many people have told me that this is what they do on Yom Kippur that I thought, well, maybe it's the last year that I'll be in California and that seems like such a California type of observance." Last year Sarah woke up on the morning of Yom Kippur intending to return to the synagogue where she had been the night before, "got all dressed and I started to go and I thought, you know, I don't really want to go, it's kind of boring and the stuff that they do, I don't know, I don't have that many associations with Yom Kippur so I kind of like when they get to the more specific things like the shofar. I don't like the stuff that reminds me of the standard service." This year she was invited to a break-fast and so spent the day thinking about the day's meaning, lest she not observe it at all and feel hypocritical at the break-fast. She "felt kind of silly" anyway, Sarah confessed. "It taught me that I can't just skip the holiday and go to a break the fast."

As opposed to Passover, which is a holiday when "you can actually have other people participate in it with you," said Sarah, Yom Kippur is "a very personal holiday, so if you're not feeling connected it's hard to observe it. You can think, 'Well, I'm observing it in my own way,' but that is not necessarily doing anything that anybody else can relate to."

Sarah's formulation of the dilemma is perhaps extreme, and her response to it—journal writing and reflection—is indeed one we heard only from residents of northern California. (Joshua, like Sarah a single person in his twenties, reported that he spent Yom Kippur this year on an island in Hawaii. It was "a really good day of reflection, good to be out there alone for eight hours. I thought that was pretty much in the spirit of things.") The dilemma itself, however—what to make of holidays that seemingly demand belief that one lacks; how to be part of a community if one's observance is utterly idiosyncratic—is widespread. David confessed to serious problems with the message of Yom Kippur. In part, he came to the idea of confessing sins "through exposure to Christianity, [and so] saw this as a sort of Jewish hangover of ancient Christianity," which he now knows is the opposite of the historical chain of influence. More important, "the notion of getting into a meditative phase in order to atone for things . . . I've never felt comfortable with this sort of stock-taking. I know it's very different for my wife. For my wife it's a family thing." Steve, a New York psychotherapist, fasts on Yom Kippur but spends the day at home, reading. Joy and her husband fast part of the day, and they do not go to synagogue but rather spend the day at a museum with their children. Sarah put the problem most perceptively: "The thanking of God or the involvement of God doesn't mean much since I really am on the atheist end of the spectrum in terms of spiritual belief. That's why the holidays that are easier for me to observe are the ones that are tied into stuff you can do and tradition and symbolic objects and stuff like that." She was speaking for many American Jews here, we believe. The counterexample she cited immediately, the holiday to which she *could* relate easily, was Passover.

Scott, a single man in his twenties who recently took a year off from work and school to study in Israel, said that the critical moment for his developing interest in Judaism came when his older sister, who had lived nearby, moved to Boston, leaving him to fend for himself on the High Holidays for the first time. "All of the sudden, it strikes me that I am one of those Jews who doesn't do anything, and then goes to services on the High Holidays. . . . I thought I was never going to become that. I was very frustrated, because on the one hand, I felt like this was important to me; on the other hand, I didn't want to do anything about it." Rosh Hashanah and Yom Kippur had to have meaning if he was going to observe them, but there seemed to be no meaning attached to them that he could accept. He and a friend resolved to spend Rosh Hashanah together studying the *machzor* (prayer book) to see what they would discover there. And

> pretty quickly I realized that there was definitely something there, something for me as a modern adult that was very compelling. . . . in a way, the reason I didn't understand that as a kid growing up was because of a certain uncomfortableness, I think, in general in Reform Judaism and specifically which my mom had with things about the service. . . . This feeling [that] this is archaic and I don't want to believe in it but I have to. So I don't believe in sin, I don't believe in God sitting there writing in a book, the gates are closed. I don't believe in those things, but [he now realized] it was inconceivable that I wouldn't be there praying.

Why so? Because, Scott concluded, "regardless of whether you believe in sin and whether you believe in God sitting and writing a book, a lot of what the High Holidays are about is setting yourself around your community, which is a very hard thing to do with other people." One had to rectify relations with others, "and then there is some stuff with God, too." Scott without pause then proceeded to a memory of saintliness described to him when he was little by his grandmother. And then back to the present:

> I had this thing that was right there, it was fairly obvious but had never been emphasized, that . . . all the people I care about in my life are people I have tension with, like telling me exactly what I think and that I had done wrong. . . . that was the moment where I connected with tradition as an adult and I realized that lack of connection was partly the way I had been relating to it.

The freshness of the realization makes it especially vivid in Scott's account. His articulation of it is extraordinarily lucid. But the coming of age

in Judaism that he describes—the realization and acceptance of connection to tradition and community—seems quite typical. Saul, too, reported
that Passover had been his favorite holiday when he was a kid, but he now
finds greater value in Rosh Hashanah and Yom Kippur than he did as a
child. "It is obvious why: I think about things differently—not that I enjoy
fasting, but I find value in it." For Nancy, who fasts on Yom Kippur as much
as her problem with blood sugar levels allows, the day is a time for concern
"with inside process, and those symbols help me." She breaks the fast with
"a group of lesbians I hang out with." They share reactions to the various
services they have attended, and tend to be involved each year around the
holidays with helping someone deal with a death—"not always HIV, sometimes cancer." Even Joshua, who spent Yom Kippur meditating alone in
Hawaii, recognized that the High Holidays "raise questions about where I
am and what I'm doing and with whom. That is one of the things about
major holidays: 'All right, who am I spending my holidays with?' I don't
know, it's a big thing. It's not like I could just pretend it wasn't happening."

These comments explain why many Jews, who have never gone through
the process of "appropriating" the High Holidays for themselves as adults,
and so have never supplied those ritual occasions with their own meanings, find observance of Yom Kippur in particular very difficult.

🎴

Finally, we want to note the ways in which *Shavuot* and *Sukkot* came to
figure in the ritual calendars of several of our respondents, individuals
who by their own accounts, and ours, would likely not otherwise have
observed these festivals. An earlier survey found that only 28 percent of
American Jews claimed to observe Sukkot "always" or "usually." It did not
ask about Shavuot. (See Cohen 1991b, p. 62.) The point of entry to our
interviewees' practice in every case was a communal activity in which the
entire family participates. We have already heard from several respondents
about their synagogue's projects of sukkah building and lulav making; we
have heard, too, of study sessions on Shavuot involving other families or,
later at night, involving only other adults. Betsy spoke about the importance of joining a community in Los Angeles that was both comfortable
and a source of guidelines for observance, enabling her and her husband
to feel that they were "bringing up our kids with other families who feel
the same." She concretized what she meant about living in a community
with the description of the annual neighborhood "sukkah walk," in which
families visit one another's sukkot on the holiday and share meals. Nancy
spoke enthusiastically about Sukkot, telling us how she followed gardeners
around town to get the needed materials for the roof, and then built a
beautiful "social action sukkah," in which the *ushpizin* (mystical guests)
were role models. When she came to Shavuot, however, Nancy said only, "I
don't eat dairy well, so that's difficult. [It is customary not to eat meat on

the holiday.] Ten years ago I was more observant than now. I don't find any events related to it." Observance with no personal meaning attached to it atrophies.

Nancy is among the more observant Jews in our sample, and so both Sukkot and Shavuot (along with Simchat Torah, Purim, and even Tu Bishvat, a sort of Jewish Arbor Day) figure in her ritual calendar. All are days she observes with some regularity, and for which she therefore seeks and finds a measure of meaning, albeit in uneven measure. Less active Jews do not undertake this search, and have more difficulty succeeding in it, particularly if their congregations are not creative in assisting them. Jews who live alone and/or are not part of a community perhaps have the most difficulty of all in making the holidays meaningful. To the degree the focus of observance is the synagogue, such observance is accessible to all who wish to participate in it. Similarly, so long as the focus of significance is thematic —freedom and oppression, say, or sin and atonement, or other themes couched in general terms—this too is widely available to everyone possessing the requisite beliefs. However, once both practice and its significance have shifted to family, the case in large measure for the Jews in our study, a great many potential participants are left out. Like Joshua and Sarah, they have a hard time figuring out what to do with the holidays—and so with Judaism—because they have a hard time finding the Jews to do it with. Aloneness at holidays is especially difficult to bear. The natural inclination may well be to distance oneself from the holidays, and from the community that celebrates them, resulting in still greater alienation. The problem is not easily overcome, and may not easily be repaired if and when such Jews find partners and raise children.

SELF IN TRADITION, TRADITION IN THE SELF

We have emphasized throughout this study the degree to which Jewish identity and observance among our sample have a decidedly personalist cast. This is evident in the accounts of ritual practice which we have just examined in at least two different but related ways.

First, moderately affiliated Jews *choose what to observe and what not to observe;* they also decide, and take it for granted that they have the right to decide, with no one able to tell them any decision is wrong, *when* to observe, *how* to observe, and *how much* to observe. The rules of tradition— which after all make ritual into ritual, separate it out from the flux of life —exist as guidelines or opportunities, but exercise little compulsion or authority in and of themselves. Jews have of course disagreed with one another since the start of the modern period about what is required for proper observance of this or that ritual, as well as about who wields the authority to decide such questions. Our subjects are clear on the second matter: authority rests with each individual or family. As many as 83 percent of the participants in our survey agreed that "it bothers me when people try to tell me that there's a right way to be Jewish." The Jews we met are simply not concerned with disputes about what constitutes proper observance. The question of what is "correct" according to a particular movement within Judaism has been supplanted in their minds by the question of what is meaningful to the individual or family performing the observance. Eclecticism is now the rule when it comes to practice. Consistency is no longer prized. Theology is virtually irrelevant.

Consider the following collection of comments, most of which we have already encountered.

> SARAH: "I do the holidays if I'm free. . . . Sukkot . . . is a holiday where I really would like to do something, but it comes so close on the tail [of the High Holidays] that ironically I have felt kind of wasted . . . so I haven't done anything for that holiday although it is one that I like. . . ."

> JOSHUA (commenting on Passover): "I think I generally find the meaning in being aware of what I'm doing rather than in exactly the sense of deprivation. . . . Even looking at the Sabbath, I break thousands of rules. . . . [When he decided recently to work on the Sabbath] I sacrificed that perfect streak of so many years of not working on a Saturday, but on the other hand . . . I don't know if that's the sort of thing I want to do in terms of keeping perfect records over long chunks of time, I don't know if that's important to me."

> SCOTT: "I am always going to be in this exploration. . . . I [once] felt like I had to do this [observe a particular holiday], because I was supposed to do this. It was like my mother wanted me to. [But then] I thought: I don't have room in my life for this sort of thing. Either I want to do it, and it is part of my life, or I don't want to do it, and it's not, and my mother will have to be disappointed. . . . The mitzvot? . . . I just don't have much of a connection with them right now."

> GIL (after describing an extensive calendar of observance and his leading role in his temple's sukkah project): "Since many holidays fall during the week, for example, Shavuot next week . . . I could rearrange my [work] schedule but it's hard. I try to attend the first day, but [the] others I don't."

> TONY: "I have tremendous difficulty with High Holiday services. Sometimes I go to hear Kol Nidre. This year I didn't."

> SAM: "Each individual has to decide the proper way to serve his religion. My way is not right or wrong, it's just my way."

American Jews, as Sarah put it with her usual directness, "do the holidays" if they are free, because they *are free* to do them or not to do them as they please. The constraints in which they operate (for example, work) are not those of the tradition or the community but a function of the Gentile environment. America moves in a much larger space and to a different calendar than Judaism, making the choice for Jewish time and space not only optional but problematic. The individual stands before the holidays waiting to be persuaded to enter into them and to pay the attendant cost in departure from the mainstream. He or she must decide, as Joshua put it, if "that's the sort of thing I want to do," "if that's important to me." Many factors enter into such decisions: prior experiences with the holidays; attachment to a community that observes them; protection of one's own autonomy; unresolved issues (not at all limited to people in their twenties) about doing "what my mother wanted me to."

Seeing oneself as an explorer, valuing the journey more than the arrival—common features of identity among the current generation of Americans, Jews and non-Jews alike (see Roof 1993 and Wuthnow 1999)—reinforce the refusal to submit to the authority of tradition when it comes to observance. So does the American (and modern) credo, voiced with stunning clarity by Sam, that it is the individual's right to decide what is right for him or her in terms of religion. There is no right or wrong way for Sam to behave. There is only *his* way.

The commitment to autonomy relates to a second aspect of personalism evident in these comments as well as in others that we encountered: *the insistence that each ritual take on a meaning which the person observing it has supplied.* Recall Sarah's desire for a haggadah "that I wanted," one that would contain only messages significant for her and in agreement with her commitments. Or consider Joshua's comment that the meaning of a given practice for him lies "in being aware of what I'm doing rather than in exactly [for example] the sense of deprivation" from eating matzo, "the bread of affliction," at Passover. "I'm never quite sure, it's a boundary that I wonder about, whether I really want to take out all of the grains and all of the beans" (which are forbidden by tradition during Passover). Suzanne could have been speaking for nearly every one of our subjects when she said, "I have to feel like it's coming from inside out, and isn't just somebody else's idea of a ritual." Sarah expressed a similar sentiment: Yom Kippur—and every other ritual occasion, for that matter—"is a very personal holiday, so if you're not feeling very connected it's hard to observe it."

These comments describe the reality of observance as the vast majority of moderately affiliated American Jews experience it. If they have come to a particular observance, it is because of an *experience of its meaning.* In most cases, that significance is highly personal in the most basic sense: wrapped up in biography and family. If the meaning disappears over time, the observance will cease. Attention will either come to focus elsewhere in the tradition—a different ritual serving as the occasion for the experience of Jewish meaning—or it will wander outside the framework of Judaism to a different setting altogether. The tradition is rife with ritual opportunities, and American Jews are perhaps more aware of them than in previous decades thanks to adult education programs and to more widespread observance, which in turn leads to still more observance by providing experiences of its appeal. But there will always be Jews who are not exposed to these opportunities or who are not excited by them when they are exposed. Such Jews will look elsewhere for significance, and Jewish rituals will in their homes go unobserved.

In the attempt to explain these patterns, we have turned both to theorists of ritual generally and to previous studies of Jews and Judaism in America. Several classical accounts remain particularly potent sources of explanation. It remains the case, for example, that ritual maintains and enhances collective consciousness in the way emphasized by Durkheimian theory. The "separation of sacred from profane, seventh day from the six days of creation," in the words of the havdalah ritual at the close of the Sabbath, serves to separate "Israel from the nations." Passover is the most obvious example. It connects Jews with their ancestors, and elicits memories of those ancestors, as Jews inside the holiday's structured performances say the same words the ancestors said, taste what they tasted, smell what they smelled. Parents savor the opportunity to pass on such a tradition to their own children, hoping as they do so that years and decades in the future the children will have their own seders at which the parents of today will be recalled. These are indeed "elementary forms of religious life," to borrow the title of Durkheim's classic work, foundation stones of Jewish identity which have become all the more crucial now that belief in a God who commands observance has so diminished. In a recent national survey of American Jews, 83 percent agreed that "during major Jewish holidays, I feel a desire to make sure my children feel connected to Jewish tradition" (Cohen 1991b).

In part, too, these ritual satisfactions are wrapped up in the holidays' role in maintaining group boundaries—the feature of ritual that is stressed by Mary Douglas in *Purity and Danger* and other works. Moderately affiliated Jews want their children to be Jews (in whatever way the children feel is right for them), and they hope both they and their children can accomplish this distinctiveness without sacrificing other parts of themselves or good relations with the rest of American society and culture. Our subjects value holidays in large part because their rituals provide positive experiences of life *inside the boundary* that the rituals maintain, thereby validating the point of keeping that boundary in place. They also find the holidays troublesome (recall Passover seders with non-Jewish family members and universalist haggadot) to the degree that the observances draw lines with which our subjects are uncomfortable. One could, following Douglas's lead, usefully chart the level and intensity of observances in relation to the actors' sense of how high and how firm the boundaries separating Jews from non-Jews should be, and how they interpret each particular observance according to that measure.

94

A distinction advanced by anthropologist Roy Rappaport (1979, 1988) is of particular interest here. Rappaport differentiates "canonical" messages, conveyed by religious practices—themes invariant across time and space—from "indexical messages," which serve to distinguish the performers of the ritual from all others, whether these be members of other communities or of the same community. Both sorts of message are problematic to moderately affiliated American Jews. "Canonical messages" by definition hold true universally. They are valid for all performers in all generations and circumstances, and are usually couched at a level of generality sufficiently vague as to make possible such universal relevance and commitment. Our subjects seem discontented with such messages precisely because their generality has rendered them trivial. They find less appeal than previous generations did in universalist themes such as oppression and liberation, desiring meanings that are at once more Jewish and more personal. Yet they would also reject (or refashion!) a Passover message that was overly particularist or God-centered. Any "highest-order meaning" of substance is likely to elicit strong disapproval; any claim to "eternal truth" will be rejected regardless of its content simply because the claim to possess such truth is deemed unacceptably arrogant.

For the same reason, our subjects reject "indexical messages" that separate them overmuch from other Jews—or, for that matter, from non-Jews—and resent being regarded as less of a "good Jew" because their observance does not conform to Orthodox norms or Reform expectations. Yet they value ritual precisely because it confirms and transmits a distinctive identity of which they are very proud. The contradictions are many—but, with the rare exceptions that we have cited, they do not trouble the Jews whose eclectic and personalist observance manages to contain them.

The determination to choose observance freely from among an available menu and to endow it with highly personal meaning is further illumined by Erving Goffman's analysis of the rituals of "deference and demeanor" which are commonly performed in the modern world, not in the context of religion but in the context of everyday life. All of us regularly offer tribute to one another, Goffman argues, and claim it in return. These rituals instruct us that "the self is in part a ceremonial thing, a sacred object which must be treated with proper ritual care and in turn must be presented in a proper light to others." They also supplant, in many cases, acts of deference and demeanor paid in respect to God. As Goffman puts it, "Many gods have been done away with," but—or rather, because—"the individual himself stubbornly remains as a deity of considerable importance" (Goffman 1967, pp. 91, 95). One finds it as hard to imagine moderately affiliated Jews separating milk from meat because "God demands it" or "the community requires it" as to see them bowing in obeisance to the "Lord of all creation" or repeating formulaic praises of the "Lord whose word brought the world into being."

There is, of course, no necessary dichotomy between obedience to divine (or communal) commands and the discovery of highly personal meaning in those actions. The rabbinic ideal with regard to ritual performance was the unity of *keva* (fixed, routine observance) and *kavvanah* (personal intention). That synthesis, however, may well have been honored over the centuries more in the breach than the observance. According to one view of things, moderately affiliated American Jews are merely shifting the balance rather decisively from *keva* to *kavvanah*, without actually abandoning either of the two. It is also true that any ritual, religious or not, must maintain a balance between the script which guides individual performance—the rules making the ritual what it is, recognizable both as ritual and as this particular ritual—and the creative originality that breathes life into the script and makes each performance unique, thereby keeping the ritual alive as one that people seek to perform. To survive, a ritual must be open enough to allow for individual intentions, interpretations, or even innovations. Jewish tradition has long supplied, and celebrated, a variety of interpretations for its many observances, and new efforts in this direction have of late been plentiful in the United States.

However, ritual must also be closed enough to remain a communal form that is shared despite the differing intentions inevitably brought to it. This is the issue raised by the patterns of practice we have surveyed. The danger of excessive closure is abandonment of the ritual. But the opposite danger, excessive openness, is no less clear—and was evident to several of our subjects. As Sarah put it, "You can think, 'Well, I'm observing it in my own way,' but that is not necessarily doing things that anybody else can relate to." Autonomy, subjectivity, personalism can go too far—precluding the experience of tradition and community that, for our subjects, is a primary motivation, meaning, and satisfaction.

❧

We believe the degree of autonomy and personalism exhibited by our subjects, combined with near-universal openness to ritual experience, stands in contrast with the pattern analyzed by leading scholars of American Jewish life a generation ago.

Marshall Sklare and Joseph Greenblum, in their classic study of Jewish life as it was then developing in the suburbs in the 1950s, proposed that five conditions need to be in place in order for a ritual to "command" widespread observance. Its message had to be formulated in *modern, universal terms*. It had to *involve no social isolation*. The practice had to *accord with the religious culture of the surrounding Gentile community* and provide a legitimate Jewish alternative to it. It had to be *child-centered*. Finally, its performance had to be *infrequent*. One can readily (and Sklare did) explain the popularity of the Passover seder in these terms. Working backward from the fifth condition to the first: the seder takes place only once a year; is directed explicitly at children; is a spring festival, temporally adjacent to Easter and concerned with analogous themes of rebirth and redemption; is performed in private space (a home or synagogue) and private time (evening) that do not conflict with work or citizenship; and, finally, declares a message unquestionably universalist in its appeal—witness the existence of "freedom seders," "interfaith seders," and "women's seders," all of which draw heavily upon the symbols and texts of the original.

Charles Liebman (1990), supplementing Sklare's analysis, theorized that American Jews, indeed modern Jews more generally, tend to minimize the importance of ritualism—investment of significance in the details of actual ritual performances—and to give most weight to moralism: the effects of a particular practice upon the spiritual and/or ethical life of the performer. Recall Nancy's notion—extremely common among Reform Jews of generations past and, as her own example proves, still evident among Reform Jews today—that Sabbath observance is subservient to a "real mitzvah" such as social justice or charity. Liebman argued further that the authority underlying ritual has shifted in the modern world, and especially in America, from God to the community.

Ritual performances are therefore better described as ceremonies than commandments. This is in fact the terminology used by Spinoza in his critique of Judaism, and accepted even by Moses Mendelssohn in his defense of the tradition and its authority. In twentieth-century America, Mordecai Kaplan, the founder of Reconstructionism and a major influence on American Judaism in all its forms, translated mitzvot as "folkways." The "commandments" became "customs" performed by Jews as expressions of Jewish culture and commitment rather than of belief in a divine commander. We saw something of this as well. Recall the linkages made by Joshua and Scott between observance of ritual and identification with the community. As Scott put it, the main business of Yom Kippur concerns one's relations with the community, "and then there is some stuff with God too." He felt he had to observe the day, despite lack of belief in a divine judge, because not to do so would declare his separation from the community—and that is not something he wished to do.

In several respects, these analyses should be modified, or taken further, in order to take cognizance of the developments which the Jews in our sample represent. First and foremost, the significance of Jewish practice among moderately affiliated Jews cannot be understood primarily as either ritualism or moralism, but as what we might call, in the same vein, "familism" (a pattern related to, but distinct from, the historical familism discussed in chapters 2 and 5). Jews value ritual because it brings them closer to grandparents, parents, partners, spouses, children, and grandchildren. They conceive of Jewish peoplehood, as we have seen, as the spatial and temporal extension of this family: *mishpoche,* to use the Yiddish word featured prominently in Jewish fund-raising appeals. They do not enter into sacred spaces and times because this makes them better or more holy. Nor is the authority for their acts communal. Rather, they have experienced holidays as a framework in which powerful meaning, cognitive and emotional, is provided. This meaning, as we have seen, is above all that of being connected to generations before and after, and includes the satisfaction and joy of membership in a community that exists around the world and does things of which American Jews are proud. Passover seders, lighting candles on Hanukkah or the Sabbath, sitting down as a family for "quality time" together on Friday night are activities invested with the deepest emotion and significance known to the individuals we studied. That is why they are content or even eager to return to these activities again and again. In part, mere nostalgia is operating here: the same motives which lead our subjects to watch old movies, pore over family photo albums, or revisit the scenes of their childhood. But we think the significance of Sabbath candlesticks inherited from one's mother and grandmother, or of a seder prepared and conducted in the manner of parents and grandparents, goes far deeper. It *commands* in a way that God and community do not. It *signifies* on a level no mere script or liturgy can match.

Second, the political dimension at work in ritual choices is somewhat different than it was previously, even if the need to find a balance between apartness and inclusion, distinctiveness and sameness, remains the same. Some members of our sample are eager for a degree of "social isolation" inconceivable to their parents, perhaps because America is now prepared to grant it without penalty, a consequence of multiculturalism and pluralism. The social interaction of Jews outside the ritual, we might say, now seems assured. Difference can safely be celebrated, and to some extent all of our subjects do so. (Otherwise they would belong to the unaffiliated and less active segment of the population, outside the purview of this study and of almost all communal life.) Certainly, Orthodoxy still involves a proclamation of essential apartness too radical for most American Jews to undertake. Nevertheless, there has been a profound change in the sensibility of this generation of moderately affiliated Jews in comparison with generations past. They are not particularly afraid of antisemitism and have little experience of it. They are also not passionately patriotic in the manner of their parents. They take for granted the legitimacy of hyphenated identity in a pluralistic society. The operational question in their minds, then, is *why* they should be different, within the broad scope for difference that America in their view provides them. Given good reasons for ritual practice, the Jews we met are willing to engage Judaism at least in some degree.

Finally, the significance of the "alternative religious culture" about which Sklare and Greenblum wrote—Christianity—has greatly altered. The great bulk of American Jews now have close non-Jewish friends, many of whom participate in ritual occasions such as the seder. What is more, a significant number in our sample reported having dated non-Jews, and in the course of those relationships confronted Christian holidays directly. An increasing number of American Jews, of course, have non-Jewish spouses, whose presence may enrich religious performances but without doubt complicates the celebration of Jewish distinctiveness.

Note, however, one of the most striking omissions from virtually every ritual calendar reported to us: Christmas. This observance is now regarded almost universally by the members of our sample as beyond the pale, and it seems to be a major object of contention between the members of intermarried couples. In our survey, 69 percent agreed that "having a Christmas tree would violate my sense of being Jewish." Among Jews married to other Jews, 76 percent agreed with this statement, as opposed to just 23 percent of Jews married to Gentiles. Christmas is the negative boundary marker par excellence. It is the observance which bears the "indexical message" on which there is most consensus—Christmas is not celebrated simply because "we are not they," and to celebrate it would declare the opposite. The Jews in our sample do not wish to make any such declaration.

By contrast, Thanksgiving is celebrated nearly universally by our subjects, and with great enthusiasm—"religiously," we are tempted to say—the only non-Jewish holiday on the American calendar that seems to be either widely practiced among Jews or regarded as existentially meaningful. New Year's Day and July Fourth are occasions for parties, if that. Thanksgiving is taken far more seriously than New Year's Day and July Fourth, because its observance proclaims the message that one can be fully a part of American society and culture, can partake of its highest ethical and religious ideals, and yet remain who one is: a Jew who is no less an American than any other (and no less Jewish) by dint of the hyphen in one's identity.

✺

This is a time, in sum, which encourages the performance of increasing numbers of rituals, and the invention of new and diverse meanings for them. America has become a place where ritual continues to offer Jews possibilities for adherence denied by creedal affirmations, and where exploration and experiment are rife. Time will tell whether the involvement with Jewish observance proves long-lasting—or whether, if it does in the patterns we have witnessed, the subjective meanings ascribed to performance will strengthen or weaken attachment to the tradition and the community which Jewish rituals until now were meant to serve. We have our doubts on both counts.

99

ECHOES OF TRIBALISM

It's not just the food. I do like the sense of belonging to an ancient
culture. . . . You can go to any corner of the world. Apparently, there are
synagogues in China. And you can hear the same liturgy. I love that tie
to something traditional and historical. . . . This is one of the ways that
you kind of hold on to . . . one of the things about Judaism that I don't
want to let go. I do like this tradition of values. Education and philanthropy are very important things to me and that's very Jewish—the
culture, the tradition.

—JOY

For centuries, being Jewish has meant something other, and something
more, than professing a religious faith; Jews have constituted at one and
the same time both a nation/people and a religious community. According to the Torah, the master story of Judaism, the Israelites who gathered
at Sinai entered simultaneously into two covenants, which bound them
and their ancestors ever after to one another at the same time as the Israelites bound themselves to God. Where Christianity, Islam, Buddhism, and
Hinduism became world religions that included among their members
individuals of diverse nationalities, Judaism remained until the modern
period the religion of one people, the "children of Israel." Its adherents
regarded themselves—by virtue of their *faith*—as members of "a *nation*
that dwells alone," and so they were regarded by others.

That has continued to be the case to some degree even in the modern
West, including contemporary America—this despite the fact that most
Jews in the United States also regard themselves as fully a part of the
American people, and would without hesitation proclaim America to be
the only nation to which they belong. As Leonard Fein and other observers

have remarked, Jews are the one American collectivity which sees itself, and qualifies, as both a bona fide religious group and as a full-fledged ethnic group. While America is home to numerous ethnic churches that serve primarily immigrant and second-generation populations, the intertwining of religion and ethnicity for Jews goes far beyond the ties characteristic of such churches, and has survived despite generational distance from immigration (Fein 1988; Glazer 1972). Jews are like Protestants, Catholics, and Muslims, but they are also like Irish Americans, African Americans, and Chicanos. In America too, it seems, there can be no Judaism without a Jewish people—and vice versa.

That is not to say that modern Jews, in America and elsewhere, have not repeatedly chafed at this linkage, and tried to shed one or the other component of their dual identity. Radical exponents of Reform Judaism in nineteenth-century America and Germany attempted unsuccessfully to transform Judaism into a community based on faith alone. Jews would be defined exclusively as "co-religionists," their nationality being that of the country in which they claimed citizenship. Secular Jews, conversely, have tried in America as in Israel to fashion a notion of Jewishness devoid of religious practices and belief. They would be Jews solely by virtue of ethnicity or ancestral culture, their religion accepted as an aspect of that culture in the past but denied any present relevance. These efforts too have met with only limited success.

Most recently, ardent Israeli secularists have been chagrined to learn that the popularity of Jewish religious practices in Israel has rendered that country the single most observant Jewish community in the world—not at all what Israel's secular founders had in mind. Jewish Israelis, it turns out, not only subscribe to a "civil religion" fashioned largely from the tenets, practices, and calendar of Judaism; this was a predictable development in a nation which sees itself as heir to the religious tradition that sustained the Jews for two millennia in exile. More surprisingly, Judaism is important to the Jewish citizens of the Jewish state on a personal level: its practices are meaningful, its God believed in and worshipped (Liebman and Katz 1997; Liebman and Don-Yehiya 1983).

We wondered if this linkage would prove equally potent among contemporary American Jews: whether a generation, integrated as never before into the mainstream of America, and attracted as never before to aspects of Jewish religiosity such as spirituality, family ritual, and personal journey, would continue to feel strongly about their membership in the Jewish people. We noted in chapter 2 that the self-conception of moderately affiliated Jews continues to carry a major component of tribalism. The Jews we interviewed maintained that they are Jews because they are Jews, period; Jewish identity in their view remains intact, irrespective of non-observance or non-Jewish marriage partners, and is transmitted automatically to children even if the latter receive no education whatever in Jewish history or tradition. Having one Jewish parent in the home, we were told, is sufficient to guarantee the Jewishness of a couple's offspring, and the Jewishness of *their* descendants, barring actual conversion to another faith, is likewise guaranteed forevermore.

But would the Jews who clung to this tribal self-conception maintain a strong sense of connection to fellow Jews of the current generation, or would they shy away from it? Would the sense of group belonging diminish —it has decreased among all other white American ethnic groups (Waters 1990)—as Jewish self-definition comes to revolve increasingly on a vague notion of spiritual journey and the practice of rituals in the home? Do American Jews today regard themselves as a part of the larger society or as apart from it? How distinctive do they really feel among Gentile Americans? How do they appraise the danger of antisemitism? To what degree do they subscribe to the ancient and fundamental premise of Judaism that Jews are different?

The answers, we discovered, are complex: a mix of tribalism and universalism not unlike the combination of tribalism and personalism, obligation and autonomy, which we noted when probing the identity of the sovereign Jewish self. As in previous chapters, we shall let our interviewees speak in their own words, and shall put what they say in the context of our quantitative survey. Before doing so, however, a few words of definition and historical background are in order.

"JEWS ARE DIFFERENT"

We use the term "ethnicity" in this study to refer rather broadly to a sense and pattern of Jewish group belonging, more substantive and comprehensive than "bagels-and-lox Judaism" or borscht belt comedians (although, as we have seen, there is far more of substance to Jewish food and Jewish humor than scholars and rabbis have commonly recognized). In contrast to the term's colloquial usage, which conforms by and large to the sort of watered-down "symbolic ethnicity" first conceptualized by Herbert Gans (1979; see also Waters 1990), the term is used here to refer to everything about being Jewish that differentiates it *formally* from a Protestant religious denomination. For simplicity's sake, and for these limited purposes only, we count as "religious" all matters of faith, ritual, and congregational membership, while we include in "ethnicity" all other communal or collective aspects of being Jewish: all manner of attachment to Jewish family members, neighbors, secular institutions, and the Jewish people worldwide. This semantic division is somewhat arbitrary, of course. For reasons already explained, Judaism and Jewishness have been inseparable over the centuries, and remain so to some degree in contemporary America. But the distinction does provide some inkling of the territory to be surveyed in this chapter, as we study a generation which has evinced more than a little discomfort with the self-definitions that have bound faith to peoplehood heretofore.

At the heart of Jewish ethnicity, we recall, is the notion of "historical familism" (Liebman and Cohen 1990). The *historical* side of the term is expressed in the extent to which Jewish religion, culture, myths, and symbols have been centered on the historical memory (factually accurate or not) of the common ancestors and experiences of a particular people. The *familistic* nature of being Jewish has embraced a number of elements deriving from the fundamental assumption that Jews are a people related to one another by ties of blood, ties which make them far more than simple "co-religionists." In this as in other forms of tribalism, *particularism* (preference for one's own kind, generally accompanied by a lesser opinion of all others) prevails over *universalism* (equal regard and concern for all human beings); *collectivism* (the perception that one derives—or should derive—meaning, norms, significance, and location primarily by virtue of relationship with the group) proves more powerful than *individualism*. Three aspects of this pattern of historical familism are of particular interest for our study of moderately affiliated American Jews.

Let us begin with the fundamental familistic assumption that "Jews are different"—distinguished from all others not only because of what they *do*, but also because of who they *are*. As such, Jews are (or should be) *familiar with one another* in the various senses of that term. One can (and should) go to any corner of the world, as Joy pointed out, and find Jews who share "the same liturgy" and the same "tradition of values." One expects and finds a common sensibility among Jews wherever they live, born of common historical experience. Jews are also familiar in the sense that they presume to know one another well and feel comfortable in each other's presence. They treat each other with familiarity (often of the sort that does indeed, as the saying goes, breed contempt): that is, they forgo a manner of polite interaction that characterizes gentle (and much Gentile) society. Observers have noted in American Jewish institutions (Woocher 1986) and the entire state of Israel (Avruch 1981; Liebman and Cohen 1990, pp. 21–26) relatively heightened expressions of familiarity such as nurturing, invasion of privacy, and the forgoing of the rules of civility—all features of "the shtetl" (real or imagined; see Zborowski and Herzog 1952) that follow on the fact or presumption of intimacy.

Jewish familism, secondly, demands *mutual responsibility*. For centuries, Jewish communities have organized endeavors of mutual assistance for Jews both near and far. Rabbis, teachers, parents, and community leaders have pronounced care for the widow, the orphan, and other sorts of needy Jews a divine obligation. Rescue of Jewish captives took precedence over practically every other commandment. Jews have long paid special heed to oppressed communities in other lands, organizing elaborate enterprises of relief and rescue such as those in recent decades on behalf of Jews in

Ethiopia and the former Soviet Union. The sense of familism expressed in this special concern for other Jews has also meant that Jews have thought it fitting and proper to extend special preference to one another in business dealings, politics, philanthropy, and other areas beyond the private sphere of kin and friends.

Finally, Jews before the modern period generally held *rather unflattering images of non-Jews and correspondingly positive images of themselves* (Katz 1961a). Jews saw Gentiles as, among other things, intellectually limited, prone to violence (both toward their own family members and to Jews), boorish, dishonest, sexually promiscuous, and easily inebriated. These images made up a view so central to the Jewish collective consciousness that it barely requires elaboration. Along with them was the presumption that *most Gentiles inherently hate Jews.* Passover, Purim, and Hanukkah, as well as the more recently established Holocaust Remembrance Day, constitute only the most prominent examples in the ritual calendar of the focus upon Gentile antagonism to Jews. (A recent joke that made the rounds on the Internet asks how one might best sum up the lesson taught by major Jewish holidays. The answer: "They tried to kill us. God made sure we won. Let's eat.") The classic rabbinic view held that "Esau hates Jacob"—wherein Jacob represented the Jewish people and Esau embodied all manner of non-Jews, but especially the Roman Empire and Christianity.

The power of that view has diminished of late in America, but it has not entirely disappeared. Notwithstanding repeated demonstrations by contemporary historians that Jews lived during much of their history with relative stability and security, the Jewish collective memory still emphasizes forced expulsions and violent waves of persecution against a backdrop of ever-present social and cultural antisemitism. This picture persists even in America, and even among Jews who have not themselves personally experienced antisemitism. It has perhaps been nourished by the unspeakable horror of the Holocaust and the continuing threat—or sense of same—to the existence of the state of Israel. Holidays still carry a subtext, never far from consciousness, that insists: "They tried many times in the past to kill us, and almost succeeded. They will try again. Be careful."

Taken together, these three elements of historical familism constitute traditional Jewish "tribalism." In somewhat weaker form all have remained concomitants of present-day Jewish "peoplehood"—the alternative term, less offensive to contemporary ears, that describes Jews whose sense of self and other has been revolutionized by the twin developments of Emancipation and Enlightenment. This transformation is well known, and we need not recount it here. Suffice it to say that modernity has constituted a grave challenge to the tenets of tribalism which held Jews heretofore. The opening of Western society to Jewish participation on an equal footing meant an end to—or at least a lessening of—the social, residential, and occupational segregation that long undergirded tribalism. Even before Emancipation commenced in the late eighteenth century, the politically autonomous communities (*kehillot*) in which Jews had dwelled for many hundreds of years had lost their authority to the centralized governments of emerging states. Jews were subject to direct taxation and conscription. Their children began to go to state-sponsored schools. They dispersed and integrated: residentially, occupationally, politically, and socially.

It was immediately apparent that traditional Jewish particularism clashed with the norms of modern Western society and would have to be adjusted. For Jews eager to gain acceptance into the societies that had until recently excluded them—and that still seemed not entirely eager to welcome Jews as full members—expressions of particularism in ritual, liturgy, and folk stereotypes posed contradictions and connoted danger. Jews laying claim to equal rights could not continue to practice apartness, let alone to presume superiority. Nor did it make logical or political sense to presume, let alone proclaim, that the Gentiles whose society they sought to join were ineluctably antisemitic. Over time, Jews internalized universalist and personalist conceptions that left no room for inherited notions of Jewish chosenness. Prayers and rituals that emphasized the elect status of "Israel" were reinterpreted or excised, part of a larger effort to calibrate and proclaim the appropriate measure of Jewish distinctiveness—in some detail (Eisen 1983).

Many Jews over the past two hundred years actively or passively opted out of membership in the Jewish group, assimilating into the nations newly inviting their belonging. At the other end of the spectrum, a small but growing number (known today as the *Haredim* or "ultra-Orthodox") worked diligently to fence out modernity in an attempt to preserve the traditional Jewish way of life intact. Peter Berger (1980) has noted insightfully that for all traditionally minded religious groups in modern times the struggle to separate from the larger society constitutes an unavoidable departure from the socially supported separation enjoyed by ancestors whose ways the descendants claim to carry forward. More recently, Menachem Friedman (1987) and Haym Soloveitchik (1994) have noted the distinctive pattern of laxness and stringency characteristic of ultra-Orthodox Jews who derive their sense of how things should be from books written by selected rabbinic authorities rather than from life—that is, from a reality transmitted (and altered) from generation to generation. This strategy, derided by Jews bent on integration as well as by sociologists convinced of its futility, is nonetheless alive and well in contemporary America, as in Israel. Its practitioners wield significant political power and exercise a significant hold on the Jewish imagination. Hasidism, whether in Woody Allen movies, *New Yorker* covers, or the psyches of countless American Jews, has come to represent authentic Judaism, the real thing, as opposed to the ersatz varieties of Judaism born of the other survival strategies employed to navigate modernity. The latter are all premised explicitly on compromise with the surrounding Gentile world and, unlike assimilation and self-segregation, are well represented among the Jews under study here.

One possibility, which Berger calls the "reductive option," involves the surrender of the norms, symbols, and practices that conflict most sharply with a group's modern surroundings. Jews remain Jews, but on terms believed compatible with prevalent notions of non-tribal religion or religion-free ethnicity. They might remove objectionable prayers or parts of prayers from the siddur (for example, passages suggesting superiority to other groups: Mordecai Kaplan banished all references to Jewish chosenness on these grounds). They might also radically re-interpret prayers and activities to bring them into line with universalist sensibilities. "Freedom seders" and "feminist seders" at Passover exhibit this strategy, as does the notion that Jews are chosen—but so are the members of every other group.

A less radical step consists of "privatization," in which the problematic belief or practice is consigned to the private sphere of family and close friends. "Be a Jew at home and a man in the street" went a popular (and oft-misunderstood) saying (Stanislawski 1988). Other analysts refer to these or closely related efforts as "compartmentalization," that is, the reserving of certain spheres in one's life for traditional Jewish activities and perspectives, while tacitly accepting that the tenets of Judaism will be silent or irrelevant in other areas. Jews would in this case feel comfortable expressing tribalist sentiments among their most intimate associates, but would feel bound by modern, universalist ideas in the conduct of their lives in the public sphere (work, politics, less intimate associations, etc.).

Still another possibility entails "re-interpretation," a feature of every tradition in every time and place but especially pronounced in contemporary American Judaism. Potentially discordant elements of Jewish culture and religion are recast to comport with the perceived demands of integration into the larger society. Alternatively, the understanding of modern culture can be recast to permit some traditional Jewish features to remain more or less intact. An example of the former move is found in the transfer of traditional Jewish concern for needy Jews, always accompanied in principle by concern for the needs of Gentiles, to a contemporary endorsement of social justice activities on behalf of all members of society and the world. "Tikkun olam," repair or perfection of the world, has for centuries been urged in the Jewish prayer book, but until the last few decades in America would not have been pronounced a major "Jewish value." An example of the latter maneuver—recasting society, or attempting to do so, in order to bring it into line with Jewish commitments—is found in the promotion by Jews such as Horace Kallen of "cultural pluralism" as an alternative to the melting pot as a grand conception of ethnicity in American society.

More and more Jews during the past few decades, opposing efforts to diminish, downplay, and minimize ethnically based differences, have come to see Jewish ethnic distinctiveness in a new and more positive light. They were perhaps influenced by the Black Power movement (Carmichael and Hamilton 1967) and the increased popularity and legitimacy of white ethnicity (Glazer and Moynihan 1963; Novak 1971). Heightened ritual observance, as we noted in chapter 4, in part betokens a greater willingness to enact Jewish distinctiveness and in part signals greater tolerance on the part of American society for such distinctive enactments. America has extended greater acceptance to Jews, and to other minorities, at the same time as Jews have achieved ever higher levels of wealth, education, and social status. All of this has made it easier for Jews who so wish to proclaim their remaining ethnic difference in whatever degree.

We found evidence of all these processes at work in our face-to-face interviews as in our quantitative survey (except, of course, for total assimilation at one end of the spectrum and total self-segregation on the other, both of which were excluded by the parameters of our interview sample). Moderately affiliated American Jews, as we would expect, are more prepared to express tribalist sentiments than less involved Jews, particularly when the latter are married to non-Jews. They are, however, less ready to do so than more involved Jews, particularly when the latter are Orthodox. The Jews we met tend to privatize and compartmentalize their tribalism, choosing certain spaces and times in which to express it. They accept the validity of familistic preferences for Jews in the private sphere of friendship with less hesitation than in the public sphere of desired government policy (and state such preferences less often overall than Jews of the previous generation). Practices deemed incompatible with participation in the larger society have long since been discarded. Others, objectionable in their original form, have been re-interpreted. Relative to their ancestors—and perhaps even to their own parents—they have abandoned historic negative images of non-Jews, particularly the notion expressed in the Yiddish saying, "Scratch a Gentile and you'll find an antisemite." Yet a degree of unease or suspicion regarding Gentiles remains.

In sum, ethnic distinctiveness—historical familism, tribalism—continues to be maintained and even celebrated, though not without lingering hesitations, anxieties, and misgivings. It is telling that a significant majority of our sample rejected the outright assertion of difference when the question was put to them in these terms. Two-thirds agreed with the proposition "My being Jewish doesn't make me any different from other Americans." At the same time, most survey participants and interviewees agreed that there is something about being Jewish that non-Jews can never understand. Few went so far as Lee of Connecticut, who said, "I'm proud to be a Jew because I'm different. Being Jewish is a strong commitment to being different." But there seemed to be widespread assent to the assertion by Amy of Los Angeles that Jews *are* different for the simple reason that they "live in a Christian country. By not being Christian, Jews are different. It's not as obvious in large cities, but there is an absolute difference."

We believe, for reasons to be elaborated below, that the survey responses reported in this chapter downplay the extent to which Jews harbor feelings of distinctiveness and insecurity. Those feelings emerged more readily, because indirectly, in the extended give-and-take of four-hour interviews. Jews remain different in their own eyes, we believe, whether they are moderately affiliated or not—distinctive, both subjectively and objectively, in ways unique to the present generation. All three of the dimensions of historic familism outlined above—shared familial sensibility; unique responsibilities born of transcendent belonging; the assumption of Gentile antisemitism—are still in place, but all have been significantly transformed.

FEW ENCOUNTERS WITH ANTISEMITISM,
AND FEWER FEARS AS WELL

Let us begin with antisemitism. The Jews we interviewed are aware that they make up a tiny fraction of the American population. It is self-evident to them, perhaps above all else, that they are not Christian. Amy's comment picks up on this theme, one that emerged repeatedly in our investigation. We will see in chapter 7 that American Jewish conceptions of God are distinctively Jewish in large part because they are not Christian, i.e., they lack the component elements of Father, Son, and Holy Spirit. More broadly, the explicitly Christian world remains a clear boundary for Jews. Even the least Jewishly involved among our interview sample agreed that, to use the words of our survey, "having a Christmas tree would violate my sense of being Jewish." No less than 79 percent of the respondents to the survey agreed with this statement. Paul and Rachel Cowan, writing about interfaith couples more than a decade ago, spoke of time bombs that explode when children in the home are old enough for their parents to confront questions of holiday observance in particular and religious identity in general. Jewish partners often became agitated over the thought that their children might participate in Christian holiday practices or acquire a Christian religious identity. We will return to this point below. Our concern here is to observe that Jews, while aware of this boundary marker separating them from what they are not, i.e., Christians, do not attribute to that marker the negative *valence* which it once possessed. They are not better because they are not Christians. No less important, they do not assume as a matter of course that Christians as a matter of course hate Jews.

This is new. The bulk of American Jews in the first two-thirds of the twentieth century—the upbeat, publicly expressed expectations of rabbis, communal leaders, and intellectuals notwithstanding—viewed the phenomenon of antisemitism with mixed emotions and perceptions. Discriminatory restrictions in the areas of employment, housing, higher education, resorts, and politics in the first half of the century, as well as numerous personal slights, offensive remarks, youthful violence, and highly publicized incidents, all served to create and reinforce the impression that antisemitism persisted in the United States. The tragedy of the Holocaust, though it happened elsewhere, heightened fears that "it could happen here." True, antisemitism in the United States ran contrary to official American ideology, and was ever less pronounced in polite society— yes, it had declined in prevalence and virulence—but American Jews saw it as persisting nonetheless. Survey evidence through the early 1990s has seemed to demonstrate an ongoing high level of concern among American Jews concerning Gentile prejudice against them, even in the United States (Cohen 1984, 1989a; Chanes 1995; Kosmin et al. 1991). This is true despite the clear finding in numerous social scientific studies and surveys of steady declines in antisemitic stereotypes among the American population (Smith 1991).

The evidence for the persisting Jewish concern with antisemitism rests primarily upon survey questions asked over the years that refer to Jews' assessment of the phenomenon as a "serious problem," as well as questions that refer to the possibility of antisemitic outbreaks in the future. Perhaps this observation may explain why our own respondents, both those interviewed in person and those in the random survey sample, seemed relatively lacking in concern about antagonism to Jews. They have not experienced serious problems, and so have no reason to expect them in the future. Quite typical were the comments of Joy of New York, who said, "I don't think I have ever experienced antisemitism. There was one incident once, way back somewhere, and now I don't even remember what it was. I should. It was probably traumatic." One or two of our older interviewees recalled antisemitic incidents from their childhoods. The following comments by Sonya, who was raised in Kansas City in the 1960s, represent the most serious reference to personal antisemitic experiences that we could find in our interview transcripts:

> I had quite a few antisemitic little incidents when I was in grade school, nothing to call the papers about, but kids really being mean. Like kids taking me to their country club, saying you can come because you're my guest, but you would never be able to belong here. It was always very clear that I was different and I felt it—in grade school, I was the only Jewish kid in my class until junior high and then there were just a few.

The findings from our personal interviews, along with the pertinent results on the survey we conducted, point to less rather than more concern with antisemitism in America, which represents a significant break with traditional images of the permanently hostile non-Jew. When asked their views on the statement "One day American Jews will probably face severe antisemitic persecution," just 28 percent concurred (only 6 percent strongly agreed). Only one respondent in four agreed that "Jews are widely disliked by Gentile Americans" (and only 3 percent strongly agreed). Even fewer (19 percent) agreed (with just 3 percent strongly agreeing) that "as a Jew, I feel like somewhat of an outsider in American society." This sentiment was, however, articulated fairly often in the interviews. So was the notion that "Jews are different," particularly (as Sonya put it) if they are personally observant: "Religious Jews are different. Non-religious Jews are not different," for the simple reason that such Jewish practices as they maintain tend to occur in private space and time. Many of our interviewees gave qualified endorsement to the idea that Jews are the chosen people, and (as we shall see in the following chapter) opinion varied on the interpretation of the Holocaust. Some respondents said the Holocaust taught a universal lesson about the evil of which human beings are capable or which God is inexplicably prepared to tolerate. Others—such as Ed of Chicago—learned from Hitler that, in Ed's words, Jews have to "watch their backs."

These results may of course co-exist with the claim that antisemitism remains an important problem for American Jews. But taken together with the earlier reported findings, they do suggest an American Jewry less anxious about their neighbors' alleged antagonism—hardly surprising given that American Jews have become comfortable with having non-Jews as neighbors, co-workers, and friends, and an increasing number have dated or married Gentiles. The newly emergent confidence in Gentile acceptance accurately reflects the positive changes in America's attitudes toward Jews. At the same time, it is likely a function of more porous group boundaries: cause and effect of a diminished emphasis on the ethnic or collective side of being Jewish.

A related change has occurred in the images used by Jews to describe other Jews on the one hand and non-Jewish Americans on the other. We were struck during the course of our conversations with how often particular, and quite traditional, images recurred, often in an oblique fashion. Among the more positive were those that cast Jews as intellectual or as possessing a certain recognizable intellectual style or as simply being smart. Some spoke of Jews as extraordinarily successful in achieving higher education and high social standing, an observation borne out by numerous quantitative studies (see for example Hartman and Hartman 1996). Others spoke proudly of Jews' strong sense of community, philanthropic commitment, and readiness to engage in activities dedicated to achieving social justice. We heard references as well to Jewish personality character-istics, as in these comments by Joy:

> There are funny aspects of my personality that my husband jokes are Jewish. I am the world's greatest worrier. I am the world's most guilty person. It's kind of the Woody Allen Jewish. It's not anything that I really learned in temple or from my parents. It's just that I am that way.

We also uncovered a variety of *unflattering* stereotypes of Jews among those we interviewed, many of which relate to the interaction between Jews and the rest of society. Steve, for example (like Joy a New Yorker), com-plained about Jews "seeing themselves as more important than other peo-ple. In some ways I find that troubling." Rachel of Chicago articulated a more widely held concern: "Clearly it is the stereotype of Jews: loud, brassy, obnoxious." Joy said in a similar vein, "I came across those few girls who were Jewish and I thought that being 'JAP-y' was being Jewish and that bothered me a lot." (JAP stands for "Jewish American Princess," an unflat-tering term for a young Jewish woman who is allegedly shallow, materially oriented, and self-centered [Prell 1999].)

The significance of these particular images can be appreciated only if we realize that they are distinctive, if not actually unique, to Jews. Members of few, if any, other American ethnic groups are as concerned with their members appearing to non-ethnics as loud, showy, and materialistic. At the same time, Jews have held these particular stereotypes about them-selves ever since their entry into modern Western societies; the images re-flect what Cuddihy perceptively titled the "ordeal of civility" to which Jews became subject as they moved upward on the social ladder with unprec-edented rapidity. Large numbers of Jewish entrepreneurs, running busi-nesses small and not so small, came to acquire the income and possessions of the middle and upper-middle classes without having first acquired the education and acculturation that generally accompanied such income. The problem, as Prell demonstrates (1999), was particularly acute in post–World War II America, coloring relations between spouses, and between parents and children, that are reflected in our interviews. The jokes about Jews' obsession with worldly success in many cases reflect a very real ob-session with worldly success. Like the nouveau riche everywhere, Jews new-ly arrived in the middle class engaged in conspicuous consumption to signal and display their newly acquired wealth and social status. But un-like other groups, Jews were also laboring to overcome centuries of exclu-sion and contemporary prejudice which had resulted in the fact that they, in mid-twentieth-century America, found their ethnic prestige at the low-est in the list of all white ethnic groups (Laumann 1966).

We found only one other major set of negative images of Jews, and it is associated with those who—objectively and in the opinion of our respondents—are most visibly set apart from Gentiles: the Orthodox. Neither our questions nor our interviewees' answers made a clear distinction between Modern Orthodox and *Haredim* (or "ultra-Orthodox"), but it seemed to us that interviewees' comments most often referred to the latter. At one time, the Orthodox of both types represented an admired segment of American Jewry. At least until the late 1960s, they stood for the highest standards of piety and Jewish commitment, even if their levels of observance and learning were seen as personally unattainable by their admirers. Moreover, unlike Israelis (many of whom resent Orthodoxy's official power and political influence), few American Jews have historically harbored deep antipathy to the Orthodox among them.

Much of that seems to have changed. Our random sample survey uncovered widespread unhappiness with Orthodox Jews. Almost four-fifths of all respondents (79 percent) disagreed with calling the Orthodox the most authentic Jews, a sign of diminished admiration. A plurality (47 percent) said that they were not grateful to the Orthodox for doing so much to maintain Jewish life. Slim majorities also agreed that Orthodox Jews are narrow-minded (51 percent) and said that they are bothered by Orthodox Jews' feelings of superiority (52 percent). One key to these negative views of the Orthodox can be found in reactions to Orthodox treatment of non-Orthodox movements in Israel. A very wide margin (80 percent to 12 percent) agreed that they get upset when Orthodox Jews in Israel try to limit the practice of Conservative and Reform Judaism there.

These data point to at least three different sources for the hostility felt for the Orthodox. One entails the tensions in Israel over such matters as conversion and "Who is a Jew?" and the standing of Conservative and Reform Judaism there. American Jews, as we will see in the chapter which follows, experience these tensions as a challenge to the legitimacy of their own Jewish identities. A second factor is Orthodoxy's forthright adherence to traditional Jewish attitudes that sharply contrast with the voluntarist and personalist values of American society generally and American Jewish identity in particular. Orthodoxy demands and claims adherence to an unchanging and binding ancient religious law, whereas most non-Orthodox Jews feel free to pick and choose among the variety of Jewish customs, rites, and ceremonies in line with their personal feelings and beliefs. Traditional Judaism (and Orthodoxy) tie Judaism to a demanding daily calendar of ritual observance, establish clear criteria for the right way to be Jewish, and enjoin Jews to reproach fellow Jews for failing to abide by Jewish law. None of these views are popular among most American Jews, nor —apparently—are the chief proponents of such views. Finally, the Orthodox—and in particular the ultra-Orthodox—are visibly and inescapably different from Gentile Americans. They thus challenge not only the authenticity of non-Orthodox modes of belief and practice but—perhaps more important—the legitimacy or viability of the accommodations made by non-Orthodox Jews to their surroundings.

Our in-depth interviews provided graphic elaboration on all these themes. Many respondents were struck by the seeming oddity of Orthodox practice and the worldview that seems to underlie it. Joy, for example, commented:

> We have some friends who are very religious. I was the architect who renovated their house. They kept a kosher home. I mean, they didn't answer the phone on the weekend [the Sabbath] and the whole bit. I wonder if I am critical of it. I guess I am a little bit. Oh man, the light switches, everything! The toilet paper holders, Kleenex holders, were built into the bathroom walls because they couldn't tear toilet paper on the Sabbath. It was ridiculous. So, I guess I am a little critical of this but not too much. It's their life, not mine.

Rachel's comments were more openly critical:

> I often wonder how it would feel if I were Orthodox and wore a black coat. I'm trying to marry modernity with Jewish tradition. I believe I can live in both worlds. They don't. So I feel like they are perpetuating a stereotype in the eyes of non-Jews. I wish more Orthodox were more open-minded.

To our interviewees, Orthodox Jews (presumably the most traditional variety thereof) certainly seem strange. But idiosyncratic behavior and appearance is not the only issue here. Rachel was concerned about the perception of Jews among non-Jews. In contrast, David expressed a concern with what may be called Orthodox cultural imperialism, the challenge to non-Orthodox legitimacy and authenticity.

> I have a lot of prejudice against the Orthodox which I try to work on. . . . I've learned a little about why people are Orthodox, but to me it's still pretty strange. It doesn't bother me as long as they don't make me do something. They can do whatever they want. . . . If they wanted to take over Hillel [at the university where David works] and make Hillel into Chabad [the outreach arm of the Lubavitcher Hasidim], I wouldn't be too involved in Hillel.

Some Jews, clearly, are still different in the eyes of contemporary American Jews, and alarmingly so—signaling the fact that the latter have not completely lost awareness of their own difference. Our respondents did not give voice to negative stereotypes of Gentiles, but they did articulate positive stereotypes of fellow Jews. They expressed no concern with anti-semitism, but repeatedly used images of Jews that betrayed anxiety lest Gentiles find Jews too Jewish. Tribal loyalties, in short, are not as they used to be. But the awareness of group difference remains keen.

MEMBERS OF THE TRIBE

Most moderately affiliated Jews also continue to think of their relationship to other Jews as a matter of belonging to a group that extends "vertically" through time and "horizontally" through space. In this sense, we may speak of "transcendent belonging," a feeling of deep connection to previous generations and future generations as well as to Jews of today who are scattered around the globe. As Sonya told us, "I don't always feel like I belong, and sometimes I resist belonging, but bottom line, I have this huge need to feel like I belong and I think I get it more from the Jewish world." In a similar vein, Rachel commented, "I have more in common with Jews [than with others], a shared history." Steve—who like Joy and Rachel is among the less involved Jews in our sample—said what he likes about being Jewish is that he is "a member of a group that I feel good about." What is it about being Jewish that is most important to him? "Just again feeling a part of the group. Seeing that as my identity." How important is being Jewish in his life? "Only somewhat important . . . the times that are religious, I mean the holidays, and [if] there was a group that was against Jews I'd be strong and stand up and feel strong about who Jews are. But it is not a big part of my daily life. I have not given a lot of thought to it."

Such sentiments—and the complexity they betray—are widely held. In our survey, 94 percent agreed that "Jews are my people, the people of my ancestors." Almost as many (90 percent) agreed with another statement evoking transcendent belonging: "Being Jewish connects me with my family's past." Similarly, 96 percent said they were "proud to be a Jew." The survey asked respondents to assess the importance of several items to their sense of being Jewish. As many as 84 percent regarded the item "The Jewish People" as very or extremely important. In our interviews, Peter (a self-employed professional from New Haven who is married to a non-Jew but is intent upon providing his sons with bar mitzvah ceremonies) spoke warmly of his family's historic connection with being Jewish. From there it was an easy and graceful move for him to conceive of all Jews as members of his extended family or tribe:

> It is the extended family in the most extreme example. To my knowledge, every marriage in my family that has gotten me to this point has been a Jewish marriage, so it is natural to think of Jews in general as my family. I mean, maybe it's just a term or a semantic thing, but it is sort of a tribal thing. Maybe that is just my term for the biggest family.

Appreciation for a transcendent, historic connection with Jewish people and culture emerged repeatedly in our interviews. Gita, one of our less traditional interviewees, nevertheless could readily say, "I like being part of a culture that goes back so far. I like learning about the history of the Jews. Despite great oppression, Jews have survived." In this remark she echoes a parallel sentiment endorsed by nearly all (94 percent) of the respondents in our survey, who agreed with the statement, "Jews have had an especially rich history, one with special meaning for our lives today." Gita went on to express the other dimension to Jewish belonging: the "horizontal" connection with contemporary Jews in far-flung communities around the world. "When I travel I like to find out if there is a Jewish community in the place where I am going and to visit their synagogue." We heard such sentiments repeatedly. They betoken more than what Philip Rieff (1966) has aptly termed "the pleasure of agreement." For Jews, participation in a history stretching back three millennia means rejoicing in collective survival against the odds and achievement out of all proportion to the Jews' small numbers: a mystery that, even without belief in divine providence, constitutes a powerful "signal of transcendence."

The particular circumstances of one's upbringing and prior experiences leave enduring imprints upon how one conceptualizes Jewish belonging and attachment. Individuals who grew up in majority environments, as well as those who grew up in areas with only a small number of Jews, claimed that those particular circumstances permanently influenced the way in which they saw themselves as Jews and the way in which they continued to seek connection with other Jews. Gita, who now lives in Berkeley, described the impact of having lived in New York, the area with the largest concentration of Jews in the United States:

> I think I am now and I will always be a New York Jew no matter where I live; that's just part of who I am. I love being with other New York Jews when I find them. I like going back to New York. I feel very much at home there even though I wouldn't like to live there.

In contrast, several interviewees—mirroring Amy's comment about the greater visibility of Jewish difference in small towns—told us stories of how experiencing a minority social situation stimulated appreciation of their own distinctiveness. Ken, a Los Angeles filmmaker in his early thirties, is in this respect not at all atypical:

> I went to Columbia; it was a very Jewish world. Then I went to Phillips Exeter Academy to teach. I expected to be an outsider and I was, but it was a welcoming place that encouraged diversity. Ten to twelve percent of the kids were Jewish. I did feel isolated. I put up a mezuzah on my suite —one other counselor came up to me and revealed that he was a Jew. I started an affair with a non-Jewish woman who was very serious about me. She read books about Judaism. I told her I was uncomfortable—I felt maybe that I should go find my people. Almost the same week I got a letter from HUC [the Reform rabbinical school] inviting me to a weekend for potential rabbinical students at Cincinnati. Why me? I decided

to go . . . I met the woman I went to Israel with [later on]. We began a relationship. I got involved helping the chaplain to Jewish kids at Phillips Exeter. But it all started at the moment when I said, *"I need to find my people."* (Emphasis added)

Ken experienced his minority status at Phillips Exeter keenly, and recoiled from the prospect of marriage to a partner who, unlike him, belonged to the majority culture. He was far from alone in this. Quite a few interviewees explained to us that dating non-Jews, or close romantic relations with non-Jews, had provoked their search for Jewish belonging. The Cowans, in their work with interfaith couples, married or otherwise, also report numerous instances of heightened Jewish attachment or the start of a process of exploration stimulated by relationships with non-Jewish partners. Intermarriage and interdating, we found, serve to focus the mélange of tribalist and "post-tribalist" elements previously examined.

Indeed, the ambivalent relationship many Jews bear to the Jewish group, the lingering sense of familism along with the diminished emphasis placed on group solidarity, all emerge clearly in narratives of how our interviewees came to marry their husbands and wives. Somewhat typical were remarks offered by Reuben. Asked about whether his future wife's religion was a concern of his, he responded:

> I think it was. . . . But I would say not the most important aspect. I think what it [her being Jewish] did, it did in much more of an insidious way, in that you recognized as we started spending time together there was a certain kind of common language. It had to do with knowing how to pronounce gefilte fish and knowing, essentially, what a seder is about. Immediately there is a sense of shared language. And that certainly was the case when the discussion came about children, the feeling you wouldn't have to worry in terms of with which religion they would identify. . . . It meant that there was a whole class of scary things [like child-rearing] that you say, this won't be scary because we have this common bond.

Several observations are worth noting here. Insofar as Reuben attaches importance to his partner's Jewishness, it is not because of a grand ideological or religious principle. Rather, he thinks in highly personal terms relating to shared language, culture, and ethnicity. In this regard, he makes explicit reference to food and the Passover holiday—the specific aspect of Jewish ethnicity that brings the family around the ceremonial dinner table (and stands in opposition to family Christmas celebrations, in which many Jews refuse to participate). Note, too, how shared language becomes especially important in the premarital discussions of child-rearing, i.e., the continuity of vertical belonging. We will return to this theme at the chapter's conclusion.

For many, the attention given to the dating partner's Jewishness clearly

increased when thoughts turned to marriage, although the matt
entirely cut-and-dried. David's ambivalence at the time is appare
recollection:

> I clearly felt very comfortable marrying a Jewish girl. I had nor.
> girlfriends and had been quite serious about a couple of them, not to the
> point of getting engaged or anything, or even discussing that, but I clear-
> ly would have contemplated marrying a Gentile. At one point, I had a
> Mormon girlfriend. I could not have married a Mormon who would have
> wanted me to be a Mormon.

For David as for many others, the absolute outer limit to ethnic flexibility
was the need to personally remain a Jew, recalling the observation made
earlier that Christianity remains a foreign territory that Jews resist enter-
ing. That issue aside, David felt a greater comfort with Jews, but, again,
there was no strong principle or ancestral obligation mandating that he
marry a Jew. Debby, a homemaker in her thirties who lives in suburban
Detroit, expressed a more unambiguous position on the matter:

> I dated both Jews and non-Jews in college [at the University of Michigan,
> which had a large Jewish student population]. I looked at non-Jewish
> guys as those you played with, and Jews as the ones to have serious
> relations with. Once I was out of college, I dated only Jews, except the one
> before I met my husband.

Family issues—the prospect of marriage, thinking about child-rearing—
served to make Jewish dating partners more attractive, if not essential.
However, even for Debby, even with her professed commitment to dating
Jews when she was serious about finding a husband, the last romantic
partner before her husband was non-Jewish. We are not in any way making
light of Debby's concern for establishing an unambiguously Jewish family.
Rather we wish to note a common feature of contemporary American
Jewish life: that even Jews with serious concern to marry a Jew often find
themselves in relationships and marriage with non-Jewish partners. Apparently, their attractive features, at least for the time, outweighed the short-
coming of their "non-Jewishness."

Our interviewees' modal stance—explicitly favoring Jews for reasons of
ethnic comfort—may be contrasted with that of individuals for whom Jewishness was altogether less important, and stands in contrast as well to the
position of those for whom being Jewish was more critical. Brad, a clinical
psychologist in Manhattan, provides an example of the former in this
interchange, which combines a declared universalism on principle with a
preference for Jews on a purely personal basis:

> INTERVIEWER: "Did you find either Jews or Gentiles to be attractive or
> unattractive?"

BRAD: "I judged people on a more independent basis."

INTERVIEWER: "So when you decided to get married, was your future wife's religion at all important to you?"

BRAD: "I was very happy that she was Jewish."

We may infer that Brad viewed the first question as calling for an expression of ethnic particularism, and so provided a quick universalist reply. The second question was couched in more personal terms, enabling him to provide an answer expressing personal preference without implications for conduct in the more public sphere of the larger society. (Brad understood the word "religion" in our question to mean "ethnicity"—neither partner was observant—in accordance with contemporary American Jewish parlance.) Joy professed even greater indifference in her choice of husband: "I never had a Jewish boyfriend until my husband. His immediate predecessor was Persian. I lived with him for about four years. I sort of thought I was going to marry him, but I didn't. Then I met [her current husband] and he won me over."

Joy, Brad, and many others whom we met portrayed the choice of a Jewish spouse as a matter of a socially probabilistic happenstance. They reported having a weak preference for a Jewish mate at the time, but said that preference was not so strong as to rule out serious romantic relationships with non-Jews. Social networks, probably heavily consisting of Jews, operated to provide them with their future Jewish husbands and wives. Sociology was more influential in this regard than psychology, or, more precisely, social networks played more of a role in producing in-marriages than did an explicit ethnic motivation. The latter no doubt also played its part, consciously or unconsciously. We of course cannot precisely fathom the depth of preference for Jewish romantic partners and, eventually, spouses. (We also tried, with little success, to learn if our interviewees found Jews more or less physically and sexually attractive than Gentiles.) Perhaps, for complex psychological or cultural reasons, interviewees presented themselves as more autonomous—more independent of the blandishments and demands of parents, other family members, and the Jewish tribe as a whole —than they actually were. We cannot know for sure, since all we have are their own self-portrayals, but we remain skeptical about the claim of indifference to the spouse's ethnicity—in part because we heard it so often.

There were exceptions to this pattern; some interviewees, possessing a clearer sense of Jewish involvement in their lives when they were dating, provided more vigorous and explicit expressions of interest in their prospective spouses' Jewishness. Betsy explained that she had married her husband because:

> his way of "Jewishing" was similar to mine. We grew it together. He was studying with a rabbi in Fresno and . . . I joined him in studying. We

talked about kashrut and decided we would be doing it at home, but [would] eat out [of the home] milchiks [dairy products]. We gradually got more observant.

For Betsy, as for many others, Jewish involvement is a dynamic process. The appeal of her husband, at least in retrospect, was that he too presented a fluid but committed version of Judaism, a model that she found personally compatible, if not attractive.

Jewishly more committed individuals, like Betsy, searched for spouses whose Jewish identity approximated their own, a difficult task given their own state of Jewish flux. The more committed seemed to have devoted more effort to thinking through the type of Jew whom they needed to marry. Scott, a young single man at the time of the interview, illustrates this pattern:

> The main thought on this dating/marriage/Jew thing is that my life has been in transition for the last five years. I feel like I have been in a state of flux and a state of learning. I certainly realize that I am not going to rest somewhere where I can easily say, "This is the kind of Jew I am, and therefore I need this kind of person." . . . I am always going to be in exploration, and so it will be difficult to do that with someone who does not identify with that in some respect. I don't know if someone who is not Jewish can really identify with that. It is more a question of who I am in the sense that being Jewish is a fundamental part of me, and so my partner needs to be able to identify with that. I don't have this clear thing that people who aren't Jewish can't do it.

Several points about this comment are striking. First, we need to recall that Scott has recently become more involved in Judaism, having taken time out of his life for exploration of his religious identity and traveled to the spatial center of the Jewish group to do so. He is unusually reflective about a process of deepening Jewish commitment, and even avows that "being Jewish is a fundamental part of me." Against all this, his theoretical openness to marrying a non-Jew is startling, or rather *would* be startling for someone of his parents' generation who was so Jewishly involved. It is not unusual for his own generation, as we have seen, which tends to think about Judaism in more personalist and individualist terms. These allow Scott at least to contemplate the possibility of marrying a non-Jew despite increased adherence to the beliefs and practices of Judaism.

The other feature of his comment that bears noting, no less typical than the first, is the high level of subjectivity, reflectiveness, and dynamism (some may say "plasticity") that characterizes his Jewishness. Scott seems to contradict himself on the matter of whether he would, indeed, contemplate marrying a non-Jew. Being Jewish at this point in his life, and perhaps forever, is about search, exploration, growth, and change. It is not about commitment. True, at the age of thirty-two, and thus among our youngest interviewees, Scott is less fixed than most in his commitments. He is still not seeking an enduring conception of Judaism, nor does he expect to find one. But the sovereignty of his self, indeed the very notion of a self in perpetual quest, is, as we have seen, not at all unusual. Nor is the fidelity shown to modern American conceptions of romance, which argue that anyone can fall in love with anyone, thereby finding fulfillment for the persons who they "already are." These notions bear profound implications for the nature and force of group belonging.

A small number of interviewees by contrast provided evidence of being heavily influenced by Jewish norms and social contexts when they met and pursued romantic partners. Ken, for example, met his wife through a prayer group in Los Angeles.

> They had a guy who . . . fixed me up. He invited me to lunch with his sister, his wife's sister, and a third woman. [W, one of the three] told her entire life story on our way home from shul. I met her at another lunch date afterward and saw her at a Hanukkah party. I decided to marry her in part because the peaks and valleys of her life matched mine.

Lynne eventually married a "very good friend from the kosher kitchen" at college. "We were best friends and he is now my husband," she said, even though at the time they met, "both of us had non-Jewish significant others."

The prayer group and the kosher kitchen provided the setting, the back-drop, that made meeting another Jew more likely. However, in contrast with what we suspect were patterns of a previous period in the postwar American Jewish community, neither participation in an intensive prayer community nor affiliation with a kosher environment in college was sufficient to *necessitate* traditional commitment in other spheres of Jewish life. Such participation, though, did betoken a level of Jewish involvement, at a time of openness to finding a mate, that increased the chances the mate would be a Jew. Both Lynne and her future husband were dating non-Jews at the time they met at the kosher kitchen, further proof that American integration and all it entails—personalism, voluntarism, autonomy—co-exist with heightened Jewish activity, all the more so before one has reached maturity. One meets other singles in both Jewish and non-Jewish settings. Jews in such situations may eventually find themselves married to Jews, or they may not—we follow the passive voice used by our subjects, despite our suspicion of it—depending on which social context manages to produce the contact that leads to romance and marriage, and in which context the new couple decides to spend its time together.

One final example should make this lesson clearer still. Liz of New Haven, like Lynne very active in her Jewish community, met her husband-to-be in another circumstance structured by a Jewish context.

> I met K within the year that my father had died, shortly after I got back
> to school. . . . December was my father's Yahrtzeit [anniversary of his
> death]. . . . Well, you look in [the town where she was in school] and see
> if you can find a Yahrtzeit candle. K went off, drove to [a nearby city], and
> got me a Yahrtzeit candle. He came back with a prayer book, and we lit
> this candle in my dorm room, and he cried with me.

The sense of connection to the tribe runs very deep here; Lynne experienced it at the moment of most profound loss and disconnection. Note,
however, that the importance of the Jewish partner is not rooted in religious obligation per se but in personal emotion born of loyalty to family.
It is a matter of direct vertical belonging, and of shared language and
experience with the fellow Jew who understands that sentiment immediately.

❧

Before considering the sense of mutual obligation elicited by this sense
of personal connection, we want to examine one other sort of personal
relationship in which American Jews of the current generation exhibit a
complex pattern that diverges somewhat from the pattern documented by
sociologists several decades ago: friendship.

Almost half the respondents in our survey said that most of their closest
friends were Jewish, though we suspect that for many the balance of Jewish
to non-Jewish friends was probably the same as for Rachel, interviewed in
Chicago: "I'm tempted to say [the ratio was] fifty-fifty, probably more are
Jewish than not. But I have a large group of non-Jewish friends from [my
husband's] work and from school." We noted earlier the special sense of
familiarity that one experiences with members of one's own ethnic group,
the feeling that some patterns of communication are better understood
and appreciated by members of the in-group than by others. A slim majority (52 percent) of respondents in our survey agreed with the proposition "I feel that, as a Jew, there is something about me that non-Jews could
never understand." We regard this statement as setting a fairly demanding standard of the concept under discussion, stricter, for example, than
"Generally, Jews understand me better than non-Jews." Only half of the
Jews polled subscribe to it.

Brad expressed the notion of presumed familiarity when he commented:

> I definitely find friendships [with Jews and non-Jews] to be different,
> because there's the shared crazy stuff about growing up Jewish, like
> having a Jewish mother, and certain things are almost indigenous to
> Jewish people, and I find it quite humorous. I think you can sit down in
> a room and tell who's Jewish and who's not just by hearing the things that
> people say.

Joshua, who lives in Berkeley, joined the pleasure of easy communication with another advantage of friendship: the trust of fellow Jews.

> To me it comes down to questions of trust, like would you trust someone to stay in your house after you meet them. I think in terms of those questions of trust, I tend to arrive at a place much quicker if they're Jewish, whereas otherwise there is a greater degree of trying to figure out who someone really is. . . . I guess I sense a certain camaraderie with a number of Jewish artists who I sense are somewhat similar to me in terms of being male, and Jewish, and artists and left-wingers, who also identify with religion. I see four or five people spread over the country; it's like a small club.

Scattered evidence over a variety of surveys suggests that the more intimate the relationship, the more likely Jews are to associate with one another. Thus, Jews are more likely to have Jewish spouses than Jewish friends, and more likely to have Jewish friends than Jewish neighbors. One demographic study reported that Jews report more Jewish spouses, proportionately, than (to use the term adopted by some social scientists) "POSSLQ's" (persons of the opposite sex sharing living quarters). Similarly, questions about one's "three best friends" produce higher proportions of respondents with mostly Jewish friends than do questions about "close friends" or "friends" which are unqualified.

Several of our interviewees said they maintain more intimate friendships with Jews than with non-Jews. These relationships may be emotionally richer, less segmented, and less compartmentalized. Saul, a New Haven physician in his forties, said:

> To me there's always been a bond with fellow Jews that simply is not there [with non-Jews] no matter how nice or outstanding a person these other people may be. When it gets down to real friends, I've always felt I could always count on my Jewish friends because there was always a real bond there.

Henry, a European-born New Yorker in his sixties, provided a particularly vivid accounting of the difference between his Jewish and non-Jewish friendships, one which may in part be a function of his generation and origin:

> I do have non-Jewish friends and some of them are very close to me, but, I don't have *non-Jewish families* that I am friends with. To give you an example: I have a [non-Jewish] friend . . . who was a colleague of mine and we became very close friends. . . . [But] I have absolutely no opinions about his family and I don't think he has any opinions about my family. We happen to like each other very much, because we have common interests, we have a lot of common things on intellectual levels, we both love Beethoven, we have an affinity for certain conductors, we like music. . . . But I have absolutely no affinity to his friends, his family. It's a

friendship not anchored into anything else but our personal sympathies. . . . With my Jewish friends, I love their families, I love their kids. There's a relationship with these things and it goes much deeper. So, yes and no. Yes, I have non-Jewish friends, but on a wider scope, we do not have the same relationship that I have with my Jewish friends.

Note that the mark of Jewish friendship in this case is the connection to actual family, which in Henry's experience can occur only inside the large extended family constituted by the Jewish people. It is a "bond," as Saul put it, a source of what Joshua called "trust," that comes only in the context of a lasting bond which transcends particular circumstances. Over three-quarters of our survey respondents agreed with the statement "Jews have a permanent bond." The word came up frequently, in many contexts, in our interviewees' descriptions of their relationship to other Jews.

Several individuals spoke explicitly of what may be seen as the flip side of the special relationship with Jews: the difficulty in establishing comparable friendships with non-Jews. Rebecca, a homemaker in Chicago, said that most of her friends and all her closest friends are Jews because:

> There is a kinship, a common bond, an understanding of one another at the same level. I feel most connected and closest to those who are Jewish. I have friends in the community who are not Jewish, though they are not my closest friends, except one who is a Japanese-American and grew up in a Chicago neighborhood with lots of Jews. My other friendships . . . are not as deep. I go out socially with non-Jews, but I don't feel as connected to them. They don't understand my holidays and vice versa. They're invited to our open house in our sukkah. I ask them questions about their holidays. During Passover, my daughter was invited to a friend's house for dinner. We discussed how she felt, what she would eat, and she said, "Don't worry, [Mrs. Brown] knows it's Passover." But I worried she would not understand what it meant. My daughter ate what was served.

The themes we have developed here and in previous chapters intertwine in Rebecca's remarks. Her selection of friends bears implications for family practices, and both relate to Jewish holidays, particularly to matters of food. For more involved Jews, friendships with other Jews are laden with opportunities for shared experience of holidays and worship, while relations with non-Jews are neutral in this regard, and may even pose difficulties. Only one person in our sample—Sonya, a young woman from Texas whom we met while she was studying in Jerusalem—spoke of actual "trepidation" around non-Jews, anxiety that there is something to be "defensive or even scared about." Nor did we find the sense, prominent among the Jews surveyed by Sklare and Ringer (Ringer 1967) in the late 1950s, that Jews were obligated to serve as "ambassadors" to the non-Jewish world and therefore could not let down their guard when around non-Jews; they had to stay on best behavior. (See also Eisen 1983.)

Quite the opposite is the case. More Jews today than previously count non-Jews among their friends, and more count non-Jews among their closest friends. When asked about the importance of various activities "for a person to be a good Jew," just 3 percent of the respondents in our survey thought that having mostly Jewish friends was essential and only another 17 percent thought it desirable. Only a third agreed with the statement "I relate easier to Jews than to non-Jews," and even fewer (25 percent) were prepared to say, "I feel I can count more on my Jewish friends than on my non-Jewish friends." But, for all that, a sense of greater ease among Jews remains, evident particularly in the interviews, where rapport with the Jewish interviewer and the sheer length of the conversation perhaps elicited greater honesty. Either way, American Jews still confess to feeling greater ease among Jews, and some confess to feeling unease among non-Jews. Both sentiments testify to the enduring power of familistic ties that bind.

TRANSCENDENT RESPONSIBILITIES

Further testimony to that power—likewise far from straightforward—is provided by the continuing sense of personal responsibilities toward other Jews, obligations that go beyond what one owes to human beings as a whole or to Gentile neighbors close at hand. Several of our interviewees expressed an unequivocal sense of obligation to help perpetuate Judaism or the Jewish people. Liz of New Haven remarked:

> I think it is miraculous that the Jewish community has survived through all of the persecution, and I think we have a very special story to tell. I think we offer the world something very special. . . . I would hate to think that we wouldn't continue to flourish and grow. I just feel it is my part to do my part to perpetuate an incredible people.

Esther, a past president of her Reform temple, said, "I think there is a very, very strong need to keep the Jewish people alive and to continue Judaism just generally." Truth be told, we are not at all sure of the extent to which these sentiments of personal responsibility for perpetuating Jews and Judaism are widely shared or deeply held. Most of our respondents would provide qualified endorsement of such views, but as we have seen in our subjects' views on intermarriage, commitment to "Jewish continuity" is not at the top of most respondents' personal Jewish agendas. It is of some significance that both Liz and Ruth have held leadership positions in Jewish communal life, and so stand at or over the high-end border of our sample. In the contexts of synagogue and federation, concern for Jewish continuity is widespread, and the rhetoric of the organized Jewish community constantly emphasizes the personal responsibility of every Jew, especially Jewish activists, to work for the perpetuation of Jews and Judaism;

Woocher's study of American Jewish civil religion, though dated in other respects, still very much applies in this one. But we wonder how far it extends.

Only a small number of interviewees, for example—these too among the more Jewishly involved—could easily articulate a sense of personal responsibility toward fellow Jews of the present day. We asked how they felt when they read or heard about Jews fleeing from places like Ethiopia. Sonya articulated the classic response sought by Jewish philanthropic leaders, one that recognizes Jews' special responsibility to needy Jews and translates it into charitable giving:

> I like the fact that the community feels like we are all in this together; we are helping each other. I do remember that my mom, quite surprisingly, gave quite a bit when the Ethiopians were getting out, and she herself had this real guilt thing that we didn't do anything as a community during the Holocaust, and that we needed to do something now. That really struck me . . . it affected me to the extent that, during Operation Exodus [which worked to bring Jews from the former Soviet Union to Israel and the West], I put in a hefty sum. . . . I think I do feel a special responsibility, actually.

Lynne's response on this point likewise stands out as relatively unusual for its forthright articulation of obligation to contemporary oppressed Jewry. Her remarks are also notable for their recognition of the extent to which her stance *is* at odds with currently prevailing norms:

> I have a real strong sense that Jews come first. That sense is very much a source of embarrassment to me in social discourse. For example, when Jews were being taken out of Ethiopia, I think I was in law school at the time, many of my Jewish friends and I thought this was just the greatest thing since sliced bread. Here we are! We did it again for ourselves. We went into Entebbe. This is my people and there are all these things to be proud of in my lifetime. Things that I see as miracles.

Few respondents in our face-to-face interviews were prepared to offer such unqualified endorsements of Jews "helping other Jews," as Sonya put it. The survey data lend further support to the inference that the familial favoritism she shows is not very widely endorsed. Only a minority (47 percent) could agree with the statement "I have a special responsibility to take care of Jews in need around the world." We have no doubt that several generations ago, among Jews emerging out of traditional European settings, such a statement would have elicited near-universal agreement. Even through the 1970s and 1980s, official community rhetoric emphasized Jews' responsibility to aid other Jews in need, with such collectivist slogans as "We Are One" and "Keep the Promise." The recent memory of the Holocaust and the creation of the state of Israel may have elicited widespread assent for these calls to unity. Today's campaign strategists must offer more personalized and personalist slogans, as in "For ourselves. For our children. For Israel. Forever." Some Jews still feel responsible for assisting other Jews in need, but both our qualitative and quantitative evidence points to a shrinking of their numbers, even within the last twenty years.

A further mark of the same tendency is the universalist cast of Jewish concern for social justice, carrying on a change in Jewish attitudes and practice initiated as soon as Jews began to make their way in the mainstream of American society. Rabbis and communal leaders, while stressing obligations to fellow Jews, encouraged involvement in civic and philanthropic causes aimed at rectifying ills in the larger society, and not just at caring for the needs of the Jewish community. Indeed, the association of American Jews with social justice activities, particularly during the 1950s and 1960s, has assumed mythic proportions in the community's self-conception, and not without a basis in reality. Jews have figured prominently in all mass-based left-of-center American social movements in the mid and late twentieth century. Their involvement in these causes has been so widespread that it must be regarded as a constituent and distinctive element in American Jewish ethnicity.

These activities probably exercise less sway over the consciousness of American Jews than they once did; social justice activities today certainly appear less visible and powerful than they were in the heyday of the civil rights and antiwar movements. The agenda of Jewish organizations seems less overtly liberal in its orientation and, indeed, culturally and politically conservative voices seem more numerous and articulate now than two or three decades ago (Friedman 1995). Recent quantitative research has demonstrated that Jews are not particularly liberal in many areas beyond what would be expected on the basis of their educational achievement and geographic location (Cohen and Liebman 1997; Liebman and Cohen 1996). The members of the community have "turned inwards," toward "continuity" and "local needs," pushing matters such as education and synagogue life to the fore and relegating universalist causes to the sidelines—perhaps because less affiliated Jews are involved in and contributing to precisely those causes.

That said, we certainly did encounter both strong and widespread expressions of universalist values in our in-depth interviews. We asked our subjects whether they "react differently towards the persecution of Jews than towards the persecution of people in general?" Gita's response represented a widely held point of view:

> It's very upsetting to me to see any people being oppressed by another people and to see genocide happening in another place. The ethnic cleansing in the former Yugoslavia was very upsetting to me, and it didn't matter whether it was Croatians or Muslims or Jews who were being attacked.

In fact, the most partisan universalists among our interviewees, those who were particularly committed to social activism with a liberal bent, saw themselves and those like them as differentiated from most other Jews. Suzanne's comments are particularly apt. After noting that her degree of concern for others can probably be traced to her Jewish upbringing, "the Jewish tradition and my family," she continued:

> It's important to me to not only think about Jews getting killed, or treated badly. Everybody gets treated badly in this world. . . . Most Jews, when I talk to them, seem to have this tremendous focus about how Jews are the victims of this, and I'm always struck by how everybody, many minorities here and around the world, suffer this same thing. So I think that is why I feel different[ly] and I don't really understand why that is, but it is usually translated into my mind that this is another incidence of people hating other people and I think that's just terrible. I don't think I get so caught up with the idea that antisemitism is so much worse than any other prejudice.

Consistent with these remarks, three-quarters of the respondents in our sample survey agreed with the statement "I feel as moved by the oppression of non-Jews as by the comparable oppression of Jews." Only 18 percent disagreed, and of these only 2 percent disagreed strongly. We have no directly comparable data from earlier times. However, the small number disagreeing, and the tiny number disagreeing strongly, stand in stark contrast to the results we would have anticipated among Jews at mid-century, to say nothing of their immigrant parents and their traditional grandparents living in Europe, Asia, or North Africa.

At the same time, we need to underscore our earlier remarks regarding the universalist bias built into the survey responses. In personal interviews, our respondents seemed more willing to acknowledge special feeling for the oppression of Jews. Leonard Fein, commenting on comparable disparities between qualitative and quantitative data a decade ago, related the divergences to the tendency of survey respondents to provide "what they take to be the 'acceptable' answer. There is, in other words, an apparent break between our instincts and our ideology, for despite our [overly universalist] answers, we do, indeed, feel more keenly the oppression of other Jews, the attacks against them" (Fein 1988, p. 194). Extended conversation gives "instincts" more time to surface.

The situation is complicated still further by the fact that many Jews, like Suzanne, attribute their universalist concerns for social justice to their distinctive Jewish upbringing. Once again, the pertinent survey results are equivocal. Just 45 percent of respondents agreed with the statement "Because I'm Jewish, I identify with the powerless, the vulnerable, and the underdog." Perhaps more would have agreed had we asked whether being Jewish *contributes to* such feelings rather than causing them in and of itself. It may be that sentiments connecting Jewishness with universalism are not widely held in the Jewish population at large—but it also may be that such sentiments are deemed "unacceptable" and so are not voiced, perhaps because they stand in contradiction to the respondents' lingering sense of tribalism.

Whatever the actual extent of universalism, the phenomenon has for decades been potent and widespread enough to have brought about a serious qualification in adherence to the traditional concept of Jewish chosenness. On this matter our respondents, like American Jews earlier in the twentieth century, were openly conflicted. A good number of our interviewees rejected Jewish claims to unique election outright—and then in the same breath qualified that rejection. Betsy commented, "I think each group has its own things that make them special. We just happen to be descendants of people who got the Torah." David, like many others, wrestled with the issue in our presence. He knows that the idea

> has two sides to it—chosen with special obligations as well as chosen with special privileges. I'm a universalist intellectually, so the notion that Jews are special or Jews take priority or Jews come first is a little bit at odds with my general secular ideas.

Others struggled but tipped the balance of conviction in the opposite direction. Stuart replied: "I have studied it [the idea of chosenness]. It means increased responsibility. Not necessarily increased benefits, and maybe increased opportunities. It doesn't mean that you are closer to God." On these terms he accepts the notion, but only on these terms.

Still others put the emphasis on another feature of chosenness that has troubled Jews since they began to enter Gentile societies in large numbers: the demand for exclusivity. "There's a certain aspect of chosenness that I felt very uncomfortable with," said Reuben, "a certain aspect of separating from the others." In like fashion, Dave cited the ideas as a bar to full integration:

> I work very hard not to believe that being Jewish makes me special because I feel one of the values that's coming at you all the time is inclusiveness. That's a hard one to balance with chosen people, but I think you have to do it.

Jews' (or Jewish) universalism emerged among our interviews in one final way: the equation of Judaism as such with ethics, a familiar theme in Jewish thought throughout the modern period. In the "what is a good Jew" question, dating back to Sklare and Greenblum's research, respondents have consistently placed being ethical and moral at the top of their list of essential characteristics. In our own survey, 67 percent saw leading "an ethical and moral life" as essential for a person to be a good Jew, and almost all the rest declared it desirable, winning more support than any other item on the list. When we asked Hank, "As a Jew, what sorts of obligations or responsibilities do you have to yourself, family, community, and society?" his answer illustrated this position clearly (if not quite purely):

> I don't think in terms of Jewish. My wife and I always had the feeling we raised our kids well. You don't steal, you work, and you don't get divorced—family values. My kids know you just don't marry non-Jewish girls. If you get married, you don't beat your wife. We don't smoke, we drink minimally—that's the way we live.

Brad, reflecting on his career choice, connected being Jewish with empathy:

> I think that the choice of practicing psychology is related to being Jewish, and it's there that the concern for others has come out. There is something about the ability to empathize and see things from other people's perspective. It seems to be somewhat Jewish.

Suzanne, as we saw, associated Judaism with opposition to violence and care for the needy; Stuart, invoking traditional Jewish vocabulary in its Yiddish inflection, said that:

> The essence of Judaism is *rachmanis* [mercy; sympathy] and if I don't have it, I'm not a Jew. I've seen lots of Jews without it; they're not real Jews. This may be an embarrassing judgment, but that's it. [In my mind], you're a Jew even if you don't honor Shabbat or go to holiday services, but not if you don't have *rachmanis*.

Such associations were common in our interviews. "You have to do it— to take care of the poor," said one person; another said her responsibility as a Jew was "social action and doing things right. We have to do things, do the right things." A third linked this commitment specifically to the Reform movement, which especially stresses, in her words, "social consciousness, social responsibility, making the world a little better for others. I wish I knew more about the traditions . . . the most important things are ethics and social consciousness."

It is worth noting that the identification of Judaism specifically with social justice work falls short of being the majority view. On the good Jew question, just 9 percent saw "work for social justice causes" as essential to being a good Jew and another 41 percent termed it desirable (as opposed to "leading an ethical life," deemed essential by 67 percent). In what may be a sharp contrast with mid-century American Jewry, just 21 percent saw being "a liberal on political issues" as desirable to being a good Jew, and only 3 percent termed it essential. The strongly universalist, politically progressive, and social-activism-oriented combination remains a significant voice within American Judaism, but it by no means embraces a majority of American Jews. Moreover, our survey found that just 41 percent agreed with the view that "being Jewish means being especially compassionate."

Some who disagreed may have noted the non-compassionate Jews and compassionate Gentiles around them, and as a result expressed an empirical rather than a normative judgment. Most, however, were probably testifying to the mixture of universalism and familism that we have noted throughout. Jews are obligated to be compassionate to others, but to say that Jews actually live up to this obligation would be to say in effect that they are more ethical than others; that they are in this sense better; that they are, in a word, chosen. That, as we have seen, is not a sentiment which many American Jews are prepared to express, in interviews or surveys, and one which few may actually feel.

❧

The enduring but altered patterns of historical familism that we have described provoke the question—in observers and subjects alike—of what these attitudes and behaviors portend for the future of American Jews as a distinctive group, a future that no one we met seemed to contemplate with total indifference. The issue arose most directly when we discussed the choices that our subjects' children are likely to make as Jews, and how our respondents regarded the prospect of their children choosing against Jewish identity or involvement. Here too, as we would expect, there was no little ambivalence and a great deal of overt contradiction. Particularist and universalist commitments vied for dominance, and feelings on the subject were rendered still more complex—and poignant—by the widespread sense that there is little a parent can do to influence the choices of his or her children in any case. Life in an open society means that group boundaries are weakened and transgressed. A person may not be quite sure on which side, if either, he or she stands, and even less certainty is available about one's children.

All of our interviewees, as we have seen—including those who seemed to have the lowest level of Jewish commitment—balk at the idea of crossing the line demarcating Jewish ethnicity by joining a non-Jewish religious group. Many expressed opposition to celebrating the symbols of such a group, for example a Christmas tree. But when it came to the Jewish choices made by and for the next generation, the boundary issue arose with a vengeance and often proved difficult. That was especially the case with Jews who had married non-Jews, whether or not the latter converted to Judaism. Karen, an accountant in suburban Boston, experienced few of the internally generated hesitations or externally generated opposition (e.g., from parents) reported by other interviewees who contemplated marriage to a non-Jew. Yet, even for her, then as now a fairly non-observant Jew, the identity of her children loomed large.

> The fact that [my husband-to-be] wasn't Jewish was not an issue. My parents adored him. . . . Neither of us was into religion. He was raised Presbyterian and was into meditation. I didn't want a rabbi to perform the wedding and he didn't want a minister, so a justice of the peace did the wedding. . . . As our family developed, we got involved in the synagogue. He had said right away we could raise the kids Jewish.

The subject of child-rearing had apparently arisen before Karen's marriage. Either she had raised the matter or her non-Jewish partner had done so, out of concern for an issue he perceived to be important to his future wife. In either event, the Jewish continuity of her family weighed heavily, in a way that the Jewish continuity secured by building a home in partnership with a Jewish husband did not. Karen was ready to forgo the latter, but not the former.

Edward, a Chicago lawyer, distinguished still more sharply between concern for his wife's Jewish identity and that of his children.

> My wife was born Presbyterian. We were married in a civil ceremony. She converted to Judaism before our first child was born. . . . Frankly, I didn't care if she converted or not. I never had any doubt my home would be a Jewish home, and that my kids would be brought up Jewish. I clearly spelled that out prior to getting married, and if she had not converted, then the kids would have [converted] at birth.

Apparently Edward made no connection at the time between his wife's religious identity and her role in shaping the Jewish character of the home. It was "important that she was not Jewish, but not important enough to keep from marrying her." Many things go into a decision about marriage. Being a Gentile "did not tip the scales." But failure to agree on raising Jewish children would have been "a deal-breaker," as would insistence on a Christmas tree in the home. Edward's wife-to-be conceded on these key points, and has since converted.

Several interviewees did not see intermarriage as in any way problematic. Joy was unconcerned about her children marrying non-Jews, even as she expressed the hope that they would learn enough about Judaism to make an intelligent choice about its relevance to them, the value of autonomy clearly trumping that of tribal belonging.

> I won't be upset if they marry out of the faith. I would be interested in their learning enough about the religion to know whether it's for them or not, and also to absorb the cultural stuff. That's important to me.

Ethnicity—"cultural stuff"—can be learned. Universal values can be practiced whether or not one remains a member of the tribe. Religion—"the faith"—seems to demand less permeable boundaries. Joy's phrasing of the dilemma reveals the ambiguity of her predilection toward some—but not too much—membership in the Jewish group.

We were somewhat more surprised by the seeming neutrality on the subject expressed by Gil, one of the most Jewishly active individuals in our sample. Recall Gil's comments in chapter 3 about how his daughter stimulated his own Jewish involvement, which now includes a proud commitment to synagogue life and raising Jewishly committed children. Notwithstanding these sentiments, Gil too harbors no strong antipathy to intermarriage:

> In terms of marrying outside of Judaism, I don't think it would be a major disappointment. Marriage is difficult and you don't have to make it more so by marrying outside your religion. But there are people who intermarry and convert. I know people with varying degrees of differences. I think that falling in love is not easy, and if they find somebody they love, and they're not Jewish, that's okay for me . . . maybe for N [his wife], too.

To a traditional Jew, combining intermarriage with a highly active Jewish life seems inherently contradictory, if not almost impossible. The very act of marrying a non-Jew is in itself a betrayal of deeply held ancient prohibitions. Moreover, as we have seen, Jewish practice takes on special meaning and greater likelihood of being undertaken in the context of an involved Jewish family. The presence of a non-Jewish spouse, who presumably lacks the knowledge, interest, and commitment to Jewish practice, would seem to undermine the chances for a supportive Jewish family context; all the social scientific data tend to support this. Gil knows all this, and that is perhaps why he seems to tolerate the prospect of intermarriage by joining it to the hope for conversion of the non-Jewish spouse. He is, nevertheless, conflicted—and far from alone in his belief that Jewish commitment and intermarriage can, theoretically, co-exist. Molly, likewise among the more observant Jews in our sample, shared this view.

> I'd love to see [my children] marry Jewish people because I'd like their Jewishness to stay important in their lives. I would be hypocritical to demand it because I didn't do it—and I have a wonderful family. I would be able to approach it if they married a non-Jew and say these things to them, and I would hope to be able to bring their lives into this community. Our lives have taken a turn in terms of depth and breadth of Jewishness, but before it was still a Jewish household, less than some and more than others, but still a Jewish household. It matters to me more that they continue to live as Jews and that their children be Jews.

Several themes are contained in these remarks. One is that intermarriage has become so widespread that opposition to it seems to lack "plausibility" (in Peter Berger's lexicon). Our survey data reveal the withering of opposition to intermarriage. Just 60 percent could agree with the rather bland, undemanding statement "Jews should marry Jews." The sample split evenly over the observation that "in-marriages . . . tend to have fewer difficulties than intermarriages." On the good Jew question, just 28 percent regarded "marry[ing] a Jew (or a convert to Judaism)" as essential, though another 39 percent did term in-marriage desirable.

A second theme coursing through Molly's remarks, and many other personal interviews we conducted, is the inalienability of being Jewish even in the circumstance of marriage to a non-Jew. For the intermarried, one's home is "still a Jewish household" even if "less" Jewish "than some," but "more" Jewish "than others." Note, however, that Molly does concede that she and her husband's "lives have taken a turn in terms of depth and breadth of Jewishness" as a result of his conversion. This is a good she treasures, alongside the universal value of having "a wonderful family," Jewish or not. In the end, she is unequivocal in her hope that her children live as Jews and that their children do so too—regardless of whether their partners share this commitment. She does and does not recognize that the depth of one's life in any respect, and certainly with regard to religion, varies dramatically with the commitment of one's partner.

In the event that one's child marries a non-Jew, almost all would produce a warm, welcoming reaction. Rejection for most was out of the question (only 27 percent of survey respondents said they would oppose the marriage), though some said they would try to convince the non-Jewish spouse to convert. A very few of those who were most Jewishly involved said that they would (in Stuart's words) "sit down with them and say that their kids' religious identity is incredibly important. They should work that out and if they can't, they shouldn't get married." This is a markedly minority sentiment—because marking the minority in this way conflicts with universalist values of autonomy and ethics that our subjects universally share. Dave probably put it best when expressing his hopes for his children.

DAVE: "I want them to be caring people. I want them to be people that get involved. I don't want them to be people that sit back and let the world wash over them. Whether I'd be unhappy or not if they married non-Jews is a really difficult question; obviously it's the most difficult question for any parent. I think from the people I know in my family and my wife's family who have married non-Jews, and there are very few, they have not lost their integrity or what makes them special regardless of the relationship they've maintained or not maintained with the organized Jewish community."

INTERVIEWER: "But in terms of how you would feel if they decided to marry non-Jews, your answer is that if they stay good people, you would prefer that they marry Jews. Is that what I'm hearing?"

DAVE: "Absolutely."

INTERVIEWER: "But if they stayed good, caring, compassionate people— that would be the most important thing?"

DAVE: "Absolutely."

It could hardly be otherwise, perhaps, for a moderately affiliated Jew of the current generation. Internal conflict is inevitable. On the one hand, minority identity can be—and is—asserted more visibly in multicultural America than in the melting pot to which earlier generations of American Jews sought to integrate. Greater distinctiveness is tolerated at century's end than ever before, and more—among our sample of Jews, at least —is being enacted, especially in the private sphere. Even some of the more recent critics of strong ethnic identity in America permit greater latitude for ethnic persistence than did their intellectual predecessors (Hollinger 1995). The three dimensions of historical familism that have marked the Jewish tribe for centuries have remained in place, along with modern adjustments further adjusted to suit the greater openness of postmodern America.

On the other hand, however, modern norms of universalism and autonomy remain very much in force as well, and Jewish selves are far too mobile and fluid in every respect to abide without complaint inside any boundary that cannot be crossed. Group identity cannot but weaken when Jews increasingly find themselves on both sides of ethnic boundaries. The claims of the tribe continue to be voiced, however, despite the fact they must now be so carefully negotiated. In no small measure, as we have seen, even those claims continue to be obeyed.

6

THE RETREAT OF PUBLIC JUDAISM

There are some people who are more organizational types than I am. I
think that is a good thing to do. Especially if the organization does good
things. . . . As you are mentioning this, I am sort of thinking about why
we haven't been involved with the Jewish community. I think it's because
I don't see that the need exists there. I think there are other organizations that need us more. The people that the Jewish organizations
benefit aren't in as much need as the people that we are helping.

—BRAD

In May 1967, millions of American Jews were transfixed by events un-
folding in the Middle East. Israel stood on the brink of war, threatened by
Arab armies on all its borders. The drama was also being played out in
the United Nations, punctuated by the memorable eloquence of Israel's
ambassador, Abba Eban, as well as in the corridors of power in Washington, where Israel's representatives sought American diplomatic and material support. To many American Jews, the threat to Israel's very existence,
the possibility that millions of Jews might perish, and the seeming indifference (or overt hostility) of the world's major powers aroused painful
memories. It had been only twenty-two years since the few survivors of the
Holocaust were liberated from the concentration camps and the full horror and tragedy of the Nazi atrocities were revealed.

What would soon be seen as the "miraculous" victory of the Israeli army
in the Six-Day War set in motion a rather remarkable period in the history
of American Jewry. Israel moved to the fore as the most compelling cause
in Jewish life and became the centerpiece of fund-raising and of political

activism. The cause of Israel pushed aside the civil rights agenda, liberalism, and even the fight against American antisemitism as the major public issues of American Jewry's vaunted organizational infrastructure. Philanthropic campaigns reached new heights, exceeded in turn several years later by the campaigns during the Yom Kippur War of 1973, another time of palpable threat to Jewish survival. These developments also helped to recruit thousands of lay and professional activists—many of them affluent, well educated, and thoroughly Americanized—to the Jewish organizational world.

Two additional issues soon came to capture the attention of those activists. The first, beginning in the 1970s, was the plight of Soviet Jews oppressed in their own country and denied the right of free emigration to Israel or the West. The other issue, which came to the fore at about the same time, was the Holocaust. Remembering and memorializing the Shoah through museums, school curricula, books, university courses and chairs, conferences, the arts, and manifold acts of public recognition became a major cultural and institutional focus of American Jewish life. The Holocaust and Israel became, in the opinion of many observers, the "twin pillars" supporting American Jewish identity. They certainly dominated Jewish public activity, epitomizing the struggle for survival against great odds that served as the major leitmotiv of "civil Judaism" (Woocher 1986; Novick 1999).

Indeed, the three causes could be (and were) seen as alternate applications of the same fundamental principles. Jews constituted one people with an obligation to come to one another's aid in time of danger. The United Jewish Appeal's slogans of the time, such as "Keep the Promise" and "We Are One," blatantly appealed to this keenly felt sense of shared obligation. So did the rallying cry "Never Again." American Jews' failure or inability to come to the aid of the victims of the Nazis served to heighten the resolve of the generation of the 1960s and 1970s to "never again" allow Jews, wherever they might be, to fall victim to persecution. Israel's defiance of the perceived odds in 1967 and 1973 was taken as paradigmatic of what Jews could and had to do, time and again. American Jews, by fighting for the survival of their fellow Jews elsewhere, would in turn justify and work toward their own survival, against the odds of assimilation.

It was in this period, too, that politically active Jews dramatically altered their method of approach to elected officeholders. In the postwar period (1945–1967) Jewish lobbyists and the groups behind them had pressed their objectives through moral suasion and coalition building, often with other liberal advocacy groups, especially civil rights organizations. Jews took great pains to frame their particular interests in terms of a broader public interest. The fight against American antisemitism, for example, was never presented as a matter of special pleading, but was depicted in conjunction with other causes that sought to rid American society of prejudice, discrimination, and intolerance of all kinds. After 1967, by contrast, Jewish activists changed both their tactics and their principled stance. They moved more assuredly and independently to present their concern for Israel and Soviet Jewry as matters of importance to Jews as Jews. They also came to pressure officeholders more vigorously. Jewish activists rewarded their elected friends with significant campaign contributions and punished their political adversaries by supporting potential opponents, often with considerable success.

These causes, and the methods employed to pursue them, constitute what we might call the "Jewish public sphere," an area of concern and activity that can be distinguished clearly from the intimate private sphere of self and family. It is also distinct from institutional worlds such as the synagogue and the Jewish community center. These, while certainly public in one sense, are geared to meet the local and highly personal needs of individuals and families. They also serve their clienteles one at a time or in small groups. Major philanthropic organizations, such as the UJA and the Jewish Federations, and politically oriented agencies such as the Anti-Defamation League or the pro-Israel lobby (AIPAC, the American Israel Public Affairs Committee) work on a very different plane, toward very different ends.

Our argument in this chapter is that the forces of personalism and privatization we have explored thus far, and the diminished salience of ethnic identification examined in the previous chapter, have exerted a major impact upon Jews' engagement with the public sphere in recent years. That engagement, measured both by the comments of our interviewees and by the responses of our national sample, has noticeably and sharply declined. The Jews we met and surveyed differ markedly from their predecessors in their perception of the public sphere; they differ too in the degree to which that sphere serves as the fulcrum of their own Jewish identities. We will chart this transformation of attitude and practice by examining our respondents' views of the three arenas which still dominate the Jewish public sphere: the Holocaust, Israel, and the federations. In each case, we will find, personal Jewish meaning, as mediated through family, stands forth clearly as the paramount concern. Activity in the Jewish public sphere is approved or undertaken only to the degree that it serves that concern—a change that clearly bears consequences of major importance for the Jewish community.

THE HOLOCAUST: JEWISH IMPACT, UNIVERSAL LESSONS

There is no question that the Holocaust looms large in the consciousness of our respondents, or that they relate to the Holocaust in strikingly personal terms. When asked if he ever thinks about the Holocaust, Scott replied:

> Yes, I think about the Holocaust a lot. The Holocaust is a very present thought for me. Going to the Holocaust Museum in D.C. was an important thing in terms of my thinking. It really brought me to the connection of the role the Holocaust plays in my life and my thinking, how important the Holocaust is; it's probably, in many ways, the seminal historical event in my consciousness.

The personal dimension of the tragedy for Scott encompassed a sense of very personal loss. Some respondents mentioned particular family members (most of whom they had never seen) who perished in Europe, or family members known to them who had survived the concentration camps. Yet even some of those without a direct connection to a specific relative who had survived, or died in, the Holocaust spoke in terms of a loss of *extended* family. A few considered how they themselves would have coped with the danger, the hardships, and the impossible moral choices that would have been forced upon them had they been there. In this vein, Lynne effected a personal linkage between herself, the Holocaust, and the state of Israel that we believe is quite typical among American Jews.

> I have had a very strong sense that I belong in Israel from the time I was very young, and it didn't come from my parents because, to this day, they would be horrified if I brought it up. A second very strong sense is the Holocaust. Something in me is very attached to this idea of a particular child that lives through the Holocaust that I don't know. Those two things are very important. I don't know where they come from.

Not surprisingly, the Holocaust carries with it implications for Jewish identity which at times are very keenly felt. When asked about the relative importance of several concepts and symbols to their sense of being Jewish, 85 percent of our national survey sample marked the Holocaust as "very important" or "extremely important." This combined percentage exceeded that for all other items in the survey question, including God, the Jewish family, the Jewish people, and American antisemitism. Fully 65 percent agreed, elsewhere in our survey, that "my feelings about the Holocaust have deeply influenced my feeling about being Jewish."

Among our interviewees, some readily moved from personal identification with the tragedy to draw implications for their own lives as Jews. Sonya, a woman in her thirties who was raised in Kansas City, Missouri, and has worked in the past for a well-known Jewish communal advocacy organization, was especially articulate on this point:

> A lot of my Jewish pride was a defensive reaction to negative things. My personal experience was being called kike and kids pushing me off the swings and that kind of stuff. But the bigger picture for us was that *we were*

killed during the Holocaust. I would like to say that I was mostly influenced by positive things, but I think I had a negative upbringing, like, I better stick together with these people [Jews]. And I also sometimes feel like I have an obligation to be a committed Jew in some way because of all the people that were killed. Sometimes I have even convinced myself that I needed to have children because of it . . . I think a lot of my Jewish feelings were so based on the negative. I identified with these poor little martyred children: poor them, poor me, we are all in this together.

The excerpt testifies to Sonya's highly personal identification with the victims of the Holocaust ("we were killed"), and to the way she draws personal lessons from the tragedy that are connected with her being a Jew. Though for her the power of the Shoah exceeded its power for most other people we interviewed, Sonya unquestionably was not alone in articulating a sense of personal obligation to Jews and Judaism in the wake of the destruction of European Jewry. Nor was she alone in regarding her own feelings in relation to the Holocaust as being in part "based on the negative." Paul, a Los Angeles architect in his sixties, reported that

I once identified myself as Jewish in that way [in terms of the Holocaust]. During college, when I was not living very Jewishly, I had an affair with a non-Jewish woman. It was quite serious. I started thinking that Hitler is no reason to be Jewish.

These two individuals were not the only ones to explicitly tie the Holocaust with unattractive conceptions of being Jewish. They seem to suggest that a Jewish identity too closely tied to the Holocaust is seen by our interviewees as insubstantial, superficial, and a distortion of Judaism. Stuart, a Los Angeles screenwriter of about fifty, linked the Holocaust to an inordinate and unhealthy fear of Gentiles.

Has the Holocaust had an effect on being a Jew? For the first part of my life, so much of my Jewish identity was tied up in paranoia.

The quip "Even paranoids have enemies" seems to enjoy a special currency among American Jews, referring to the very real enemies Jews have faced in recent memory—whether during World War II or from Arab adversaries in the Middle East or from antisemites closer to home. Yet in the comments just cited, paranoia seems to connote the belief (which is mistaken in the eyes of the speaker) that Jews are widely disliked by Gentiles in general and American non-Jews in particular. Just 25 percent of those polled in our survey agreed with the assertion that "Jews are widely disliked by Gentile Americans," and just 3 percent agreed strongly with the claim. For Stuart as for others we met, the Holocaust has had the unsavory impact of drawing Jews apart from non-Jewish Americans to an unnecessary degree, and this consequence may be one of the reasons that thinking about the Holocaust provokes such discomfort.

Indeed, for some, the Holocaust arouses so much discomfort that they make a studious attempt to avoid thinking about or encountering it at all. When asked whether the Holocaust had been an important issue for her, Suzanne responded:

> It's been an issue in the sense that I have avoided it because I couldn't find any way to hold it before, so I dealt with it by trying not to think of it. If I were to think about it, I would be so undone that I couldn't live. That's how I [dealt with] suffering altogether for years, which was to try not to see it.

Suzanne's comments picked up yet another strain in our discussions on the Holocaust. While the Shoah certainly etched a powerful imprint on the consciousness of nearly all our interviewees, many attested to an encounter limited to adolescence. This is certainly when the initial encounter with the magnitude of the Holocaust took place. Joshua, now in his early thirties, reported that when he was fifteen or sixteen years old, a lot of his friends "just wanted to listen to music and do drugs or have parties or whatever." He, by contrast, would find himself thinking frequently about the Holocaust. Sonya too reported:

> In fact, I was a little bit obsessed with it [the Holocaust] when I first found out about it in about the sixth grade. I remember at Hebrew school, which was such an awful educational system, my teacher made us read a fiction book about it, and then I think I read every single adolescent fiction book there was about the Holocaust. They were based on reality but were fiction. It was a pretty formative topic for me and I was quite obsessed with it.

Martha, now in her fifties, also used the word "obsessed" (twice) to describe her relationship to the Holocaust as a youngster. And, underscoring the centrality of family discussed in chapter 3, she linked her reaction to the Holocaust with some rather unflattering images of her parents:

> I've sort of obsessed about the Holocaust since my childhood. I can't separate the two [being Jewish and the Holocaust] . . . I was obsessed with reading novels as well as historical information. I began to be aware of it in junior high school; I still am affected. I think there was guilt about being someone who was not affected and was not alive to fix it. I was angry with my parents about not having done something about it. I think, in a certain sense, I could be part of this family experience; this is sort of sick, but I think it's true.

Dave, a writer in New Haven who is about forty, was most explicit in limiting the impact of the Holocaust to his adolescent years:

> In college I went through a big Holocaust period. Everybody goes through their turmoil, and there was this sort of Rubenstein death-of-

God sort of thing. But I disengaged from the Holocaust very much in the last ten or twelve years.

Dave was referring to the controversial conclusion by the Jewish theologian Richard Rubenstein that God's failure to rescue Jews from the Nazis meant that "God is dead"—in other words, that notions of providence must be abandoned.

We are led to surmise, though without very solid evidence, that Dave is far from alone in both respects. The impact of the Holocaust was most keenly felt by many of our respondents in the teen years—and for many, perhaps most, the Shoah has since faded in significance. It was not a topic to which our interviewees ever readily referred; without explicit prompting it did not come up. This is so, no doubt, because of the inherently difficult nature of the subject matter, but also perhaps because of the personally threatening implications of deep-seated Gentile hostility toward Jews. Our interviewees largely rejected formulations of the significance of the Holocaust which focused on the Jews as victims of Nazi genocide or which placed this persecution in the larger framework of antisemitism throughout the ages. We did not hear more than one or two echoes of the well-known view by the Jewish philosopher Emil Fackenheim that the Holocaust carries profound lessons about the eternally "singled-out" condition of the Jews. "What does the Voice of Auschwitz command? Jews are forbidden to hand Hitler posthumous victories. They are commanded to survive as Jews, lest the Jewish people perish." Our interviewees tended rather to draw universal lessons about the nature of humanity as such, believing with Fackenheim that "they are forbidden to despair of man and his world, and to escape into either cynicism or other worldliness, lest they cooperate in delivering the world over to the forces of Auschwitz (Fackenheim 1970, p. 84).

One exception was Esther, a homemaker and communal activist in her sixties, whose remarks echoed Fackenheim's approach rather directly. She said of her development as a Jew:

> I wanted to have a strong Jewish identity. I felt that we needed to preserve the Jewish people to make up for what Hitler had done.

Others among our interviewees seemed to straddle the "universalist-particularist" divide. Reuben, for example, a Manhattan writer, suggested as a lesson of the Holocaust that Jews' vulnerability is tied up with that of others, and actions that protect other minorities will also serve to protect Jews:

> I think that one always needs to be prepared, and I think one needs to speak out against bigotry and racism because even though it's not directed at Jews, today it's this group, and tomorrow it could be the Jews.

However, the vast majority of interviewees drew more universal lessons from the Holocaust experience. Betsy, in keeping with a common American Jewish association between antisemitism and the cultural and political right (see Cohen 1984, 1989c), pointed to the need to be wary of fringe groups which, in her view, threaten certain non-Jewish minorities far more than they actually threaten Jews:

> Beware of cult following. At times I do think it could happen here. The Christian Right, the KKK could come back. It [persecution] might be directed against Asians or blacks. Not Jews. Not a holocaust, but attitudes toward immigrants now are bad. There possibly could be a holocaust, but it's not likely.

Many did not see the Holocaust as a peculiarly Jewish tragedy at all. When asked what lessons she derived from the Holocaust, Amy responded:

> The lesson is don't trust your own government fully without questioning it. You have to speak out for what you believe in at all costs. There's not enough effort looking to help outside of the Jewish community, for example places like Bosnia. I believe [what is happening in Bosnia] will come to rival the Holocaust in the end.

We did not hear very much about the Holocaust as a Jewish tragedy bearing profound political implications for the collective existence of Jews as a people. No one placed the Holocaust in the context of Jewish history or linked it to centuries of antisemitic persecution. None spoke, as Israelis do with regularity, of the need for Jewish military and diplomatic power to thwart those who might embark upon another attempt to visit mass destruction on a Jewish population. Only one seemed to draw the lesson—popular in the rhetoric of communal organizations—that such organizations are required to ensure that the slaughter of Jews will not recur. Instead, the Holocaust was consistently presented to us as a *human* tragedy, albeit one that is personally very painful because it touched one's own extended family. Most interviewees readily drew critical universal lessons that aim at preventing similar tragedies from befalling other minority groups, who were often seen as more vulnerable today than Jews. The heart of our respondents' Jewish concern clearly lies elsewhere—and, they are convinced, rightfully so.

ISRAEL: A GROWING DISTANCE

Since the inception of the Zionist movement, the organized American Jewish community has pursued a largely two-dimensional relationship with the Jewish community of Israel—at first the pre-state settlement or Yishuv, and, since 1948, the state. One dimension of their relationship has consisted of lobbying Congress and the president to extend economic, military, and diplomatic support to Israel. The other dimension has been fund-raising to support pressing social welfare needs that largely flowed from the rescue of Jewish refugees and their resettlement in Israel. More generally, the funds were meant to lend material support to a society that was perceived as having to expend a disproportionate share of its resources on security needs. Israel was perceived as the bulwark of Jewish survival in the second half of the twentieth century, with American Jewry playing a key role in ensuring that the state had the wherewithal to perform that function.

Both the relation between the two Jewries and the perception of that relation have changed dramatically in recent years. The quantitative and qualitative evidence we collected for this study, in line with numerous other indicators, supports the notion that American Jews have been experiencing increasing alienation from Israel. Our sense is that this alienation is exacerbated but not caused by recent political and religious events. The ultimate cause is more deep-seated. Once again, the priority for American Jews is *individual* Jewish meaning, and the question is whether Israel enhances or detracts from that meaning. All too often, we found, Israel has been judged on this score by our respondents—and found wanting.

The limited extent to which Israel actually figures in the private lives of American Jewish consciousness was underscored for us by two focus group discussions conducted by Cohen in 1995 with parents of Hebrew school youngsters in a suburban synagogue in New England. Both sessions opened with responses to very general questions on what parts of being Jewish the participants found attractive and unattractive. None of the participants in either focus group so much as mentioned Israel during these initial conversations, each of which lasted about half an hour. This failure was all the more startling in that the moderator had moved to Israel about three years earlier from the same community, a fact well-known to the focus group participants. Then, after he asked the participants why they had not referred to the Jewish state, they vigorously claimed to feel strongly about it. For these focus group participants, at least, Israel carries little real import in the private sphere of Jewish identity, the part that is closest to their inner core.

The results of our survey point in the same direction. When asked about their emotional attachment to Israel, just 9 percent answered "extremely attached" (as opposed to 13 percent in a similar survey in 1988), and only another 18 percent said "very attached" (versus 24 percent in 1988). In other words, a total of just over a quarter (27 percent in 1997 versus 37 percent in 1988) defined themselves as at least very attached to Israel. When asked about how close they feel to Israelis, 8 percent said to a great extent (against 19 percent in 1988), and 41 percent answered to some extent (versus 54 percent in 1988). About a third do see Israel as "extremely important" to their sense of being Jewish, with another third ranking it "very important." But this places Israel well down on the list of symbols and concepts that seem to resonate with American Jews. By contrast, about half the respondents said that Torah, High Holidays, the Jewish family, American antisemitism, the Jewish people, and the Holocaust were very important to their sense of being Jewish. It also represents something of a decline, even relative to findings a few years ago. In 1998, in a national survey of American Jews sponsored by the American Jewish Committee (American Jewish Committee 1998), fully 74 percent agreed with the statement "Caring about Israel is a very important part of my being a Jew." With respect to their ideas of "the good Jew," just 20 percent in our survey thought it essential for a good Jew to support Israel. Even fewer (18 percent) had similar views regarding visiting Israel in the course of one's life. For most respondents, these behaviors were at least desirable, but about a third, in fact, found them entirely irrelevant to their concept of what a good Jew does.

How do we explain the cooling of American Jewish ardor for Israel? One change, surely, is the loss of the factor that had served to fuel attachment to Israel heretofore. The once-beleaguered Jewish state no longer seems to require the financial and political assistance it once did. Israel's army is strong, its economy booming. Fear for Israel's (i.e., Jewish) survival has abated. American Jews no longer feel that Israel needs their help to the same degree, and feel less compelled to offer it.

Nor can American Jews relate to the complex reality of Israel's dynamic society with the same facility that they can relate to the myth of Israel: the larger-than-life picture of exiles ingathered, David fighting Goliath, deserts blooming, life triumphing over death. Few American Jews read or speak Hebrew, and not many more read Hebrew literature in translation or seek out Israeli films with subtitles. The subtleties of Israel's political process and ethnic mosaic elude comprehension far away, and are not covered in any detail by general or Jewish American media (Eisen 1998b). Israel, in short, does not force itself on American Jewish consciousness, except as the source of political and religious turmoil which we shall discuss in a moment. American Jews for their part seem not to mind the resultant distance. As Joy put it:

> I certainly notice it. I have an ear out for it more than I might for some other country. Yes, I notice it. I don't follow it very closely. I don't look for it and I can't name all the politicians that are important although I could name a handful.

Two recent developments may have contributed to the lack of desire to "follow it very closely." The first is the troubled state of the "peace process," which at the very least has made Israel a source of unease for American Jews and posed the threat of rupture with the U.S. government. The second is the refusal of ultra-Orthodox groups in Israel to accept non-Orthodox forms of Judaism as legitimate. At worst, these developments have led some Jews—at odds with Israeli government policy on the matter and troubled by the influence of the ultra-Orthodox—to distance themselves from the state of Israel altogether.

Paul expressed a view common to many, perhaps most, American Jews when he said, "I'm a strong supporter, but I'm not in a position to be a senior adviser in terms of what we should do." Most American Jews by all accounts see themselves as pro-Israel. They harbor some ill-defined doubts, confusions, or objections to the state's current policies. Yet they resist aligning themselves with American Jewish groups and informal networks that publicly dissent from official Israeli government policy—whether out of a sense of professed ignorance, as Paul's remarks suggest, or, more tellingly, out of a sense that they lack the moral standing to dissent. Others, however, did not shy away from criticism in our conversations, even after confessing their ignorance about the details of Israeli politics and society. Joy, for example, told us:

> I think there are many different cultures that can lay a claim to Israel's soil as their own. I think the Palestinians have been displaced. I think that is terribly unfortunate and I don't think that should happen. I think that some kind of home for the Palestinians is correct. So, I am glad that Israel is finally doing something in that direction. I don't know if this is the answer, but at least some progress is being made.

Peter objected strongly to the militarism associated in his mind with Israel. Though perhaps unavoidable, in light of past and current confrontation with her Arab neighbors, the militaristic aspects of Israel are nevertheless unappealing to this New Haven architect, community volunteer, and father of three boys:

> The Arab-Israeli conflict is something that I find very hard to access. I feel ambivalent about it. I think the sites would be phenomenal to see the history of it. But the militarism of it, it's always there. There is a strength and a vigor about it that I have trouble relating to because I am an American.

It is of some interest that Peter traced his ill feelings to his identity as an American. In a similar and more explicit fashion, Suzanne made a clear distinction between her identity as a Jew and her identity as a "citizen of the world." The former undergirds her identification with Israel; the latter leads her to take issue with Israel's approach to its conflict with the Palestinians and other Arabs, producing an explicitly stated ambivalence:

> My feelings about Israel are very ambivalent. There is a part of me that is very identified with being Jewish and feels very powerfully towards Israel and its continuing, and is protective about it. But there is this other part of me that feels like a citizen of the world that's going, "This isn't

working, is there some other way?" and I feel very confused. I mostly feel identified with Jews there, and in a way I just don't know how to feel about it, and so it's a real tough one for me. I can't just completely say, "Yeah, this is it." I think I would like to see some resolution there. I have felt much better since there has been some movement towards peace there, but I haven't personally felt like I need to go there.

Nancy drove home this point, articulated by a good number of our interviewees (disproportionately located, we suspect, in such bastions of liberalism as Manhattan's Upper West Side or the San Francisco Bay Area). Like Suzanne, she explicitly applied a progressive perspective to Israel and found the Jewish state in some ways deficient:

> Some aspects [of Israel] are wonderful, like having our holidays, but Jews are the people of the Book, not of land. There is a distortion of understanding around the role of the state of Israel. It feeds into stuff around the Holocaust. A lot of it is valid, but part of it we don't understand like when we become oppressors, or when we become fanatical about killing each other or our leaders who begin to move towards peace.

For David, it is the perceived prominence of right-wing political forces, especially when associated with what he regards as the "Orthodox lunatic fringe," that drives him to distance himself from Israel:

> Frankly, even being vaguely associated with the Orthodox lunatic fringe in Israel, the [far right-wing] Kach groups [who call for the expulsion of Palestinians], and [Ariel] Sharon [a leading right-wing political figure known for his hard-line stands toward the Arabs], [I] have to say when Israel does something like that, that it's not my Israel. I'm not responsible for that.

David's adverse reaction to the combination of religious with nationalist zeal was not at all unique among our interviewees. They find this combination threatening in its U.S. manifestations as well. Nor is David's reluctance to be held "responsible" for what Israel does unusual. David understands that his own fate as a Jew is bound up with Israel; he remains a strong supporter of the state and is far from one-sided in apportioning blame for the lack of peace between Israel and its neighbors. But David does not want, in his words, to be held "responsible" for Israel—either by his own conscience or, we suspect, by Gentile Americans. Israel must help American Jews to feel good about being Jews if they are to feel good about—or close to—Israel. In Suzanne's words, they "would like to see some resolution there." For the moment, they do not. As Matthew put it, "How is Israel going to find its way into the future? That's very problematic."

The same could be said of the conflicts between Orthodox (and particularly ultra-Orthodox) Jews in Israel and Conservative and Reform Jews, who are currently barred from performing weddings, issuing divorce decrees, or conducting conversions. Over the years, notwithstanding the importance of the peace process to Israel and of the historic involvement of American Jews as advocates and lobbyists for Israel, the religious question has captured even more attention than the peace process among American Jewish rabbis and communal leaders, as well as the rank and file. One reason for the discrepancy is the strong sense of denominational identity among Conservative and Reform Jews in the United States, as well as their resentment of traditionalist Orthodox Jews. In addition, American Jews more readily assume they have more moral standing in debating, criticizing, and intervening in Israel's decision-making processes affecting religious issues than in those affecting Israeli security. Sylvia, a New Yorker in her sixties, told us she was "very much for the peace process," and believes that "Americans should have input into that." But she was far more emotional when it came to perceived religious discrimination. "I am very, very upset about the religious stranglehold that all these coalition parties have on making Israel's decisions. I think that Americans can have an influence, certainly not in politics, but in policies in the religious sphere."

The basis for the struggle over religious policies lies in the near monopoly of official state recognition afforded the Orthodox rabbinate in Israel. The so-called status quo arrangement, dating back to the years before and just after the establishment of statehood, in part reflects the major historic divisions of Jewish Israel into three major camps: the religious, the secular left, and the nationalist right. For years, non-religious Jewish Israelis, who arrayed themselves on a spectrum ranging from the moderately observant to the militantly secular, conferred religious legitimacy and authenticity upon the traditionalist population and its rabbis. Unlike American Jews, Israelis were not inclined to establish alternative and competing religious ideologies, communities, movements, synagogues, or liturgies. As a result, Israelis have little indigenous basis for providing state recognition for forms of Judaism, or their rabbis and Jewish religious institutions, other than the Orthodox. Resentment among secular Israelis against the more traditional Orthodox has certainly grown in recent years for a variety of reasons—including this community's lack of service in the Israel Defense Forces, their studying for years in yeshivas and making limited contributions to the economy and the national treasury, and the attempt to apply Orthodox norms to various parts of Israeli life. However, most of this resentment has not been channeled into calls for more support for non-Orthodox approaches to Judaism.

In contrast, Conservative and Reform Judaism in the United States are major sources of self-definition for American Jews. Almost four-fifths of all American Jews identify as Conservative or Reform, and the comparable proportion reaches 85 percent among members of synagogues (Lazerwitz et al. 1998, p. 40). For American Jews, therefore, especially those who are not Orthodox, controversies in Israel over religious questions strike at their very identity as Jews, challenging their right as individuals to decide what sort of Jews they will be and contesting the authenticity of the Jewish choices which most of them have made. At various points, Israeli political and religious leaders have been embroiled in heated debate over such issues as whether converts to Judaism who were converted by non-Orthodox rabbis would be regarded as Jewish under Israeli immigration law, or whether non-Orthodox institutions should receive government funding in the same fashion and to the same extent as that received by comparable Orthodox institutions; or whether sexually mixed prayer groups, most often associated with Conservative and Reform movements, would be permitted to pray within sight of the Western Wall. These and similar issues touch directly upon the Jewish subgroup identities of moderately (and actively) involved American Jews, almost all of whom identify with a major Jewish denomination. It is thus no surprise that as many as 80 percent of our survey respondents agreed with the statement "I get upset when Orthodox Jews in Israel try to limit the practice of Conservative and Reform Jews in Israel." The slight is taken personally. Reuben touched the heart of the matter when he said:

> What I have become much more aware of is how, despite being a somewhat observant Jew, Israel is the one place where I would have the most trouble practicing my brand of Judaism because it's not recognized by the state of Israel.

We learned in our conversations that many American Jews feel that Israel symbolically belongs to them, or should; perceived denigration of Conservative and Reform movements, ultimately at the behest of highly traditional Orthodox groups, thus seems equivalent to stealing Israel away from them, from the Jewish people as a whole, and limiting symbolic attachment to the Orthodox. Writing about these matters in 1989, Cohen explained the reactions to questions on the pending "Who is a Jew?" legislation in Israel among a national sample of American Jews thus:

> The theme running through these responses is one of fear of potential rejection by Israel. Respondents felt that, by passing the proposed legislation [so that Reform and Conservative converts to Judaism would not count as Jews for purposes of citizenship], Israel would be rejecting their brand of Judaism, their family members [especially non-Jewish in-laws and many of their children], their friends, and their claim to a special attachment to the Jewish state, which they regard as a center and refuge for all Jews, not just the Orthodox. (Cohen 1989e, p. 48)

American Jewish sentiment about Israel, then, needs to be understood against the backdrop of antagonistic feelings toward the Orthodox, and in particular the more traditional or *Haredi* Orthodox. American Jews do feel much better about the Modern Orthodox than about the "ultra-Orthodox"; the most recent research on the matter is, in our view, still pertinent (Cohen 1989e, p. 48). However, the simple term "Orthodox" tends to connote for many the more traditional branches of Orthodoxy, an association no doubt responsible for some of their considerable disaffection. Several items in our survey indicated that this disaffection is not only significant but likely growing. At one time, at least until the late 1960s, the Orthodox stood, in the eyes of many American Jews, for the highest standards of piety and Jewish commitment, even if their commitment and learning were seen as personally unattainable for their non-Orthodox admirers. Unlike Israelis, many of whom have long resented Orthodoxy's official power and political influence, few American Jews have historically harbored deep antipathy toward the Orthodox among them. This seems to have changed in recent years. Almost four-fifths of the respondents in our survey (79 percent) disagreed with calling the Orthodox the most authentic Jews. A plurality (47 percent) said that they were not grateful to the Orthodox for doing so much to maintain Jewish life. Majorities also agreed that the Orthodox are narrow-minded (51 percent) and that they (the respondents) are bothered by Orthodox Jews' feelings of superiority (52 percent).

These data, then, point to fairly widespread feelings of aversion to the Orthodox. The latter's forthright adherence to traditional Jewish attitudes sharply contrasts with the voluntarism characteristic of American society generally and American Jewish identity in particular. Orthodoxy sees Judaism as demanding punctilious ritual observance, establishes clear criteria for the right way to be Jewish, and enjoins Jews to reproach fellow Jews for failing to abide by Jewish law. None of these views are particularly popular among most American Jews, and neither—apparently—are their chief proponents. Our interviewees told us repeatedly that they deplore internecine conflict among Jews, and that they resent being judged as less good Jews because they are less observant or less believing. Their resentment of Orthodox claims to Jewish superiority in America carries over to feelings about the Orthodox in Israel, and, more generally, to images and feelings about Israel. How can their relation to Judaism be strengthened by the denial of legitimacy to the forms of Judaism they practice? And that, as we have seen time and time again, is the bar of judgment before which Israel, like the Holocaust, must pass.

It is telling, we believe, that significant numbers of American Jews still explicitly regard Israel as an important part of their being a Jew, despite all the factors that tend in the opposite direction. The question, of course, is why. How does Israel nourish American Jews' sense of themselves as Jews? The following comments by Brad, one of the less Jewishly involved among our interviewees, are helpful in pointing to the answer. We asked about the type of Jew that he would like his soon-to-be-born son to become. In response, Brad answered:

The issue about being religious doesn't matter. I would definitely want him to go to Israel. That was very, very powerful for me. I think I would want him to understand a lot of the history of the story and identity . . . the strong identification about being Jewish. That's going to be crucial. That's why Israel is very important. Now my parents never went to Israel, and I have been trying for several years to get my mother to go and now I feel she has some interest in going. I feel on some level she doesn't want to focus on Judaism, but I think she will have to face that by going there. She would much rather go to Paris or somewhere else than go to Israel.

Whether in terms of his son's future, his mother's present, or his own past, Brad connects Israel to struggles over Jewish identity. He wants his son connected to the state, as he is, because he wants him to understand "the story." That, for Brad as for many others, "is why Israel is very important." Several interviewees told us that Israel is important to them as "a safety net," a "sanctuary" in case Jews should face persecution elsewhere in the world. Others spoke of their pride in Israel's military prowess. Still others said they felt completely unconnected to the state. As Dave put it:

If I never get there, I don't think I will have been completely unfulfilled. It's not like I need to go to feel completely Jewish.

Dave is not someone totally divorced from Jewish interests who, as a logical consequence, lacks any significant interest in Israel. Rather, in contrast with others in this study who exhibited a moderate level of Jewish involvement, he feels remote from Israel, even to the point—highly unusual in our encounters—of claiming little interest in visiting Israel. It is all the more important that we attend to the point Dave is making, which explains why it is no longer uncommon to find lukewarm-to-cool attitudes to Israel co-existing with warm-to-passionate feelings about being Jewish. The question is what he and others like him need in order "to feel completely Jewish," to be "fulfilled" as a Jew. When Israel contributes to that end, they value it highly.

Hence the combination, evident in this comment by Nina, of fond recollection of a visit to Israel years ago alongside evidence of near indifference at the time of the interview:

When I was there, it was overwhelming day to day. But I don't feel a real connection to it. Sometimes I feel bad about that. I don't have a huge connection. It's not the first thing I read about in the papers.

Nina's current indifference is even more striking in that she is among the minority of American Jews who have actually visited Israel, and she had a particularly positive experience to boot. Proponents of the Israel experience as a Jewish educational enterprise will no doubt be disheartened by such comments; but, in fairness, we found many more examples of individuals recalling their trips to Israel as exciting events in their lives. Sylvia said, "I just loved it . . . just loved it. Loved being in Israel. I loved it more than I thought I would." Interviewees emphasized various aspects of the experience, all of which were in some way connected to their emergent Jewish identities. While each stressed a particular manner in which Israel played to their Jewish sensibilities, we have no doubt that each also experienced, to some degree, the sorts of emotions reported by their counterparts.

For Saul, whose Jewish involvement marks him as significantly more traditional than most in our set of interviews, Israel represented a comfortable religious environment, the bringing to life of Jewish history, and the pleasure of not standing out as a minority:

> I guess being in Israel was just a fantastic experience and it was just a very comfortable Jewish atmosphere. One could walk around with a *kippah* [skullcap] and it was not something you have to think twice about. It really was a good way to tie me to the past. I think I may have read *The Source* by Michener on the airplane going over, and being able to read this and then walk around and see these places just made a tremendous impact for me. That trip to Israel was probably one of the most powerful pro-Jewish experiences that I had.

Brad too found that he was moved by the feeling of ties to the distant Jewish past.

> One has to confront the fact that you have a wall or something and you see this piece of rock that people have been praying at, you know, for so long, and you have to confront a sort of mysticism. That actually holds some appeal to me.

Sarah, who grew up amid a small Jewish minority in a small city in Texas, stressed relief at being part of the majority for once:

> Oh yeah, I loved that [my first visit to Israel]. I thought that was great. I had never seen a Jewish bus driver or all of that kind of stuff. Just the idea that everybody around you is Jewish, it was such an opposite. I had such a strong awareness [growing up] that no one around me was Jewish, but that I was standing out as being a Jewish child. I didn't have that much experience at that time. It seemed so noteworthy that everyone around you was Jewish, and you didn't have to have a sort of tense feeling that something bad might happen, or that people somehow might cross you and you would have to stand up for something.

Surveys report that about two-thirds of American Jews say they want to go to Israel, nearly double the number who have already been there. Yet at the same time, several considerations inhibit the fulfillment of these intentions. One factor is, of course, concern about safety. "I'd love to take my family, but it's too scary for me now," said Rachel. For others, the trip has simply not meshed with family schedules as yet. "I know I have to go," said

Joy. "We will go. When the kids are older." More often, we heard a generalized interest in going unaccompanied by any definitive plans to do so, as
in these comments by Paul: "I would like to go. I would have a feeling of
coming to a second home. I have heard so many things about it, and my
friends felt strongly [about being in Israel]." The lesson is explicit. Israel
resonates sufficiently with American Jews' sense of who they are as Jews—
part of a people with a history, a minority people that has finally become a
majority in one place in the world, a religious people that began its encounter with God at sites in the Holy Land—to provoke a desire to visit. It
is not just another vacation spot in their eyes, or merely a place rich in
historical meaning. It would mean a homecoming of sorts. They have
heard a lot about the place, and know it is valued by their community. But
Israel is not central to who American Jews are as Jews—and so the need to
visit it, or learn about it, or wrestle with its importance to the Jewish people,
is far from pressing.

JEWISH ORGANIZATIONS: REMOTE AND IRRELEVANT

The American Jewish organizational infrastructure is both highly elaborate and highly professionalized, and has long been seen as a distinguishing feature of American Jewish group life. The organized community
embraces numerous functions and sorts of institutions. It includes synagogues, Jewish community centers, federations and other fund-raising
bodies, fraternal organizations, community relations agencies, Zionist organizations, old-age homes and services, family and children's agencies,
vocational services, youth groups, schools, institutions of higher learning,
museums, newspapers and magazines, other cultural agencies, and bodies
serving still other functions. Each functional area is characterized both by
local institutions and continental umbrella organizations. One researcher
conservatively estimates the annual philanthropic contributions to this infrastructure at $4.5 billion (Wertheimer 1997), and to that figure must be
added fees for services and other sources of income that further expand
the size of the national Jewish political economy.

The expanse and significance of organized Jewish communal life is
such that it is fair to say that no other major religious or ethnic group
supports a voluntary organizational life as elaborate, variegated, or prodi-
gious. Today's Jewish communal agencies derive from a long history of
Jewish communal organization that characterized Jewish communities in
the Diaspora for centuries.

Indeed, large numbers of American Jews are attached to one or another
piece of this organizational infrastructure. Almost half (48 percent) of the
survey respondents claimed membership in a synagogue. Jewish community centers represent the next largest point of affiliation, a distant second,

with 14 percent reporting membership (other studies suggest a somewhat higher level). Even more (27 percent) reported that their household has participated in a JCC-sponsored program in the previous year. About a third (32 percent) of American Jews belonged to some other Jewish organization. Combining these figures, a clear majority of American Jewish households (56 percent) report membership in a synagogue, JCC, or other Jewish organization. As many as 42 percent report having contributed to the UJA/Federation campaign in their local communities in the previous year (as against the actual numbers of donors, this figure is undoubtedly exaggerated). A recent study of Jews in Greater Boston, a region not especially noted for extraordinarily high levels of communal affiliation, found that as many as 82 percent of adult Jews in the region professed some sort of connection to a formal Jewish institution (Israel 1997, p. 87).

Yet, even amid widespread belonging to Jewish institutions, the evidence—both quantitative and qualitative—suggests a rather narrow base of commitment (aside from the synagogue). We asked our survey respondents to assess the extent of their attachment to several institutions. Just 11 percent said they felt very or extremely attached to a local Jewish Federation/UJA, and just 18 percent felt that degree of attachment to any other Jewish organization (other than the synagogue, JCC, or federation). In addition, somewhat over 40 percent of respondents agreed with each of these survey items:

• "Many Jews in synagogue or Jewish organizational life are hypocrites."
• "The organized Jewish community gives too much recognition to the wealthiest Jews."
• "I find Jewish organizations largely remote and irrelevant to me."

The comments of our interviewees were consistent with these findings. Joy expressed a typical lack of passionate commitment to Jewish charitable giving. "Our [family's] charities are not Jewish ones. We send a check to UJA and stuff like that every year, but it's not significant." We did not find the sense of connection to the organized community commonly expressed by members of their parents' generation two or three decades ago. Sylvia, whose praise of her synagogue was heartfelt, and who told us how much she loved her stay in Israel, was sharply critical of most Jewish organizations:

> There is no sensitivity about what people need. They need organizations that give them a purpose and a meaning. When my husband was involved with the Weizmann Institute of Science, that was very focused and they knew why they needed money and what kind of research, and that's easy. But that's something easier to get involved in. Smaller. Particular.

Sylvia's attraction to the smaller and more "focused" reflects a drive for personally meaningful experiences, largely unavailable in organizations. The statement is also important for what it did not say. It apparently never

occurred to Sylvia—or to any other of our respondents, for that matter—
to see Jewish organizations as a locus for friendship, a place where they
could socialize with other Jews in an easy and relaxed atmosphere. Such
were clearly the perspectives and interests of the previous generation(s).
Conversely, the ease with which Jews make friends with non-Jews today
(and their prominence in American institutions) deprives Jewish organizations of the opportunity they once exploited to provide Jews with a safe
and comfortable arena for socializing, or for recognition and positions of
leadership.

Dave wove together a number of themes explored in this chapter when
he told us:

> I'm not sure if I want my charity to go where it goes because it goes to
> a lot of organizations that are maintaining the status quo of the Jewish
> power structure in Israel. Why should I send money to places that end up
> politicking against my interest? I'm a Reform Jew and a lot of the places
> that the Federation's money goes to in Israel don't want me to have any
> rights.

Like many other Jews we interviewed, Dave approaches the matter of ties
to the Jewish public sphere very personally. He expresses a good deal of
autonomy and independence, feeling little need to effect a tie with other
Jews or with Judaism by way of philanthropy or organizational activity, and
is utterly unimpressed with the size and success of the Jewish Federation.
He is concerned about the impact of his money. As a Reform Jew, he is
annoyed, to say the least, with Israel. Most important of all, he calibrates
the extent of his obligation to the memory of the Holocaust, to engagement with Israel, or to participation in Jewish philanthropic and organizational activities in accordance with his needs as a Jewish self in search of
fulfillment. The public sphere, we might say, bears the burden of demon-
strating its importance to Jewish loyalties nurtured and focused elsewhere.
We now shift our focus in that direction.

GOD AND THE SYNAGOGUE

God is . . . an angel on my shoulder. God is something like a best friend.
A day doesn't go by when I don't have a literal conversation with God
about something. . . .

—LYNNE

I feel like I have some sort of personal relation with God. Sometimes
when I talk to myself out loud, and say why don't I make a serious effort,
and think of things I need to do, it borders on prayer, talking to God.
. . . Maybe there's an element of real prayer in that . . .

—TONY

People ask me why, if I'm not religious, I go to shul . . . I came to the
conclusion that it was very important for me to do something for myself,
and it's the only time of the week that I truly get lost in thought for
three hours and let my mind wander and get caught up in the melodies.
. . . I have a lot of faith in God. My Jewishness . . . has seen me through
some difficult days. God has seen me through difficult days.

—LEE

The most striking finding of our study in connection with God and the
synagogue is that, for the most part, the Jews we interviewed do not make
any straightforward connection between the two. They believe in God—
far more than we expected, or than survey data about American Jews led
us to believe. They are also surprisingly content with, and even fondly
attached to, their synagogues. But they told us time and again that they do
not come to synagogue expecting to find God there, or stay away because
they do not. The words in the prayer book do not particularly interest
them. The God described and invoked in those prayers is very different
from the one in which they believe—too commanding, for one thing, and,
in ways we shall explain, far too "Jewish." They are distinctly uncomfortable with the act of prayer. And yet they pray. This combination of unease
and devotion, enthusiasm and disquiet, came through repeatedly in our

interviews—making for a pattern of alienation and belonging not easily unraveled or reversed.

Consider Gil, for example: one of the more highly involved members of our sample, as well as one of the most articulate—a physician of about fifty who lives in suburban Boston with his wife, a financial analyst. Their children are both away at college. Gil is an avid reader, plays piano, and enjoys gardening. He grew up in a fairly affluent family, attended a Conservative synagogue and its Hebrew school as a child, and credits his grandparents, his rabbi (who "singled me out in some way"), and Camp Ramah as formative influences on his adult commitment to Judaism. Like many others we interviewed, Gil recalls the home observance of his parents as sparse, his own interest in the tradition as a child far exceeding that of his family. Typically, too, his practice lapsed once he left home for college. Despite occasional attendance at Hillel functions, a summer on kibbutz, and—later—High Holiday attendance with his wife, strong Jewish connections did not resume by his account until "the arrival of my children" impelled "a stronger urge to be members of a temple."

Gil is now an active member of his congregation, involved particularly in its school and adult education committees, and speaks glowingly of the Me'ah adult Jewish education program as a transformative experience that satisfied his desire "to know more about what my religion is—to be a Jew by choice." Gil says that he "loves the tradition," and now attends synagogue services regularly. When asked about any negatives attaching to Jews or Judaism in his eyes, he complained only about factionalism, intolerance, and "a certain clannishness," the feeling that Jews are better. He now thinks of himself "more as a Jew than I used to"—no longer "an American who is Jewish" but far more "a Jew living in America." It was right after Gil made that self-identification that we raised the issue of faith.

"That's hard," he said at once. "I'm not sure I have a very coherent sense of God. Prayer comes hard for me. I think it comes hard for anybody. There are times when I think of God as being the best that all of us can be —in a humanistic, secular sense. In a sense I believe in a primal force—a spirit that causes things to happen, that set the world in motion." When he goes to synagogue Gil "is not always looking for dialogue with God." Rather he finds something "calming and soothing about the service." The two to three hours he spends in synagogue on Saturday mornings "are very meaningful, the center of the week." Concentrating on the prayers is "an important part of my week, part of the cycle I miss when I don't go." But "in terms of God, I don't know that I can say much. When I think of God personally, it is trying to strive to be the best person I can be—a concept of *tselem elohim* [creation in the image of God]—mimicking God by being the most perfect person I can be, as opposed to a greater theological sense of He who created heaven and earth and set nature in motion."

Does Gil have any sort of personal relation to God? "No. There are times when I think about my family, or worry about family or friends in trouble, and I think there is a sense of prayer there." In synagogue he thinks about the week past or the week coming up, about "ways I could relate to people better . . . [whether] I am being as good a father as I could be." He also tries to evaluate his life and his relation to other people. "I don't know if this is God-talk, but to me it is an important spiritual outlet that I spend time thinking about my role in the universe or at least in Lexington. That's in a sense my dialogue with God."

We asked if Gil had ever felt closer to God in times of crisis, and his response was telling. He felt closer to *religion* at such moments, he said, but not to God. When his grandparents died he found solace in Judaism. "I'm not sure God plays a role in that." The sense of community and family, on the other hand, mattered a great deal.

Gil's comments are exceptionally thoughtful and articulate (though they are far from unique among our sample in that regard). But his views are fairly typical. Three elements of his response are of particular interest.

First, Gil understands God as a *force or spirit that is present in the world* rather than as a *personal being endowed with consciousness and purpose*. Of the nearly fifty individuals who made up our interview sample, only seven indicated belief in a personal God who hears prayer, intervenes directly in history or the lives of individuals, or rewards human beings after death in accordance with their deeds in this life. About twenty either described God explicitly as a force in nature or spoke in ways consistent with that view. Only two or three were avowed atheists; others were too vague on the subject to characterize. In like manner, relatively few of the participants in our survey (10 percent) would say that God probably or definitely does not exist, though only a slim majority (56 percent) said, "Definitely, yes," to the statement "There is a God." These beliefs of course have direct (albeit complex) bearing on the way that our subjects conceive of the act of praying, as well as on their assent to, or interest in, the claims made about God repeatedly in the liturgies (whether Orthodox, Conservative, Reform, or Reconstructionist) of the synagogue service. Gil in fact attested a stronger relation than most to the liturgy, despite his inability to take literally its claims concerning God's creation, revelation, and redemption.

Note, second, Gil's conviction that *God is not a subject easily discussed.* "That's hard," he said immediately when asked to describe his belief. Almost every person we interviewed reacted in a similar fashion. It *is* hard to talk about God, of course, all the more so to an interviewer whom one has never met before. The matter is both immensely difficult and immensely private. We were repeatedly struck by the humility and honesty of our subjects in addressing it. We were also impressed by *how few Jewish (or non-Jewish) sources were cited in doing so;* even Gil, then in the midst of the Me'ah program, an intense course of study in the history of Judaism, did not seem to have Jewish texts or "God-concepts" ready at hand in his conceptual repertoire. He instead employed general notions selected from the inventory of contemporary American culture. For many of our subjects, Jewish notions of God were simply unavailable. For others, however, they were of no interest, or even repellent.

Finally, *despite his lack of assent or relation to the content of the prayers he utters there each week, Gil's devotion to his synagogue is apparent.* This response was typical of the more highly involved members of our sample. The vast majority of our subjects did find the synagogue attractive as an institution, even if (or perhaps because!) they attend but rarely. Significantly, they find it so despite lack of belief in the content of the liturgy. In fact, of synagogue members in our survey sample, fully 70 percent said they felt very or extremely attached to the congregations of which they are members. Some of those we interviewed, like Gil, said they use the hours spent in shul for reflection about their lives and resolution concerning self-improvement. Others spoke of the experience of community, or of contact with the tradition, or of the appeal of a particular rabbi. A few mentioned music or the sermon. It is utterly clear that prayer in the traditional or conventionally understood sense is not what brings or keeps them there.

Divergence between "latent" and "manifest" meaning is, of course, not exceptional in any realm of human behavior. We should not be surprised to find it in this one. However, if our informants are at all typical, the implications for the restructuring of synagogues are profound. We shall explore those consequences at the chapter's conclusion.

TALKING TO GOD

Lee, an insurance executive in Connecticut who is almost sixty, has been extremely active in the Jewish community (as well as in local politics) for many years. His family was not particularly observant when he was growing up; his bar mitzvah took place in an Orthodox synagogue and his confirmation in a Reform temple. "As Marlon Brando would have said in that movie," he quipped, "I cover the waterfront, I fit that mold." His own connection to Judaism at the time seems not to have come from either synagogue but rather from his grandmother, who "probably had the biggest influence on my life." Her role at Passover, with the extended family gathering at her home for the seder, is particularly vivid in his mind. Lee also remembers his grandmother suddenly crying at a song on the radio because it had been sung by Jews going to their deaths in the Holocaust, and this prompts the thought that for him too the Holocaust has been a major source of Jewish commitment. "That sort of has been the reason for my involvement in Jewish survival: so it [the Holocaust] can't and won't happen again, God willing." The motivation for involvement grew further when, after raising his children, Lee felt "I had a commitment to put something back into the community." He says, simply and powerfully, "The Jewish community has been a very important part of my life."

At first, Lee's adult involvement did not include the synagogue. That came only when he decided that it was important for his children's development that their attendance at Hebrew school be matched by his own attendance at, and leadership role in, the synagogue. (His wife was supportive of the decision, but was far less active than Lee in any Jewish realm.) Lee then began to go to services weekly. Only about a decade later, however, at about the age of forty, did he arrive at his current understanding of *why* he goes.

> People ask me why, if I'm not religious, I go to shul. . . . I came to the conclusion that it was very important for me to do something for myself, and it's the only time of the week that I truly get lost in thought for three hours and let my mind wander and get caught up in the melodies, singing the melodies which I truly enjoy. I don't really know Hebrew, I can't read it, but I sing the songs by heart. . . . My week is not complete unless I go to shul on Saturday morning.

Note this strikingly individualist formulation of the purpose of prayer, joined to a no less striking commitment to the Jewish community and its institutions. Note too that Lee, who describes himself as "non-religious," spends about three hours in services each Saturday morning engaged in serious contemplation and caught up in traditional melodies! The fact that he cannot follow the Hebrew perhaps precludes intimate relation to the content of the liturgy. But it may well foster the ability to "get caught up" and "get lost"—the space for meditation—that in Lee's mind constitutes the service's main appeal. The issues are clearly complex.

We would be wrong to conclude from what we have learned about Lee so far that he does not believe in God, or even that he dissociates God from the synagogue in the manner typical of many others whom we interviewed. Quite the opposite is true on both counts. Lee believes in God in a very personal and intense fashion. He explained that when he looks at his family, his business, all he has been through in life, he is full of thanksgiving. He thanks God that his children came out whole, and for the continuing health of his family. "I'm delighted about that and thank God every Saturday." Later in the interview, when asked what he likes about being Jewish, Lee affirmed his belief that the Jews are "the chosen people. . . . It's a heavy-duty responsibility being Jewish."

> God is a very important part of my life. What I mean by that . . . I look forward to going to synagogue. It's an opportunity to commune with God, not that you can't do it every day at home, but it takes on a greater

[meaning] for me in a synagogue setting. . . . I get lost in singing melodies and just trying to communicate: during difficult days asking for help, on good days thanking God for my family's well-being, my being, that I have a wonderful life, a comfortable lifestyle, that I'm delighted to have my health . . . I don't think, sometimes, that we take the time out in life to really appreciate what we have. I think there's an old expression, if you have faith in God your trust is well-founded. I have a lot of faith in God. My Jewishness . . . has seen me through some difficult days. God has seen me through difficult days. When everything else fails, you know you always have the good Lord above looking over you and you know that you always have somebody to talk to.

Lee commented at a later point in the interview that he had turned to God especially during a difficult divorce from his first wife. His life "changed dramatically with God's help . . . there was a motivation on my part that I felt came from other things. I really feel that we live a grand design and we're playing it out and that God has great things in store for me and I'm looking forward to that." In calling himself "non-religious," then, Lee uses the term, as do many Jews of his and his parents' generations (his age cohort may be an important factor here), to mean "non-observant by traditional standards of piety." Indeed, of all the individuals we interviewed, Lee exhibited the strongest faith in God's providential care for him personally, and expressed gratitude and petition to God most directly. Without actually articulating a relation to the *words* of the prayers, Lee made one of the strongest connections between God and the synagogue that we encountered. For Lee, God is not a force, but a personal being who hears and answers prayer (a view held by only about one-fifth of our survey sample). What is more, God is not only the God of nature and of history, but also the God of Israel, the chosen people. "I think life is a grand design. God has put us here, our cards have been dealt to us." Lee showed a confidence in himself, and life, that he attributed to the faith that God not only exists, but is active in his life: "near at hand," as the psalm puts it, to "all who call upon Him in truth."

❧

We heard similar sentiments from several others. Rachel, a social worker of about fifty who belongs to a Reform synagogue in Chicago, said that God is "a really personal thing." Her "perception of what I needed God to be comes out of unhappy childhood years," and she will always retain the picture of God formed then: "beneficent, always there and always watching over me. Even if that's not how it's supposed to be, that's how it will always be for me." God was and is, she remarks, a "very comforting notion" —believed in despite her awareness of its origin and the needs that it serves. Rachel added that she prayed a lot to God as a child, and prays now as a parent that God will watch over her children. Her view of God may not be terribly educated, she said, but it will always remain her vision. She too described herself as "not an active religious person," perhaps because Jewish obligation in her view connotes responsibility to family and society rather than observance of the commandments, but she did say that she may be "becoming more spiritual." She also agreed that the Jews are God's chosen people, not in the sense of being special but "to be responsible and make the world a better place."

Lynne, a New Haven lawyer and author in her forties, belongs to both a Conservative and an Orthodox synagogue. Among the most observant of our interviewees, she thinks of God

> as an angel on my shoulder . . . God is something like a best friend. A day doesn't go by when I don't have a literal conversation with God about something, whether it's a few words or we actually have a conversation. I will say, "Okay, give me strength now, I need to get through this." I just have the sense that God is on my shoulder and we are going to do it. I will get the help that I need . . .

She adds that traditional images of God as a male figure on a throne writing the destiny of human beings in a book year by year no longer work for her. Lynne tries when teaching Hebrew school to get the children to remember that God could just as easily be female as male.

Nor can Lynne relate to God as a judge toward whom one feels fear. "I don't understand fear of God at all. I keep coming against it because I study with Rabbi X . . . and I just don't get it. Maybe I don't understand what they mean by fear but . . . [you don't] do something because you are afraid of something." In this she resembles most contemporary American Christians, who are likewise not disposed to believe in a God who punishes people or in any way makes life difficult for them, but are rather inclined to worship a God who supports them, encourages self-assurance, and demands a discipline that only legitimates the way of life to which they are already committed (Wuthnow 1998, pp. 85, 101). Ritual observance has value with or without God. "Whereas, on the one hand, God is all-important to me, on the other hand, it's not at all important to me, whether there is or isn't a God just isn't that important to me" as a reason for Jewish practice. Lynne tells other people that she keeps kosher "because God said so," but in reality she does not really know why she does it "except that it connects me to a glorious history that I want passed on for its value in and of itself."

Lynne's position on the meaning of ritual observance places her in good company among modern Jews. Much of twentieth-century Jewish religious thought, Eisen has argued elsewhere (1998a), can be seen as an attempt to find reasons for ritual practice that is already under way. The ritual is, as it were, "out in front" of belief and continues all the while that thinkers seek, and do not find, adequate theological justifications for it. Laypeople too have demonstrated an adherence to a variety of ritual observances—circumcision, recitation of the Mourners' Kaddish, attendance at Kol Nidre prayers on Yom Kippur—not explicable by their avowed beliefs. Nor is Lynne unusual in her inability to relate to the traditional concept, "fear of God" (*yir'at ha-shem*), or her non-belief in God as the Commander of the Jewish people, despite a strong belief in a God personal enough to be the angel on her shoulder—a very traditional image indeed. The issue of divine authority among modern Jews goes back to the very beginning of Emancipation. It long predates the "therapeutic" or "yuppie" or "me generation" cultures of the past three decades, to which some have attributed the notion of a God who is there to help but has no power to command or injure.

One might be tempted, too, given Lynne's special criticism of male imagery for the divine, to ascribe her aversion to "fear" and "commandment" to a feminist distaste for hierarchy. Rachel too said she believes in a God who is beneficent but not in a God who issues mitzvot to the Jewish people. Rebecca, a financial manager in Chicago who is now in her late forties, likewise reported that she feels connected to God whenever she feels awe, but "has a very difficult time with male imagery and prayer language." We heard this sentiment quite a lot from the women whom we interviewed. However, while men did not express the same dislike for male imagery, alienation from traditional imagery for the divine—the Commander and Redeemer of Israel who appears on every page of the prayer book—was prevalent among them as well.

The God in whom our subjects believe is, in this sense, not a particularly Jewish God—or at least not a particular*ist* Jewish God. Moderately affiliated Jews in America have rather embraced universalist and personalist elements of the tradition and of modern culture. They have left aside or rejected those parts of Judaism that claim a special relation between God and the Jewish people. The particularist opening of the Aleinu prayer, we might say, which praises God "who has not made us [Jews] like the nations of the earth," does not resonate at all for our interviewees. They prefer the prayer's universalist conclusion, which looks forward to the day when God will be ruler of all the earth.

Three other witnesses to personal belief, all of whom conform to this pattern, stand out in our minds because they introduced important themes and concerns not yet highlighted.

The first concern, perhaps the most venerable of all subjects in the philosophy of religion, is the existence of evil. Amy, a non-practicing lawyer and member of a Reform temple in Los Angeles, responded to our question about God with "Oh, man, this is like an essay in college." She then confessed to mixed emotions on the subject. Amy emphasized that her relation to God, "whatever it is, is personal"; when she compares Judaism to other religions, the ones that in her view understand more about the world are those which do not rely on intermediaries. "My relation is with God and I don't have to explain myself, feel negative, hide something, cushion something." At the same time, however, Amy constantly struggles with the concept of a God who is good but does bad things. When a child in her extended family contracted cystic fibrosis, she was led to question what kind of God would allow this to happen. The pain of the matter is still raw, and led her to cry when describing it for us. Amy says the child's mother, who is not Jewish, believes the tragedy struck her because God knew she could handle it, but Amy herself no longer believes that God picks and chooses to whom to give bad luck. The event "kills the concept of a good God."

However, whereas another woman we met confessed that she ceased praying to God when her prayers for her father's recovery from a serious illness were not answered, Amy continues to pray despite her doubts. She does so "formally" at temple—"I don't think about it, I just do it"—and with real feeling and intention at Passover ("a beautiful, incredible story") and on Yom Kippur.

Nancy, a convert who was raised as a Catholic and who repeatedly emphasized lesbian and social justice agendas that she regrets are not more central to contemporary Judaism, told us that she does not understand the traditional belief in a Jewish covenant with God, and believes that anyone who does claim to understand it is arrogant. Nonetheless, she has a very personal relation with God, indeed talks to God every day in some form or other. Uncomfortable with male imagery, she imagines God as Shekhina, refuses to use the word "Lord," abbreviates the word "God" in the Orthodox way when she writes it (substituting a dash for the *o*), and, in sum, "believes in God a whole lot." Nancy reports that this could not have happened until she learned "to shake my fist at God," strengthened by the (mistaken) belief that Hanna, mother of the prophet Samuel, had done the same. Terrifying ordeals with a psychotic lover who underwent constant medical crises made it difficult for Nancy to believe in a God who was exclusively kind and gentle. She felt abandoned at that point, she says, but also carried by benevolence. One night, when things were going particularly badly, she began to sob. "I went to temple, and ran into a woman, now passed away, who was totally dear, she has an autistic son. There was something about her—she was the angel of the evening for me—to me she was the voice of God that comes through people."

Nancy adds that she believes in magic, in the mystical aspects of the world, but does not "lean on them too much." Instead she relies on her community. She believes we have access to God through prayer and meditation, as well as through observance. "If I notice a mezuzah, or eat something better in a day, observe any kind of holiness, I'm there. Keep it real simple. You don't have to literally pray . . . just check in consistently." Nor does one need to address God in personal terms. Her use of "shekhina" is not meant to substitute a mother for a father image. God can be seen as energy or spirit. Nancy's approach is at once highly personalist, extremely universalist, and grounded in Jewish sources. "Keep it simple," she says of her approach to religion. The point is not the details of belief or practice, but the "holiness."

Finally, consider Simon, a lawyer in his forties who has been a highly observant and involved member of a Conservative synagogue in Denver for some time, and who recently brought his family to Israel for a year of full-time study. The view of God he expressed was unabashedly traditional, more so than any other we encountered, and was obviously informed by his recent period of Jewish learning. Yet it somehow lacked the passion exhibited by the women just quoted, perhaps because Simon is unwilling to discuss such a personal matter with strangers, or because he has adopted the tradition's aversion to discussing God directly, or because his belief is less sure than it seems—or because he is a male, which of course bears on all the tendencies just enumerated. Asked what he tells his children about God, Simon replied simply, "I guess the most traditional answers you can give. I try to convey my personal views: there is a personal God . . . described in the Torah; you can accept it, you can understand it, and you can modify it in the sense that you can personalize it, you can make it whatever it means to you." For Simon, the events described in the Torah actually happened. "I believe that God was present in the times that the Torah said He was present." He added that he would not tell his children things "that are strictly Torah-based, because I don't know the Torah that well, but I would take some guidance from that." Asked whether he felt particularly close to God or religion in times of crisis, he stressed the latter rather than the former: the comfort of tradition, of ritual, of community, of knowing what death means from a Jewish perspective, rather than of direct consolation from God.

The "varieties of religious experience" on view in these accounts are strikingly diverse—testimony to the complexities of conviction with which contemporary American Jews are wrestling. As we would expect of such intelligent and self-conscious individuals, their belief regarding ultimate matters is never simple or straightforward. Note these paradoxes, most of them quite venerable in the history of Jewish faith: Praise of God's goodness in prayer co-exists with awareness that God's world contains much evil. Cognitive doubt does not preclude either worship or observance. Awareness that adult images of God are often formed in childhood does not prevent adults from invoking those images sincerely. Relation to a personal God is almost invariably bound up in personal relations to parents, grandparents, loved ones, and community. Recitation of prayer to God is simultaneously—or primarily—a precious occasion for personal reflection (the Hebrew verb for prayer, le-hitpalel, is reflexive).

Finally, and perhaps the only real new development in the series, believers feel completely free to pick and choose among the attributes ascribed to God in Jewish sources, rejecting those which overly particularize God in their eyes or which compel specific observances. Even the most traditional affirmations, such as Simon's, do not rule out "modifying" and "personalizing" Jewish belief, making it (in his words) "whatever it means to you." We shall now turn to individuals who do not believe in a personal God—do not believe, in other words, that God hears and answers prayer—and shall find that this sort of faith does not necessarily hinder prayer, and certainly does not deter synagogue attendance. In some cases quite the opposite is true.

❧

Three themes are especially pronounced in these expressions of belief, all of them articulated by Gil. He spoke, we recall, about the image of God as an ideal toward which he reaches when he tries to "be the best person I can be." Gil used the phrase "spiritual outlet," invoking the term which in contemporary America seems far more positive, and so more potent, than "religion" or "faith." Finally, he described God as a "force"—a notion popularized by the *Star Wars* movies and countless New Age books but also favored by religious thinkers such as Mordecai Kaplan. All three images—current in the culture, and possessing venerable origins in the canon of twentieth-century Jewish thought—are far more widespread among those we interviewed than the personal notions of God examined thus far. Like the latter, however, beliefs in God as force or spirit or ideal vary enormously.

Molly responded to our question about God with "Oh, this is an easy one! I'm considering believing in God. I think I can sometimes." The formulation is telling, and utterly typical. Belief is not a duty, not something that holds one. It is rather something that one explores, and chooses whether or not to hold. Molly has trouble with notions of God as beneficent and merciful, given the state of the world, and she confesses to being "torn" because she occasionally finds herself praying "to a being who's supposed to be in control, who I can't believe would let these things happen in the first place." She does not believe in a personal God, feels she has no right to ask God for anything, but can believe in a "historical God, the God Jews have believed in for thousands of years. . . . It's how I can say a *brakha* [blessing] without feeling ridiculous." Molly knows that her ancestors did not believe as she does (and does not). Her belief is "historical" because it emerges from the ancestors' belief, is grounded in their texts, abides inside the framework of their liturgy and rituals. A moment later Molly speaks of "an attempt to bring some spirituality into my life." All this is said slowly, thoughtfully, by a person whose journey is clearly continuing.

Would she call herself spiritual, then? "I like to believe I could go in that direction."

Karen, an accountant who like Molly is in her mid-forties and a resident of suburban Boston, said she has long been nurturing her "spiritual side" through yoga, to which she gave some of the credit for taking her back to Judaism. Yoga raised questions for her which it could not answer. She admitted, however, that "God-talk" still makes her very uncomfortable. God is a private matter. Her belief constantly changes. She does not believe in a God who wrote the Torah or "micromanages" the world; what she does believe, she continued, is not incompatible with the views of physicist Stephen Hawking. God does not answer prayers. "You put your intent out and hope it happens." Karen has recently begun to explore Jewish mysticism, and her relation to God still comes through yoga as well as through synagogue services—or enjoying a beautiful day, or sitting with her children. Once again Judaism is the framework for a universalist notion of God, and the synagogue is *a* site of relation to God but not the *primary* site.

Tony, an engineer in his fifties, reports that he did not go to synagogue more than three times from the day he graduated Hebrew school until he began to say Kaddish for his mother about fifteen years ago. He believes in God, always has believed, but has gone through different phases in trying to understand what that belief entails. "So much of it I can't articulate." Asked whether he has a personal relation to God, Tony begins to say, "I don't," and then checks himself:

> That's a good question. I like to tell myself that I have. I guess I do. I feel like I have some sort of personal relation with God. Sometimes when I talk to myself out loud, and say why don't I make a serious effort, and think of things I need to do, it borders on prayer, talking to God. When I go to services, I don't often feel like I'm praying in the sense of communicating with God. There is not much *kavvanah* [focused intention] involved there. In other ways, there is. . . . Just to be here, making some sort of effort, that's a mitzvah, doing the best that I can at the moment. I shouldn't be too hard on myself. Maybe there is an element of real prayer in that.

Once again, the personalist nature of the belief is as pronounced as the honesty of the quest and the disinclination to believe in a God who commands mitzvot in a traditional sense. Edward, a Chicago physician in his forties, made similar observations about the time he spends in synagogue. "What do I get out of it? . . . I like going to services . . . I like it—it's my own time. I almost always go by myself. It's my own time." Other reasons for going, clearly secondary, included the desire to be "part of praying and the culture."

Stuart, a screenwriter in Los Angeles, told us that his mother "has a path" that he himself lacks, but occasionally he has flashes of experience which convince him that "there is God . . . a force . . . something that is truth." Words "are nice for connecting to God" but he doesn't really need them. The only words Stuart feels are so holy they should be spoken are those of the Mourners' Kaddish. Its words are "as holy as Torah." Ken, a Los Angeles filmmaker, reported that he has lately begun to think more about God, to wonder about God's interest in the commandments and the presence of evil in the world. He conceives of God as "a warm loving spirit to reach out to when I need love and nurturing." He has "some issues with God," but most of the time "is okay with God . . . I feel really good about God." The formulation may strike some as "pure California," or as a cliché of therapeutic yuppie religiosity. But, as we have seen, the desire to feel good about God and to feel good in the synagogue are, among our sample, not limited to one region or to any age-group but rather are widespread, indeed nearly universal.

Rebecca, whose feminist distaste for male images of God we noted earlier, says that God for her means connectedness to nature. That is "one of the most powerful experiences I have had in life." She is aware of a natural order in the world despite its chaos. While she has no personal relation to God, Rebecca for some years now has blessed her children on Friday evening with the traditional priestly benediction, and says that it is "so wonderful for me to talk to God and pray to God [by means of this blessing], to feel connected."

Edward too said that he prays to God, though "I don't know who or what I pray to. I hope for things. I pray for things." God is a force, not a person: "a good idea." Because of that belief, he says dryly, "There is not a lot of money in praying." Heaven and earth were created long ago. God is somehow involved, but science describes the forces which dictate our lives. Edward is a rationalist through and through. God does not exercise providence, but religion is a source of strength. The Jews are not chosen; they are simply smarter, and so get into better colleges. The lesson to be learned from the Holocaust is "Watch your backside." Is he a spiritual person? "I don't know what it means."

Others in our sample, however, did exhibit or refer to the cluster of attitudes and behaviors that we normally associate with spirituality (experiences of awe, wonder, and thankfulness), and some did so without linking these in their own minds to God. Suzanne, the Palo Alto therapist whose emotion-laden decision to use her mother's candlesticks was described in chapter 4, has had no adult affiliation with a synagogue. She is quite certain that she does not believe in God even as a force. "Spirituality," however, evoked a series of powerful associations. "I guess it's about meaning. It came up as an issue for me after my father died and my daughter left home." The question of meaning to life was suddenly front and center, and Suzanne found herself grappling with it—and experiencing thankfulness.

She then added—the move by this point should no longer surprise us—"I've prayed a lot, but the way I now see what prayer is, that isn't what I was doing at the time when I was growing up. . . . Now, if I pray, it's about surrender and thankfulness, a deep sense of thankfulness which seems to feel wonderful." Such prayer is not dependent on words but is rather a way of saying, with or without verbalizing the feeling, "Thank you that I am so lucky to have this in my life." It is also, Suzanne continued a moment later, "about trying to find some way to tolerate an awareness of life and death. That's a big part. After my dad died, I realized that I had no way of being about life and death. I had grown up denying this could happen." The notion of God does not resonate for Suzanne, perhaps because she had been brought up to believe in a "male figure on high who runs the show down here." However, the concept is not entirely alien; she recognizes that others might feel as she does and attach those feelings to God. This is simply not a language that she chooses to use, "but it certainly is about the same issues."

The difference between Suzanne's belief and that of others we have described is a matter of shading. Indeed, the distinction between belief in God as person and as force blurs considerably as soon as we enter into the actual language used by our subjects and come to appreciate the gropings and difficulties that their words convey. For that reason, we think it would be a mistake to attribute Suzanne's lack of affiliation with a synagogue (or the lack of affiliation among the handful of outright atheists we encountered!) solely or even principally to lack of belief. A host of other factors are involved (such as, in Suzanne's case, conflicts over religion in her family of origin, strong opposition to synagogue affiliation on the part of her spouse, alienation on feminist grounds from a religion perceived as patriarchal, and a series of negative encounters with Jewish events and institutions). God is simply not what draws those we interviewed to synagogue, or keeps them away. Joy, a New York fund-raiser, told us—and tells her children—that "I really don't know" about God. She tends to associate divinity with "a common body of ethics and morals which is godlike . . . our spiritual foundation." Yet Joy also told us frankly that she has wanted for some time to join a synagogue, and has not done so only because her husband will not permit it. She would have joined despite the complaint, quoted earlier, that there is often no connection in services between "brain and mouth." Joy believes God is "sort of the great body of knowledge [including scientific knowledge] that man has access to," but there is no "all-powerful force," and certainly no "personality ascribed to that body of knowledge."

Why then, if belief does not explain affiliation and attendance, *are* people coming to services, or staying away? Exactly half of the participants in our survey agreed that "I look forward to going to synagogue," though only 12 percent said they agreed strongly with that statement. Most, apparently, find services "interesting." Only a third confirmed that "synagogue services are not interesting to me," while 44 percent disagreed and 18 percent disagreed strongly. Something is drawing Jews to synagogue, on the relatively infrequent occasions when they go. Is it simply, as Joy told us, that they love the music? The rabbi? The sense of community? To address these questions, we turn to our subjects' comments on what they do and do not find appealing in the synagogues to which they do or do not belong and go.

THE SANCTUARY

Samuel C. Heilman (1976), at the outset of his classic ethnographic analysis *Synagogue Life,* observed that the Jews whom he was observing attended an Orthodox synagogue, and thus were subject to "the imperatives of commingling." They had no choice but to be in synagogue week after week because it is required of them in a body of law which they trace back to divine revelation at Sinai. Many of the males obeyed the halakhic requirement that they attend services several times daily (Heilman 1976). Highly involved Conservative and Reform Jews, for their part, obey a similar (if less intense) imperative. For completely uninvolved Jews the opposite is true: the question of synagogue attendance rarely arises. They are unlikely ever to consider the matter, except at Rosh Hashanah and Yom Kippur or to attend a bar or bat mitzvah. Only in the middle group, the moderately affiliated, do we find Jews for whom the question of synagogue attendance and/or membership is a serious one. For these Jews the question arises again and again. Synagogue attendance is not an imperative for them, and neither is it, except in a few cases we encountered, a long-established routine. Why do such Jews come to services, when they do?

We have already heard from Joy about this subject. The music at services is what attracts her. The prayers are meaningless. She made no reference to the sermons. One gathers that she is also attracted to the public expression of the ethical and moral ideals with which God is associated in her mind, and to the possibility of making this affirmation in the company of other Jews. Sylvia, who supervises student evaluation of teachers at a college in Manhattan, is by contrast extremely attached to her congregation, and was quite specific about the reason: "I find it very stimulating . . . there is generally something that I learn . . . it lifts me up." She particularly enjoys the rabbi's talks to bar and bat mitzvah celebrants. Her only complaint about services is that they are too long.

Despite the brevity of their remarks, Joy and Sylvia identified two key components of synagogue life which were mentioned repeatedly in our interviews: music and the rabbi. Sonya, a woman in her thirties who recently left work on public policy issues in order to study in Israel, described herself as having just emerged from a "rebellion away from God and . . . tradition" that she attributed to a desire to be in "complete control." A traumatic personal experience brought home the lesson that she did not exercise such control, and so opened a path to thinking about God. Sonya is still not sure that she is a believer. Nor has her new openness to faith translated into interest in the liturgy. She goes to services, now as before, because "it is a time for me to stop out of my busy day, even though I don't really relate to the prayers as such for what they say . . . the part I enjoy the most is in the Amidah, when I do my own silent prayers, and it's not as much a petition to God . . . as an affirmation, what I want to improve with my life." What did she like about services in the United States, aside from this opportunity for reflection? "Since I was little, I always liked the songs. That is always what drew me . . . I definitely like *ruach* [spirit]. I like music and dance." What did she dislike? "The rabbi." He was neither dynamic nor charismatic, and on top of that he was dismissed by the congregation after being suspected of having an extramarital affair. "I really didn't think the rabbi was such a big role model."

The importance of music in synagogue services has long been appreciated, of course, and much of the revival currently under way in the American synagogue can without a doubt be attributed to the introduction of American, Israeli, and Hasidic melodies that have proved to have broad appeal. What may be new in the situation described by our respondents is the greater importance assumed by music, given the inability of congregants to relate to anything else in the service, most notably to the words on the page of the prayer book. If the service is Conservative, and therefore conducted largely in Hebrew, the words may be alienating, a source of discomfort. Or, as we suspect on the basis of our interviews, they may function, like the music, as background for personal reflection. To Sonya, Lee, and many others we met, that is the main activity engaged in at synagogue. Our impression is that this is true even of congregants in Reform synagogues, who are reading prayers in English. The language of those prayers does not speak on a literal level to the Jews uttering them week by week. The congregants are stirred rather by a religious experience in which the words do not play a leading role. Music, far more important in their eyes, is thus no longer a vehicle for the words (if, indeed, it ever was). Instead, words are the occasion for the music.

Rabbis are an equal or greater source of appeal (or alienation)—in both expected and unexpected ways. The major rabbinic roles might be defined, in administrative parlance, as recruitment and retention. Rabbis not only bring Jews back to the synagogue but keep them there by addressing the needs their congregants bring with them to services. (Pastoral care outside the synagogue was almost never mentioned by our respondents.) What is more, rabbis often bring Jews to far more than the synagogue, returning individuals to active Jewishness in the broadest sense, whether inside or outside the sanctuary.

Two women whom we interviewed in Detroit, both raised in and currently affiliated with Reform temples, described patterns of renewed affiliation which are quite common. Nina and her husband took advantage of their temple's free year of membership for newly married couples. They were induced to remain members by a young rabbi who had children in the same playgroup and "called a lot to invite us to things." A young adult havurah proved appealing, as did their study toward adult bar and bat mitzvah. Nina's attendance now comes mainly at monthly children's services. We gather from her remarks that a rabbi who was distant or authoritarian would not have succeeded as much as this one did, a peer and fellow parent. His persistent invitations to activities of special interest to the potential congregants proved successful. The final hook was, of course, the child of school age. But Nina now finds other meaning in the synagogue service as well. She conceives of God as a "higher power" who "gives people strength to carry on" and who, without controlling things, is connected to whatever goodness exists in the world. While "organized religion has so many bad aspects," Nina feels more connected to God inside the sanctuary than elsewhere. That is where she thinks about God, and so receives help in "deal[ing] with things."

Debby's story was somewhat different. Both she and her husband seem to have taken it for granted that they, like their parents, would affiliate with a synagogue. Because he had been raised in a Conservative congregation, they tried that option for a while but eventually settled on a Reform temple because the Conservative congregation was "too contrary to what I was brought up with." They then dropped membership altogether for a while —"money was tight"—and joined again when their children reached school age. Debby said she connects to religion primarily from a generalized "spiritual sense" rather than from Judaism, and feels no particular connection to prayer or to the institution in which it transpires. She thinks about God "all the time. I am trying to figure it out. Life is amazing." When formal prayers fail to resonate with her, "I say my own prayer. I make up my own stuff." The rabbi in this case apparently did not play a major role in their decisions, perhaps because he embodies Judaism.

Our impression is that Debby's is not the typical case. Rabbis seem to loom large in our subjects' impressions of the synagogue. Jack, a lawyer who is active in a major "secular" Jewish organization in San Diego, insisted that God is a matter too profound for him to understand. He never talks to God, "nor has God ever talked to me." Jack generally finds synagogue unappealing, goes six to eight times in the course of a year to his Reform temple, and is terribly bored there. He is vehement in his critique of services that consist of rote readings "from pages 132 to 168, top to bottom, lacking any potential to challenge, almost unbearable." It is irresponsible of the Jewish community, he says, "to fail to find a better way to learn." When Jack does go to synagogue, he brings books with him to pass the time. We infer that he has not searched for a more appealing synagogue because he is convinced that switching venues could not solve the problem he has with services. What *does* Jack enjoy in services? Why does he come?

He enjoys seeing friends from the community, and listening to "thought-provoking sermons." (We concluded, from his active interest in music, that he might find the music in some temples appealing as well.) And he joined the temple in part, we believe, because that is what Jews do—part of the communal obligation of which he spoke with great passion. "There is a community, and we are responsible for it."

For others, such as Stuart, a particular rabbi made all the difference by reaching out and establishing a personal relationship of trust which gradually drew the individual back to Judaism. This pattern came through most eloquently in our interview with David, whose Jewish journey we described at length in chapter 2. Raised in a home that featured a Christmas tree every December and inculcated a firmly atheistic view of the world, David married a woman from a Reform background and became active in the Hillel Foundation at the campus where he works. However, it was the active intervention by the rabbi and the cantor in his local Reform synagogue (strongly encouraged by his wife) that led him back to the religious aspects of Jewish tradition. Until that point, David recalls, his wife "would drag me to services on High Holidays. . . . I remember taking a biography of Napoleon with me one time, as if to declare that 'there are other ways to be Jewish than to be religious.'"

Several things happened to change his mind. He took a course about Judaism, which excited him intellectually, increased his pride, and aroused his interest. David also decided to join the synagogue, not so much because the course was given there as because membership "gave me a formal membership in the Jewish community. . . . it was a public statement of being a Jew, [whereas] slipping in and out of a Jewish service on the High Holidays was not." David also met the congregation's new rabbi as part of the preparations for his daughter's bat mitzvah, and was impressed. The rabbi, he said, "was intellectual, real smart, respected me, didn't try and dump religion on me." Rather he invited David to give a class on Jewish history at the synagogue. David then made a connection with the cantor as well: "Somebody that I could relate to who was a Jewish religious professional but who understood me. He was funny, and he was relaxed. . . . I didn't feel excluded as I had felt at services, where I never felt like I belonged." David has since been invited to participate in a number of services and has found them meaningful, though he still finds the prayers difficult to relate to, largely because "I just can't feel comfortable addressing some figure called God." More explication of the prayers by the rabbi during services, he suggests, might help. When his father died, the rabbi spent time with him that was much appreciated—particularly because he did not try to console David with messages about divine salvation in which he could not believe.

We note, once again, the importance of personal contact with the rabbi (and cantor), and the significance of palpable inclusion through a role—

in this case an intellectual-educational one—that the congregant is specifically invited to perform. Time and again we were told of the importance of such invitations, whether to chant from the Torah, serve on an education committee, or assist with financial management. In a recent study of Conservative congregants, about half cited the rabbi as a major reason for joining the congregation, making the appeal of the rabbi one of the most widely cited reasons for joining. Not quite as many respondents (44 percent) also cited the rabbi as a major reason for attending services (Cohen, forthcoming [a]).

Rabbis can clearly attract Jews to Judaism by this sort of personal nurturing—but they can also repel Jews from the synagogue by embodying the opposite of what particular Jews happen to be seeking there. Rebecca, who told us that her form of prayer consists in blessing her children on Friday evening, reported that she had been unaffiliated for a number of years before joining her present congregation. The rabbi at her parents' synagogue was "autocratic." There was no "level of comfort" in his sanctuary, no warmth. At some point early in her marriage, she embarked on a search for a synagogue to join. She made appointments to speak with a series of rabbis and educators, and was about to join one which had a strong curriculum and a wonderful education director—but she did not join because the rabbi was "remote" and the service she attended "uncomfortable." In addition, the service used too little Hebrew for her taste. Then someone suggested a certain small congregation not too far away. The rabbi was a "very warm, engaging man," who had marched in Selma and had strong social justice interests. The congregation, as she put it, had its focus squarely on "the religious aspect"—no brotherhood or sisterhood, no appeals from the pulpit for donations. Everyone in the sanctuary participates in almost the entire service. It is "warm and comfortable." She and her husband are very happy there and have become very involved.

In one form or another, with or without use of the particular images of warmth and comfort that are the obvious leitmotivs of Rebecca's comments, a large number of our subjects described the appeal of synagogue for them in terms of *community*. Some, like Jack, said they simply enjoy seeing their friends. Hank, an attorney in his sixties, said he liked "going to shul on the holidays [because] most of our friends are Jewish so it's a comfortable feeling." Tony, who returned to the synagogue after a long absence when he began to say Kaddish for his mother, increased his involvement when he was asked by a friend to join the adult education committee. His primary interest is still family education because "it feels like the only possible avenue where I and everybody else can be like grandparents." Tony's attachment to services comes and goes. Sometimes he likes it, puts up with the sermons, and "it goes by fast"; at other times he feels as if he is swimming, holding his breath, and "finally has to stop and rest for a while."

Karen, who serves as treasurer of her congregation, joined when her son reached school age, and now likes the sense of "being an insider." Gil, whose comments opened this chapter, joined his synagogue because his daughter "got a lot of love there." He began attending regularly because he felt it hypocritical to send her to Hebrew school without going to services himself, and so the family began to come weekly, as a family, to junior congregation. Their children's presence in shul every week is now "non-negotiable." Finally, there is Scott, who told us that High Holiday services for him mean primarily "setting yourself around your community, which is a very hard thing to do with other people. It's about fixing your business *ben adam la-havero* [between one person and another], mainly, and then there is some stuff with God, too." Scott also credited the Hillel rabbi at his university—"a dynamic, interesting woman"—and the "really nice congregation" he attended in Berkeley and its Saturday morning Torah study group with "strongly orient[ing] me" toward Judaism.

Others, making the same point in reverse, complained that they found synagogue a *lonely* experience, whether because they had recently moved and not yet made friends in the congregation, or because they attended without spouses who were not interested in coming, or because people in the congregation were standoffish and did not introduce themselves, let alone invite them home for meals. Brad, a clinical psychologist in Manhattan, complained that the synagogue in which he grew up "was almost like a church. People would go there with their briefcases from work and the whole thing seemed to be so unreligious and more concerned with who's wearing what that it just didn't interest me. When we looked for places to get married, the first thing they told me was how much it was going to cost me." Brad spoke highly of the rabbi he and his wife eventually found to perform the marriage ceremony, and said he liked the services at his synagogue on the few occasions when he has gone there, singling out the Torah discussions for special praise. Why does Brad not attend more frequently? "I don't know the answer to that. It's on the other side of town. It ends up being longer than I want it to be. . . . I am not a real kind of group sort of person, you know, so I think it could probably get old pretty quickly for me . . . I find it rather tedious. I don't find the prayers particularly interesting. I don't know what that means." Community in its various aspects both attracts and repels Brad; free to choose, he goes with what is most comfortable. The choice is all the easier for Brad because he lives in New York, where Jewish identity seems to many Jews easy to maintain without formal affiliation. The community is, as it were, on the streets and does not need to gather inside walls.

Family—whether grandparents, parents, spouse, or children—also figures in these comments in a variety of ways. In part, family is a metaphor for the community discovered in synagogue, powerful in its own right and of course not lacking in ambivalence. In some measure, too, family is a crucial vehicle for that community. Several people whom we interviewed reported that synagogue supplies a powerful connection to parents and other loved ones who cannot be physically present in the sanctuary—the same appeal that we found in the Passover seder. Linda, a fund-raiser in her late thirties, replied to our question about belief in God by saying that she believes "in something, not in God like a person, but a purpose to what we are doing, some kind of spirit or something out there"—and added at once that "my mother, who died ten years ago, is somewhere out there." When she prays, then, "I talk to my mother. I pray, but I don't know if it's to a specific context of God. I reflect during services on what's on my mind."

Tony attends Sabbath services in spurts, but also goes to weekday services once or twice a month to help make up the minyan. When his parents died, he went every day, and "started to get the feeling that we were in a boat together, sailing through life and the seasons. . . . It started to mean something to me, and at the end of each year of saying Kaddish I said I would keep going, and did for a month, then dropped off." Scott, immediately after his comments about wanting to set himself around his community on Yom Kippur, recalled an emotionally powerful memory of his grandmother (and the piety of her generation) connected to the lesson that "all the people I care about in my life are people I have tension with. . . . All of a sudden I thought: yeah, I can imagine that, all the people crying and trembling. . . . I think that was the moment where I connected with tradition as an adult."

Once again, the emotions are powerful, and they run both ways. Several individuals recalled going to synagogue as children in order to be with grandparents or, in one case, to get away from a very difficult home environment. "I became this sort of darling in the synagogue and it was all a great nurturing experience." These images, stored in a memory from childhood, strongly resemble those expressed by many of our subjects when asked what is drawing them, adults all, to the synagogue now.

MORE THAN THE WORDS—AND LESS

The sentiments and beliefs concerning God and synagogue articulated by our respondents emerge from a venerable tradition in Judaism concerning the multifaceted role of the synagogue. They are also in accord with powerful currents in American culture that have of late caused great upheaval in the churches and elicited significant attention from scholars.

Jews have long conceived of the synagogue as more than a *beit tefillah*, a house of worship. It has also been a house of study, or *beit midrash*, and a house of assembly (*beit knesset*, the word for synagogue in modern Hebrew). Nor has prayer in the narrow sense ever been the exclusive, or necessarily predominant, activity of the synagogue in its role as *beit tefillah*. There has always been music, of course, and the teaching of a homily;

always the pleasure of friends, family and gossip; always the books on the shelves and the conversations in the courtyard to relieve the tedium of services during which one could not summon proper intention. What is more, only a small portion of the prayers themselves consisted of actual petition to God, and almost all of that has been in the collective rather than the individual voice. Far more space in the siddur is devoted to praise of God, to recalling of the wonders performed on behalf of the ancestors, and to meditations on the ways of life and the world.

The traditional prayer book functions more as anthology than credo, containing a wide variety of images of God, eliciting a host of emotions, and encouraging a range of worldly projects to which prayer is meant to lead. Lawrence Hoffman is surely right, then, when he argues that the study of liturgy must, like those who recite liturgy, go "beyond the text" in order to encompass the multiple contexts in which liturgy figures and the multiple meanings that it carries (Hoffman 1987, 1988).

In the modern period, Jews have felt an increasing distance from the God portrayed in the traditional liturgy: Creator of, Revealer to, and Redeemer of all the world, but especially the Jews. Accordingly, rabbis composed new words for the prayer book and employed new strategies to keep Jews coming to the sanctuary. The Reform movement shortened its services, conducted them in whole or in part in the vernacular, introduced a choir and organ, tailored the service to accommodate a weekly sermon, and made it into a family affair (Wertheimer 1987). Conservative synagogues, largely opposed to use of an organ or drastic overhaul of the liturgy, appealed to new sensibilities with English prayers and sermons, and perhaps most critically of all with the introduction of mixed seating. Uplift and enlightenment became widespread aims in every denomination. Social justice or Jewish history loomed large as the subjects of synagogue sermons. The stress on community and study often eclipsed address to God, avowedly or implicitly, as the purpose of Sabbath services. America in particular has seen a number of such changes to synagogue liturgy and practice, most recently occasioned by the challenge posed by the advent of Jewish feminism. Today's Jews are not the first to innovate, but are simply reflecting and continuing modern developments that long preceded them.

We can usefully consider these changes in terms of the traditional three-fold purpose of the synagogue: prayer, study, and assembly. Our subjects seem far less interested in *tefillah* (prayer) than their forebears, and so are less interested in adjustments to the liturgy. Whereas the Reform and Reconstructionist movements have devoted enormous energy to revising and re-revising the prayer book over the years, it seems that new and more relevant formulations of the words, even feminist adjustments, might not compel those whom we interviewed. Opinion was mixed on the point. Many in our sample, women and men alike, have learned to use the words as a sort of springboard—background music in a different mode—to a religious experience that takes place with little direct relevance to the words. Although they for the most part believe in God, as we have seen, and include God in the reflection about life that they undertake during services, God is often not at the center of that reflection. Many testified that God is no more accessible to them inside than outside the sanctuary. Synagogue for them is not so much the house of God as another Jewish house, communal rather than private, in which they can be at home and so take refuge from the hurly-burly of everyday life.

The sanctuary in part functions as such a home, a sanctuary in the other sense of the word. It engages the minds as well as the hearts of its congregants around issues of value, tradition, and ultimate truth—issues not addressed often or adequately in the secular culture. Without exception, the people whom we interviewed liked *learning* in their *beit midrash,* whether during services or in classes. The Me'ah program of adult study in Boston, synagogue-based but drawing on a faculty including local Jewish studies professors, received special praise. Similar programs elsewhere also drew plaudits. Indeed, several of our subjects embarked upon their journeys back to Judaism in large part through adult education classes or the committees which organized them. These classes also create communities within the congregation, building and sustaining networks of friends who provide institutional leadership as well as a tangible reason for attendance at services. More important, the teaching of texts roots moderately affiliated Jews in history and tradition. It offers the fact and feeling of belonging and empowerment which they crave, and identifies the synagogue in their mind with aspirations crucial to their sense of self: moral, spiritual, social.

This is only one of the many ways in which synagogues serve as a house of assembly or *beit knesset:* the locus and creator of community. Another, especially meaningful to the younger members of our sample, was as a center for social action. Our respondents expected this activity on the part of their synagogues, in some cases actually demanded it, but only rarely made it the focus of their own involvement. They were more interested, as we heard repeatedly, in the "spiritual" side of things, and they valued synagogues for providing it.

Our findings strikingly resemble those in recent studies of American churches and their congregants. Roof and McKinney examined "American mainline religion"—not fundamentalist, not Pentecostal, but the sort of Christianity which most approximates the Judaism to which the great majority of American Jews adhere. They found that the churches they studied were characterized by individualism and pluralism in belief, consistent with the contemporary American culture that the churches for the most part affirm. Attendance, even among Catholics, has dropped steadily (it has been low among Jews for decades), and there has been a decided turn toward "experiential religion." Both developments, the researchers believe, should be seen as part of a larger "expressive individualism" that stresses the rationality of means and the satisfaction of individual wants, both emotional and cognitive (Roof and McKinney 1987, pp. 23, 32).

Roof, focusing on the baby boomers in a second study, finds them even more committed than Americans generally to personal autonomy and the fulfillment of individual potential, in religion as in all other areas of life. A majority of those he surveyed "indicated a preference 'to be alone and to meditate.'" Asked which was more important to them, solitary meditation or worship with others, 53 percent chose the former, 29 percent the latter. Asked whether they prefer to explore the teachings of many traditions or to stick to the tenets of one faith, exploration received 60 percent of the approval, constancy 28 percent. One individual, whom Roof describes as "deeply anchored in his church," said, "You don't have to go to church." He attended (or so he believed) because it helped him grow, and was good for his family: it taught them morality and helped them operate as a unit (Roof 1993, p. 105).

Like today's Jews, this informant is alienated by the language of obligation, whether communal or divine, despite his active participation in a community and his weekly prayers to God. His language of preference is individualist, utilitarian, and psychological, rather than normative or collective. He is in church because he wants to be—and he wants to be there because he likes it and believes it is good for him. Most of Roof's respondents, even those classified as conservative, agreed that religion is "something you do if you feel it meets your needs." Majorities also said one should arrive at one's religious beliefs independently of any church, and that one can be a good Christian without attending church at all (Roof 1993, p. 110).

Indeed, sociologist Robert Wuthnow argues in a recent study that "a profound change in our spiritual practices" has taken place in America during the last half of the century, involving a move from what he calls "a traditional spirituality of inhabiting sacred places" to a "new spirituality of seeking." The latter exchanges "spiritual dwelling" in the sacred spaces of church or synagogue for "the new spiritual freedom," individual experience, and the spirituality of the inner self (1998, p. 3). His research found that respondents who grew up before 1960 were more likely to center their spiritual lives on a particular congregation, and they also more often said that their closest friends were members of their own faith, indeed of their own congregations. Individuals are now much more "free-floating," and much less inclined to ground their self-esteem in their relation to God (p. 211). Selves, like institutions, are far more fluid than ever before. Wuthnow argued in an earlier study that such findings hold across denominations among the boomer generation. Indeed, he has argued, the diversity in American religion is now found largely *inside* the various mainline denominations rather than between them—or *outside* these denominations altogether, given the rising importance of Islam, Hinduism, and Mormonism as minority American faiths (Wuthnow 1989, pp. 15–16). Doctrinal disputes, once the source of denominational division, seem not to interest the laity very much. The truth they are seeking comes in experiential rather than propositional form.

⚜

This certainly holds for the Jews whom we interviewed. Ideological disputes over which a great deal of ink has been spilled in the annals of modern Jewish thought blur in the eclectic and fluid commitments that are now the rule. Mordecai Kaplan believed in God's existence only as a set of forces making for goodness in the world, sought a "Judaism without Supernaturalism," and ridiculed the act of prayer to a God who hears prayer as insane, given that no such being exists (Kaplan 1967). Abraham Heschel countered with a God who very much exists as a personal being to be encountered in prayer, urged a revitalization of awe and wonder in the face of this God, and condemned prayer that is merely the expression of communal loyalty or the statement of ethical ideals or the groping after connection with tradition. Belief is decisive. "If such conviction is lacking, if the presence of God is a myth, then prayer to God is a delusion. If God is unable to listen to us, then we are insane in talking to Him" (Heschel 1986, p. 62).

Our subjects were quite comfortable with conceptions of God partaking both of Heschel and of Kaplan. Their view of prayer, as we have seen, does not depend on anything resembling certainty about the nature of the deity—certainty that, they believe, is unavailable in any case. Many are quite content to engage in prayer for the reasons Heschel criticized—as well as for reasons which Kaplan could not credit. Rationales for faith hold little interest. It is enough for our subjects that they find personal meaning in what they are doing. If they do, arguments about God's presence in the sanctuary are beside the point.

This may well represent something of a change. A generation or two ago, Jews such as those we interviewed might well have found other, "secular" outlets for Jewish participation that did not require synagogue attendance. Or, when they did go to services, they might have seen that act as merely a social performance, something Jews do to express and maintain Jewish community. They would not have been engaged in personal quest, or seen the synagogue as an agent or location for personal transformation. Now, freed of the need to declare "party allegiance" to one or the other of the accepted credos of modern Jewish adherence, religious and secular, our subjects seem more content to experience what is there to be experienced and to take the meaning as it comes.

That eclecticism holds as well for the language in which faith is now couched. Some speak a language of spirituality and personal awareness. Others prefer an idiom of moral aspiration and social justice. Still others have opted for a lexicon of community and tradition. Some speak of God as person, others prefer to speak of God as force. What is new, once again, is the degree to which our subjects speak a *combination* of these Jewish religious languages, seeing no need to choose among them. Indeed, they resent the exclusion or criticism of some Jews by others because the former have chosen to believe or practice in ways that the latter find inappropriate. To them, religion is supposed to be a private matter, even when practiced in a collective framework.

This ideological openness may of course be a function of ignorance. Few of the individuals to whom we spoke about God seemed to draw on specific texts or ideas. Some had a minimal acquaintance with Jewish sources, but either were not confident enough to cite the sources with which they were familiar or felt that it would have been pretentious to do so. No one referred to religion courses they had had in college or the sources they had studied there. Lacking firsthand knowledge of the details of century-old disagreements "for the sake of Heaven" in Jewish tradition, and (like most Americans) unfamiliar with the modern philosophical literature on faith, our subjects could not very well use these sources to contend with others who believed differently. Ignorance perhaps serves the cause of tolerance. Disagreement, beyond our subjects' capability in any event, is judged bad form.

One might also see the reigning pluralism as indicative of a certain lack of passion where faith is concerned. We found a degree of correlation between emotion and gender, as one might expect: women were more expressive of their faith and more interested in its expression, men stiffer and less articulate. Nowhere, however, did we find any sense of acute emotion where God and the synagogue are concerned. This feature represents another continuity with American Judaism in all its varieties, as it has existed until now and continues to exist. For all that our subjects care about these issues, passion is directed elsewhere, and only entered our conversation about the synagogue when it bore on those areas: family, suffering among Jews or in the world, personal traumas and achievements.

Eisen has argued that the paucity of Jewish theological works in America until recently can be attributed first of all to the particularistic function of theology. Systematic religious thought articulates the distinctiveness of one faith community and its relation to God—and ours is a time when neither the elite nor the laity of American Jewry has wished to stress particularism to that degree. Theology is also discouraged because it requires mastery both of the variegated sources of the Jewish tradition and of the contemporary philosophical literature. There are few Jews with the requisite training in either area, let alone in both. Finally, theology generally emerges as reflection upon the life of a particular faith community, and the community which might stimulate such reflection—and did, in past eras of Jewish history—is, in all cases but the Orthodox, sorely lacking in contemporary America (Eisen 1982). In all three respects the moderately affiliated Jews whom we interviewed seem very similar to the elites of the community, only more so: less interested in particularistic affirmations, less learned, less possessed of a rich communal life on which to reflect.

What our subjects do have, and so stress both to themselves and to us, is personal experience. They respond favorably in the synagogue to any enhancement of that experience which leaves them free to choose—and grow—at every stage. The study of Jewish texts is one such opportunity for personal growth, but the others mentioned in our interviews all have a similar aim: the transmission of inspirational spiritual teachings; the deepening of connection to family; the comfort of felt community; the strengthening of relation to God. The synagogue is not the main arena of Jewish life for most moderately affiliated Jews. Nor is it the place in which they tend to seek God or find God. It is, however, the place where, as Edward put it, each can have "my own time"—alone but in community. They remain the selves they are, while attached to generations and millennia. They sacrifice no attachment to the larger culture or society, but sit in a distinctively Jewish time and space. What is more, they sit there with their families, and not only with them: they are connected to God, that which is Most High, though they are not required to believe or practice anything in particular. This is a precious sanctuary indeed.

CONCLUSION

We undertook the research for this study with two main purposes in mind.

First, we sought a better understanding of the meaning of Judaism and Jewishness to the moderately affiliated Jews who today constitute the bulk of American Jewry. What was happening with this population? Were they simply abandoning Jewish involvement? Or—as we suspected—were they, in part, establishing new patterns of belonging? Were they withdrawing in ever larger numbers from religious and secular Jewish affiliation? Or —again, at least in part—were they rather distancing themselves from the Jewish public sphere in favor of new interest in the private ritual settings of home and synagogue? American Jewry, we believed, was no longer carrying forward the modern master-story of heightened individualism, reduced community, and growing secularism. Something else was occurring as well: a postmodern story of "local narratives," "multiple life-worlds," and fluid movement among commitments by fluid selves, embarked on personal journeys that never end.

Second, we wanted a surer grasp on what these emergent patterns of attachment and significance portend for Jewish life and institutions in the decades to come. Scholars, communal professionals, and Jewish lay leaders have all grown accustomed to a more or less unilinear story characterized by steady movement "leftward" on the denominational spectrum. Orthodoxy, in that account, gives way ineluctably to Conservatism in the following generation, and thence to Reform and, eventually, assimilation. But what if the picture were more complicated? Suppose—as we found to be the case—there has been a deliberate blurring of ideological boundaries rather than the replacement of one ideology with another. What are the likely consequences, positive and negative, of a principled eclecticism when it comes to belief and practice, of steady or growing interest in ritual observance rather than the regular decline in observance found in earlier decades? What would be the effect, on Jewish individuals and communities alike, of a near-total lack of interest in either denominational loyalties or communal organizations?

The Jews we interviewed offered accounts of their own journeys and behavior which are fraught with contradictions. They are resolute in rejecting the Jewish choices of their parents, yet childhood upbringing remains a powerful predictor of their adult involvements. They care little for Jewish organizations, but are far from indifferent to Judaism and things Jewish. Our encounters with them time and again revealed great passion—and also great ambivalence. They take their Jewish journeys very seriously and regard Judaism as an intrinsic part of their identity. But they are also determined to protect the options and prerogatives of what we call the "sovereign self, " including the option to journey far from Judaism and to leave that part of themselves completely behind. And yet they also for the most part retain important ties to Jewish ancestors, express enduring loyalty to the Jewish people, and articulate a strong desire to discover and create meaning in the context of the Jewish tradition.

All of this makes the present estate of American Jewry somewhat hard to characterize, and the American Jewish future difficult to predict. In this final chapter we offer reflections aimed at shedding further light on both these matters. We shall begin with a brief summary of our findings, and then consider two major issues involved in the understanding of those findings: the novelty or lack thereof in the patterns we have discerned, and comparison of these patterns with recent studies of other American ethnic and religious groups. We shall then turn in conclusion to inferences about the likely impact of these developments on both personal attachment and communal strength in the decades to come.

SELF, FAMILY, AND COMMUNITY

The main thesis of this work, suggested in its title, can be succinctly stated: More and more, the meaning of Judaism in America transpires within the self. American Jews have drawn the activity and significance of their group identity into the subjectivity of the individual, the activities of the family, and the few institutions (primarily the synagogue) which are seen as extensions of this intimate sphere. At the same time, relative to their parents' generation, today's American Jews in their thirties, forties, and early fifties are finding less meaning in mass organizations, political activity, philanthropic endeavor, and attachment to the state of Israel. In broad strokes, that which is personally meaningful has gained at the expense of that which is peoplehood-oriented. American Jews today are relatively more individualist and less collectivist. Taken as a group, their patterns of belief and practice are more idiosyncratic and diverse, less uniform and consensual. No less important, they regard the ever-changing selection of Jewish activities and meanings from the broad repertoire available as part of their birthright as Jews. They celebrate the autonomy of this choosing and do not worry about its authenticity. Indeed, they welcome each change in the pattern of their Judaism as a new stage in their lifelong personal journeys.

We arrived at these broad conclusions after examining in detail both national survey data and intensive in-person interviews. Throughout the research, our principal concern has been the understanding of moderately affiliated American Jews: those who are neither unusually active in conventional Jewish life nor among the most uninvolved in terms of ritual practice, formal institutional affiliation, or social networks. Accordingly, while the nationwide survey we conducted reached Jews at all levels of involvement, our personal interviews were far more focused. None of those we met in person was Orthodox; only a few were among the organizational or philanthropic leadership of JCCs, Hadassah and other Jewish groups, or Conservative, Reform, and Reconstructionist synagogues. In line with our interests in the American Jewish middle, we also largely excluded from our in-person interviews those at the other end of the Jewish identity spectrum: those with no current connection with organized Jewry, or those with only the weakest of connections. Most of our interviewees ranged between thirty and fifty years of age: the age-group which comprises nearly half of adult American Jews. Almost all were married, and nearly all of these were married to other Jews.

The texts of the forty-five solo interviews we conducted with them, and of two group interviews (with fifteen individuals in all) conducted early on in our research, made up the primary evidence on which this study is based. We supplemented and contextualized these reports with the aforementioned random sample survey of a national cross-section of 1,005 American Jews, as well as with other secondary literature on Jews and Gentiles in contemporary America, some of which we ourselves have authored.

The starting point of our analysis was and remains *the sovereign self:* confident of its unalterable Jewish identity by virtue of birth to at least one

Jewish parent and asserting an unquestionable right to choose how, when, and whether it will enact that identity in practice. The self—albeit in negotiation with others, particularly other family members—is the ultimate arbiter of Jewish expression. Since every Jew is free to make his or her own decision in these matters, no one can judge the morality, let alone the propriety, of another person's Jewish choices. Jewish selves now expect to be encouraged by Jewish professionals and institutions to change and develop in their own way, free of outside interference, and with the support of those near and dear to them.

Moreover, because today's Jews believe that Jewish identity is inalienable, i.e., that they will always remain Jewish no matter what choices they make, they exercise enormous latitude in what they choose to do and not do Jewishly, assured that they need have no fear of losing themselves in the process. Jewishness for them is an absolute. It cannot be increased or lessened by observance, in-marriage, communal affiliation, or any other normative behavior. They feel no need to express or enact their identity in regular activity. Judaism is rather an "inner thing," a point of origin, a feature of experience, an object of reflection. The Jews we interviewed are not opposed in principle to undertaking more Jewish activities; indeed, many have opted to set themselves more frequently in the context of Jewish groups or institutions. However, they see no compelling need to do so, no necessary correlation between actions such as these and the persons they already are and forever will be.

Certain actions, however, are precluded in their eyes. The sense of self would be compromised by any behavior that implied denial of the persons they believe themselves to be: converting to Christianity, for example, or ceasing to care about suffering in the world, or abandoning self-consciousness and personal journey. What is more, the selves we have described are at rare moments aware that they are not nearly as independent as most of them claim. As one commentator on an earlier draft of our work wrote, "[T]he 'self' in the case of moderately affiliated Jews is not nearly so independent as most of them passionately believe. . . . To an astonishing degree, it turns out, moderately affiliated Jews are actually shaped and constrained by their past—their parents, their grandparents, their experiences growing up, and . . . their level of Jewish education (or lack of same)" (Cohen and Eisen 1998, p. 73).

In this and several other respects, even while uncovering much that seems—and is—genuinely new in the patterns and meanings of Jewish selfhood in America, we were struck by the *conventionality* of much that we were hearing and seeing. Incessant proclamations of free choice where Jewishness is concerned were carried to a degree of "protest too much." Now, as always, adult involvement bears the imprint both of the starting point of the Jewish journey and of the varied opportunities for experience available at the times and places where they are sought.

The most critical role in the formation and expression of Jewish identity, moving outward from the center of the self, is played by the *family*. The self does not operate on its own, but rather in ongoing conjunction with intimates. The nuclear family, in particular, plays a vital role in shaping Jewish commitments in childhood. It also provides the prime arena for the expression of adult Jewish involvement. Of particular importance in this regard, we found, are grandparents, parents, spouses, and children.

Respondents recall their grandparents with great affection and admiration. For the most part, they see them as loving exemplars: positive and authentic Jewish role models. (Whether today's grandparents will serve the same role for today's youngsters remains to be seen. It is also not clear —or important—whether the memories of grandparents reported to us have any basis in fact.) In contrast, and not surprisingly, our interviewees' feelings about their parents are more complex, laden with powerful and ambivalent emotions. Parents offer a variety of Jewish role models, some positive, some less so. One or the other parent may have been the stronger or weaker influence. The two may have reinforced messages of Jewish socialization or sent messages which contradict one another. Some parents continue to play significant roles in the Jewish lives of their adult children and grandchildren. Almost all occupy a significant place in the respondents' Jewish cognitive and emotional construction of self.

Spouses constitute another major influence on adult involvement. They constitute the major partner to negotiation over how to conduct Jewish life at home, and of course help to shape the Jewish selfhood of the children. Generally, it is women, as wives and mothers, who are the partners more emotionally invested, physically present, and ultimately influential in conveying Jewish identity. Men, whether as husbands or as fathers, do and care far less (though we did find several examples of the reverse pattern). Consistent with well-established survey evidence, children provide both a need and a stimulus for Jewish involvement. The Jewish engagement they provoke gets played out both within the home and outside of it, in the institutions that serve the socialization of the children and the Jewish life of the family.

Holidays celebrated throughout the year, with observance heavily focused on the family at home, therefore constitute the master script of Jewish involvement. The features that today's American Jews find most compelling and memorable in holiday celebration are those connected with families of the past (grandparents and parents), families of the present (especially when gathered at the dinner table), and families of the future (imagined and planned for through the presence of children and grandchildren). Central to all these observances is the preparation and joint consumption of food, which stands at the nexus of love and tradition, family and festivals. Sabbath and Passover in particular are associated with specific foods and with specific (usually female) family members who prepare them, or did so in the past. Family is thus not only the site and vehicle for holiday observance but its most important meaning and motivation. It is what Jews celebrate and ponder when they get together on ritual occasions.

Jews are drawn to holiday celebration at home, moreover, because they feel free to improvise the details of observance at will, skipping those acts or scenes that carry little obvious personal meaning or significance, and adding or emphasizing others. The Jews we interviewed proudly and self-consciously choose the rituals they observe in terms of that which is personally enjoyable or fulfilling. They seek out that which enhances family experience, and endow whatever they do with interpretations compatible with their place in society and their social values. Far from rejecting a particular ritual act because they do not literally believe in the words said, they feel free to alter the words or transform their meaning. The innovations they recounted to us range from minor changes in ritual practice to wholesale replacement of well-established behaviors grounded in the Jewish tradition of centuries.

In making these changes, the Jews we interviewed seemed far less influenced than their parents' generation by concerns for impressing Gentiles with the acceptability, value, and morality of Judaism. Today's Jews have already attained the highest levels of education, professionalization, and affluence of any American group their size. They take for granted the complete integration into the larger society which earlier generations of American Jews sought in vain. Their aim in transforming Jewish rituals seems rather the attainment of personal meaning unavailable elsewhere— meaning compatible with their own spiritual, aesthetic, and moral expectations. Such meaning—which for many carries a sense of ultimate purpose in life—is most fully attained in the company of the family members with whom their selfhood is most intertwined.

This resurgence of interest in the Jewish ritual calendar, combined with unparalleled participation and integration in America, makes possible the creation of selves at once more Jewish and more American than before. It therefore raises the question of whether and in what ways the Jews we studied have abandoned traditional Jewish *tribalism*. This concept, which we have also termed "historical familism," may be operationally defined as the sense that Jews differ from others, that they understand one another better, and that they can and should rely on one another in times of need.

Some interviewees continued to express a greater degree of comfort and compatibility with their Jewish, rather than their non-Jewish, friends. Most, in fact, even testified to a sense of transcendent belonging, finding great meaning in their membership in an historic, familistic people that extends backward and forward in time, and outward in contemporary space to all corners of the globe. At the same time, however, most have abandoned many of the assumptions about themselves and other Jews that marked a decidedly more particularist Jewish past. They are uncomfortable, to say the least, with the traditional concept of Jewish chosenness. Many explicitly reject giving needy Jews priority over others in equal need. They have special affection for spouses, friends, and community members who are Jewish. However, they are loath to endow the Jewishness of these ties with explicit value and meaning. Most express the hope that their children will choose to find meaning in Judaism as they have done, but believe they do not have the right, let alone the ability, to direct their children to live in the company of Jewish friends, neighbors, organizations, or rituals.

Nowhere is the departure from Jewish tribalism so vivid as in these Jews' attitudes toward intermarriage. Almost all of the respondents we interviewed were married to Jews, most of whom were also born Jewish. Nevertheless, many expressed only a mild preference for the in-marriage of their children, and even those who vigorously endorsed in-marriage did so more on the basis of the anticipated happiness of their children than in terms of traditional survivalist ideology or obligation to God or tradition. Many reported having dated non-Jews seriously before marriage, and almost all numbered non-Jews among their closest friends.

It is no wonder, then, that they preferred universalist and personalist meanings in Jewish observance to particularist and collectivist meanings; no surprise, either, that they exhibited rather ambivalent attitudes toward several of the most potent expressions of contemporary Jewish tribalism: the Holocaust, Israel, and organized Jewry. In all three areas, we find evidence of fading interest, emotional distancing, and expanding universalism.

Those we interviewed and surveyed certainly report strong reactions to the Holocaust, confirming its continuing importance to the shaping of Jewish identity in contemporary America. At the same time, many of those we spoke to regard learning about the tragedy as having been significant to them in their adolescence, but less meaningful to them now, in their adulthood. Some drew "lessons" from the tragedy regarding the threat of antisemitism and the need for Jewish survival, but far more—in keeping with widespread American attitudes (Novick 1999)—derived universal lessons concerning God or the human propensity to evil. Some even spoke of putative Jewish "lessons" that they find objectionable, specifically rejecting teachings that run counter to the universal principles that make the Holocaust meaningful to other Americans. For no one we met was the Shoah a primary locus of identity.

This finding, we should note, is at variance with our own and others' survey data. We suspect that the latter may not measure depth of concern or sensitivity with sufficient precision. Large majorities of Jews have clearly been affected by the Holocaust. They consider concern with the Holocaust essential to being a Jew. But their depth of feeling on the matter is apparently far from uniform. Our interviewees, belying the survey data, evinced only moderate concern with antisemitism in general, and what we might call a contained reaction to the Holocaust. Neither subject evoked strong expression of emotion in our conversation. Neither is at the center of our respondents' Jewish activity or meaning.

That is all the more true of Israel. Our interviews confirmed our prior suspicion that the 1967–82 period should be seen in retrospect as one of unusually enthusiastic American Jewish involvement with the Jewish state. The young to middle-aged Jews we interviewed in the 1990s have clearly retreated from a passionate engagement with Israel. Whereas just one to two decades ago, American Jews cast Israel as eminently (and, at times, desperately) worthy of their vigorous philanthropic and political support, our respondents find both sorts of activities intrinsically less interesting or obligatory. Israel appears to today's Jews to be less needy of their help; at the same time, issues of war and peace—once seemingly clear-cut—have become more nuanced, subtle, and even confused. Many of those we met felt that their personal Jewish identities as Conservative or Reform Jews in America have been called into question by controversies in Israel pitting ultra-Orthodoxy against other streams of Judaism.

This decline in passion for Israel is but one of several factors underlying a related decline in Jewish organizational life. There seems less need for protection against antisemitism or support for the Jewish poor. Moderately affiliated American Jews today feel little compulsion to participate in a Jewish organizational life in which they see little value. The economic, social, and political forces that once made these diverse organizations seem valuable and vital to large numbers of American Jews are today far less potent. We found much less investment in the sorts of institutions that characterized and distinguished organized American Jewry in the middle of the twentieth century, whether these be large membership organizations, politically oriented agencies geared to the defense of Jewish interests, large-scale philanthropies (the UJA and Federations, recently merged and renamed the United Jewish Communities), or Israel and all that pertains to it (e.g., the Zionist organizations). The Jews we interviewed are relatively more invested in the institutions that serve their personal, spiritual, and familial needs, ideally all at once. These are pre-eminently synagogues, schools and other education programs, and Jewish community centers.

Synagogues are of particular interest in this regard—in part because, in a context of declining Jewish ethnicity, the religious sphere can be seen as more acceptable than ethnic or national conceptions of being Jewish in America. As several scholars have noted, synagogues provide a venerable and appealing context (or cover) for the expression of Jewish ethnicity (Sklare 1972; Glazer 1972; Fein 1988). Jewish religious institutions also gain appeal, at the expense of secular organizations, to the degree that Jews participate in the widespread revival of interest among the baby boomer generation, in spirituality and personal quest (Roof 1993; Wuthnow 1998).

Our findings in regard to God and synagogue are not straightforward. Most Jews with whom we spoke did express belief in God, whether as personal being or as cosmic force for creativity and good. Many interviewees told us they had experienced God's presence, in prayer or elsewhere. However, they like other Americans held rather undeveloped and untutored understandings of the God in whom they believe. We found relatively little evidence of America's much-heralded spiritual stirrings in our personal interviews, belying the claims to the contrary in our survey. (Here as elsewhere, we trust the accuracy of three-hour personal interviews more than the yes/no responses of the surveys.) More important, perhaps, we also heard few echoes of traditional Jewish conceptions of God (articulated in the prayer books of every denomination). Few believed in a commanding God who revealed the Torah and who maintains a special relationship with the Jews.

In fact, the only clear sign of a specifically Jewish God that we came across, one distinguishable from the God worshipped by other Americans, was the total absence from these conceptions of Jesus. However, even this distinction may be blurring. Wuthnow reports (1998, p. 128) that "most Americans say they pray generally to God or a supreme being rather than specifically to Jesus or Christ." If so, American Protestants may be moving toward Jewish notions of God, just as American Jews may be moving toward Protestant constructions—individualist, moralist, universalist—of religious identity.

Of some curiosity is the extent to which God and synagogue function separately in the hearts and minds of the Jews with whom we spoke. Even relatively frequent worshippers at Conservative and Reform services express little interest in the Jewish God or in the liturgy that supposedly addresses this God. They do not come to services in search of encounter with God, and so are not disappointed when they do not have such encounters. They attend rather to be in palpable community, or out of family interest or obligation, or to soothe and nourish the harried self, or to connect with selected elements of Jewish tradition. In this, as in all else, the decisive factor seems to be personal experience. Today's American Jews are not much interested in the putative truths about God or the world transmitted on the pages of the prayer book. They respond strongly to whatever enhances the self's development and fulfillment, whether it be text study, social action projects, Yom Kippur fasting, or an inspirational Sabbath sermon. Having experienced meaning in this way, they are ready and willing to return for more, at a time, place, and frequency of their own choosing.

THE IMPACT OF AMERICA

What are we to make of these findings? To what extent do they signal truly new developments in American Jewish identity and/or patterns unique to Jews as distinguished from other Americans? Alternatively, to what extent are these developments continuous with and predictable from the recent Jewish past and/or recent patterns of ethnicity and religion in America generally?

We have found significant elements both of continuity and of change. Social scientists have wondered for more than a decade whether Western societies have entered a period of "late modernity" or have made the transition to a different constellation of circumstances that merits the name of "postmodernity." The answer best suited to the complex facts of the matter has often been "both." So too can we say that American Jews have evolved a group identity that is characteristic of late modern religion, culture, and communal forms—and have also developed new patterns that seem to us best described as postmodern. Something has taken place since the late 1980s or so, we believe, that differentiates this subperiod of American Jewish life from its predecessor. At the same time, many of the trends we observe seem to be extensions of those observed earlier by previous students of American Jewry. Both the continuities and the changes, finally, seem to parallel developments traced by scholars of American religious and ethnic groups other than the Jews.

The modern Jewish story, inaugurated by the entry of formerly segregated Jews into the larger society, is well known. Whether Emancipation (as this process is called) "came to" the Jews, as it did in Western and Central Europe, or the Jews "came to" Emancipation, as in the migration to America, the individuals affected by it needed to confront two new and critical sets of choices. One regarded the nature and extent of their participation in the larger society. The other concerned the nature and extent of their engagement in Jewish group life. Modern Jewish existence, shaped by these choices, has been characterized for the past two centuries by many or all of the following features:

• A compelling drive to enter and integrate into the larger society.

• Lingering insecurities and anxieties about Jewish acceptance, occasioned by and stimulating continued social separation, and necessitating organized collective action in defense of Jewish rights, interests, and culture.

• Rebellion against premodern, segregationist features of Jewish life and culture, with accompanying rejection of religious rituals and tropes perceived as fostering exclusivity or precluding Gentile acceptance.

• Innovation in religious and cultural life to bring both in line with prevailing norms, albeit in dialogue with a tradition that has retained a measure of authority, and in search of the continuity required to supply authenticity.

• Contention among the various ideological camps, religious and secular, which struggled to advance their particular views of Jews and Judaism, and to protect both from their adversaries.

• Individual freedom to choose among the variety of Jewish elements supplied by the tradition, in accordance with patterns laid down by the competing ideological movements.

We cite these features of Jewish modernity in order to demonstrate how much American Jews and their understanding of what it means to be Jewish have changed in recent years.

• Jews no longer seek American integration. They have in full measure achieved it, and as a result can consider options (such as day schools for their children) once viewed as threatening to Gentile acceptance. Moreover, notwithstanding survey results that point to ongoing Jewish concern over prospective American antisemitism, today's Jews behave as if their position in the society is secure. Hardly any of our respondents could recall significant personal encounters with antisemitic prejudice or discrimination. They are fully a part of the larger society—and the larger society's norms and expectations, after generations of internalization, are now fully a part of them.

• No less important, rebellion against the oppressive authority of premodern rabbis and communal authorities has long since become unnecessary. (This despite the echoes of rebellion still evident in resentment against "the Orthodox," and the pervasive assertion of autonomy.) Rabbis and communal institutions can and do continue to offer guidance for behavior and belief. But they are no longer viewed as custodians of authority or as gatekeepers to personal authenticity. For that, one looks inward, to the experience of the self.

• Historic social boundaries and sweeping ideologies are both in fast retreat, among Jews and non-Jews alike. The lines dividing Jews from Gentiles have become less distinct and more porous. At the same time, the lines dividing Jews into a variety of movements, religious or otherwise, have grown less significant, and even bothersome. We might say that Jewishness is both more assured and less significant (unless one chooses to make it so). The various adjectives modifying Jewish identity seem of far less moment, just as the legitimacy of difference in general has gained acceptance in America—and lost most of its ultimate significance (Hollinger 1995).

• Finally, while Emancipated Jews have always had the freedom to select favored elements from within the repertoire of Jewish life, present-day Jews do so with what may be called a subjective vengeance. "Pick-and-choose Judaism" is certainly not new to American Jews. However, previous generations arguably felt far less secure in asserting the unquestioned legitimacy of abandoning or transforming tradition in line with personal predilections. Nor did they feel as comfortable doing so as frequently as each "personal journey" requires. The only criterion governing this selection today is what is meaningful to the self and the family members closest to the self. There is no longer any need to claim obedience to higher authority (as ethics once trumped law in the arguments of Reform Judaism), and no need to rebel against such authority on grounds of historical development (as Conservative Judaism criticized Orthodoxy, and Reconstructionism criticized Conservatism). Where their parents' generation struggled against and rejected unpalatable aspects of Jewish tradition, contemporary Jews simply adapt and transform these elements, as eclectically and idiosyncratically as they please, and do so without undue self-consciousness.

This, we believe, represents a change of some significance. In Robert Merton's terminology (1968), the surreptitious thief (the violator of established norms) has turned into the unknowing revolutionary (the reviser of prevailing norms). Today's Jews reject the notion that Judaism places demands upon them. Some even told us that Judaism *requires* them to choose those options that they find most personally meaningful.

Thus, despite concern that unqualified application of the term "postmodern" to contemporary American Jews may somewhat distort the phenomenon at hand, and despite evidence (to which we shall return in a moment) of substantial continuity with modern patterns that have held for almost two centuries in America and elsewhere, we believe that Judaism in America, as the new century begins, exhibits ample signs of the elements now widely viewed as constituting postmodernity. Local narratives have in significant measure supplanted global claims. Jews happily inhabit "multiple life-worlds" rather than one, ascriptive collectivity. They move contentedly among commitments formerly held to be exclusive, and among the fragments of their selves, neither claiming nor seeking wholeness.

And yet, for all that—though perhaps logical inconsistency is itself a feature of postmodern selfhood—the Jews we met retain powerful ties to their personal and collective ancestors. They express affection for and loyalty to the Jewish people. They search and find new meaning in Jewish tradition. They even exhibit a significant degree of belief in God, though the God they believe in differs from the one portrayed in the blessings they recite at home and the prayers they say in synagogue.

Nor are these the only continuities evinced by our interviewees with past generations of American Jews. We were repeatedly struck by the conventionality of much that we were hearing in their reports, even amidst the change on which we have focused. Two major features which are unchanged merit review here.

The *link between childhood and adult levels of Jewish involvement,* mentioned above, is the first case in point. Upbringing remains a powerful predictor of adult Jewish involvement, though not of the nature of that involvement. The latter bears the imprint of varied Jewish journeys, and individual development of course remains as idiosyncratic and unpredictable as it has always been. Children raised in the same household by the same parents, now as before, grow into very different kinds of Jews as adults. Nonetheless, homes populated by parents and grandparents to whom Judaism mattered, effective role models such as teachers and rabbis, positive experiences in school and summer camp, Jewish friends and dating partners— all play a part in nurturing adult commitment. Our interviewees spoke more often of Judaism as something to which they had *returned* than as something they had first discovered or arrived at as adults. This sense of return to origin seems to play a major part itself in the meaning carried by Jewish commitments.

Another continuity from the patterns of previous generations of American Jews is no less striking—and more surprising: *Many of the conventional indicators of involvement, used for decades by sociologists of American Jewry, still tend to appear as a "package" in contemporary Jewish lives.* One would expect that a major reconfiguration of the attitudes and behaviors that make up Jewish identity would produce different relationships among the various dimensions of Jewish involvement. In particular, if subjectivity is indeed more critical, then we ought to see the emergence of an increasing number of Jews who report high levels of subjective commitment to being Jewish without accompanying evidence of participation in conventional Jewish activities such as rituals, prayer, and affiliation with a synagogue. These new configurations, however, fail to emerge in the data we have studied. The "package" of indicators still appears, as a package. In other words, the presence of several standard beliefs or practices still implies the presence of others in the set; the coherence of beliefs, ritual observance, communal affiliation, informal ties (in-marriage, friends, neighbors, etc.), and subjective commitment to being Jewish persists and endures.

Among our sample of moderately affiliated Jews, we were therefore able to make straightforward distinctions between Jews on the "higher end" of involvement and those whose infrequent practice and weaker identification with Jewish tradition render them quite similar to those who are entirely uninvolved. We looked for examples of wildly uneven patterns of commitment—both among our personal interviews and in our quantitative survey evidence—and failed to find them. In either context, those who claimed that being Jewish was very important to them almost always reported several sorts of concrete (and conventional) activities.

In sum, then, while much distinguishes the beliefs and attitudes of contemporary Jews from those of their parents' generation, much also connects the generations and links both to earlier periods of American (and modern) Jewish history. We believe we have identified something more than a modification or minor alteration, but it amounts to less than a revolution or transformation. Words such as "shift" or "development" seem more suitable to the phenomenon at hand. If we have described a postmodern vision of the American Jewish future, our investigation also points to an incomplete and far from comprehensive transition to that future. American Jews may have moved in the directions indicated, but they have arrived at no clear end point and—by their own accounts, as well as our own—may well switch directions again in the years to come. That is all the more likely if developments in American society and culture as a whole mandate such changes. Therefore, before considering the likely future direction of American Jewry, we turn to comparison of this population with other religious and ethnic groups in the United States.

❧

Jews are both like and unlike Christian and white ethnic contemporaries in several important ways.

Jewish selves, for example, seem to draw on the same sources for their notions of personhood, in response to the same existential dilemmas, as do other modern individuals analyzed by philosopher Charles Taylor. Enlightenment rationalism, romantic expressive individualism, and enduring loyalty to religious tradition all play their part. The Jews we met, in Taylor's words describing the modern self, "anxiously doubt whether life has meaning, or wonder what its meaning is." Among modern individuals, Jewish or otherwise, "some traditional frameworks are discredited or downgraded to the status of personal predilection." No less important,

> [t]here is always something tentative in their adhesion, and they may see themselves, as, in a sense, seeking. They are on a "quest." . . . Not only do they embrace these traditions tentatively, but they also often develop their own version of them, or idiosyncratic borrowings from or semi-inventions within them. (Taylor 1989, pp. 16–17)

We likewise found among our sample confirmation of recent psychological research into the nature of identity as such. The Jews we met, like many others in America today, seem to hold a view of self "as a multifaceted and dynamic entity—active, forceful, and capable of change." Social identities (e.g., Jew and American), role identities (parent and professional), and individual attributes (caring, just) are integrated or combined without integration, in shifting combinations. The point is that

> [a]lthough terms such as identity and self-concept suggest a single, monolithic entity, phenomena like identity and self should be viewed as plural and diverse even within the individual. . . . it is no longer feasible to refer to the self-concept. . . . Within an individual's collection of con-

ceptions of the self, some are tentative, fleeting, and peripheral, others
are highly elaborated and function as enduring, meaning-making or
interpretive structure that help individuals lend coherence to their own
life-experiences. (Oyserman and Markus, pp. 190–191)

The Jews we met tend to place Jewish commitment at or near the center of that which is enduring in their "self-concept." Jewish tradition is a "meaning-making" and "interpretive structure" through which they seek coherence in their lives. However, unlike American Jews a generation ago, they see no need for a hard-and-fast distinction between the Jew and the American "inside" them. They feel no need to decide which of the two they will "be" or to sacrifice one in order to achieve the other. Indeed, they can envision no way even to think about these things except at boundary moments (a prospective intermarriage, for example) which threaten the blurring of identity components with which they are comfortable.

Similarly, while the Jews we interviewed cling to an ideal of wholeness, they generally practice a studied pluralism of commitment inside the self. They are pleased when their "social identity" as Jew is joined with their "role identity" as parent to produce a sense of transcendent meaning inside their home and family. However, they are generally uncomfortable when that social identity intrudes on professional roles or political allegiances. They do not practice law or medicine as Jews, they told us, or vote as Jews. Overwhelmingly, when we asked how they would want to be described by their friends, it was not as good Jews but as good and caring human beings.

One team of researchers captured well the paradox of this self-conception in speaking of contemporary American Jewish identity as at once "unambiguous" and "segmented." Jewishness now "constitutes only one segment of personal identity," exists alongside others, and shapes and is shaped by them, but "the multiple aspects of identity coexist independently rather than coalesce," and "neither the extent nor the intensity of the Jewish segment of personal identity is fixed" (Medding et al. 1992, pp. 18–19). That is why, as we too found, Jews can "assume or hope that intermarriage will have little effect on their Jewish feelings and commitments." For their identity is unalterable and unambiguous, and so need not find expression in one's activities, intimates, or home.

It might well be, as psychologists Markus and Kitayama argue, that ethnic, national, and religious groups vary in the way they conceive of the self. American Jews show signs of the more communal and less individual notion of self that these researchers found among their Japanese (but not their American) subjects. Their sense that Jewish is simply who and what they are, an essential and inalienable aspect of self, represents an enduring attachment to "historical familism" and as such a departure from the rigorous individualism depicted in recent literature about the self in contemporary America (e.g., Bellah et al. 1985). They differ in several other crucial respects as well.

Most prominently, Jews do not seem to choose Judaism, or choose among competing forms of Judaism, primarily in terms of belief. Hoge et al. found in their study of Protestant baby boomers that religious belief is a major reason that people chose one church over another. But virtually none of the moderately affiliated in our sample—whether Conservative or Reform or Reconstructionist or currently unaffiliated—would have assented to Jewish equivalents of the traditional beliefs the Hoge study used to distinguish among the varieties of Christian adherents (Hoge 1981, pp. 60–62). Nor did the rare belief among our sample in a God who created the world, revealed the Torah, and exercises special providence over the children of Israel correlate with higher ritual observance or communal activity. It would not be true among any but Orthodox Jews, therefore, that "the strongest predictors of the Baby Boomer's [synagogue] involvement are religious beliefs" (p. 168).

The peculiarities of Jewish identity, in particular the absence of a focus on God, lead us to doubt whether there is much hope for the "creative potential of liberal theology" that Roof holds out as one possible aspect of renewed "mainline religious life in America" in coming years (Roof 1983, p. 147). The Jews we met enjoy thinking about God and seem to have worked out inchoate theologies that enable them to feel comfortable in synagogue and ritual settings. However, they see no need for formal theologies that would systematize and rationalize their beliefs. Theology remains far less important to them than it is to Christians. *Tradition* functions as their "god-term," and it is not clear that Jews would want a faith any more certain than the one they already have—for it would necessitate a submission to authority from which they recoil. What matters to them in the absence of such faith are experiences of meaning in family and communal contexts that leave them free in other respects to be the selves they want to be. They are quite comfortable with the status of seeker after an ultimate truth they never locate. It goes along well with their strong attachment to voluntarism.

That voluntarism in matters religious follows a venerable American pattern. Echoing de Tocqueville, Stephen Warner has noted that "religion in America has historically promoted the formation of association among mobile people." Indeed, it "serves as a refuge of free association and autonomous identity." Voluntarism has always been at the core of this association; salvation—in the broad sense of an ultimate good unavailable elsewhere—has always been its aim. Hence, "the religious groups that seem to work best in cosmopolitan America are those that recognize the mobility of their members, and bring them into contact with great cultural traditions by incessantly and elaborately recounting the founding narrative" (Warner 1993, pp. 1059–60, 1078). That narrative—especially the Exodus drama, recounted at American Jewry's favorite holiday, Passover —remains as powerful as ever. But, so is the reluctance to sacrifice the freedom of association or non-association, the mobility of adherence, the autonomy of identity.

Jews may in fact differ from other Americans—Protestants in particular—in the degree to which their identity is rooted and expressed in rituals such as Passover, celebrated primarily with the family at home. While it is true, as we have noted, that our interviewees retain sovereignty with regard to ritual practice, and insist upon the discovery of personal meaning in each observance as the prerequisite for observing it, we are not sure that Gans's concept of merely "symbolic religiosity" adequately characterizes the practice of those we interviewed and surveyed. His categories presume distinctions between religious and secular, individual and group, consumption and participation, "symbolic" and "real" which the Jews we met refuse to make—for good reason.

"If the Passover seder, and even the High Holiday dinner, are mainly family meals in a Jewish context," Gans writes, "but people who attend feel that their religious identification is nevertheless enhanced by them, they would be an increasingly significant example of symbolic [as opposed to actual] religiosity" (1994, pp. 585–87). This misses something important in the reality we have depicted: when Jewish meaning is the instrument and object of the exercise, "symbol" is at its heart and meals with the family are usually the center of the action, the major purveyor of ultimate significance and purpose. "Quality time" with Judaism, as with family, is regarded by those we met as more meaningful than long hours spent doing things peripheral to the sense of self (including, perhaps, "non-symbolic" religious activities such as attendance at synagogue services). That is all the more true when Jewish and family quality time are one and the same. Most American Protestants, by Wuthnow's account, now have this religious "quality time" available to them only at Christmas (1999, p. 35).

In this respect we might say that Jews conform to the widespread American sentiment that personal experiences rather than institutional norms are what matter most. But they diverge from other Americans in having a long-established and religiously sanctified pattern of behavior in which this experience can be had on a regular basis. Jewish meaning is routinely and legitimately accessible to them, in concert with those most dear to the self, in the privacy of their own homes.

Passover observance also binds Jews, even as they observe it at home, to all the other Jews around the world who are celebrating the ritual meal at the same moment in the privacy of their homes. This paradoxical linkage of individual to group activity may also represent something of a divergence from prevalent American patterns. Jews seem to be resisting the trend toward the rapid attenuation and eventual disappearance of white ethnicity (Waters 1990); for all the weakened sense of tribalism, powerful "echoes" of it remain. Among moderately affiliated Jews, we are not seeing the reduction of group identity to what Gans famously labeled "symbolic ethnicity" (1979). Even intermarriage, often held to be the most certain indicator of ethnic disappearance, has not entirely eliminated either the sense of identity or the practice of ritual among Jews, though it has weakened both significantly.

Jews—in this respect like other white ethnic groups—cling to the "persistent notion that ethnicity is a primordial, biological status," a matter of *identity,* even as their ethnic *affiliation* is—and is known to be—"manifestly voluntary" (Hollinger 1995, p. 40). Their increasing disaffection from communal institutions and general reluctance to make particularist affirmations of belief likewise conform to the larger American pattern. Yet American Jews have also displayed a renewed level of comfort in recent decades with rituals and other activities (such as sending their children to Jewish day schools) that serve to highlight Jewish particularity. What is more, they apparently believe in—even if they do not always enact—the combination of "voluntary" and "involuntary affiliation," of "respect [for] inherited boundaries" and activity on behalf of "solidarities of wide scope," that Hollinger approvingly labels as "postethnic." His recent and influential analysis "urge[s] more attention to religiously defined cultures and suggest[s] some of the consequences of looking upon religious groups as 'ethnic' and upon ethnic groups as 'religious'" (p. 14).

For all their many departures from the ways of their ancestors, the American Jews we interviewed continue to look upon themselves in precisely that way—and their doing so arguably sets them apart from other ethnic and religious groups in America, however much it serves to align them with Hollinger's theory. Jewish religious belief and practice, even when attenuated, now as always bespeak and reinforce ethnic loyalties, however much the latter have been weakened, even as these ethnic loyalties demand and receive enactment in religious rituals and expression in religious symbols. American Jews by and large seem content with this degree of difference from the general pattern. American society—torn between pluralist affirmation of the value of difference and concern that multicultural diversity will rend the social fabric—seems content to encourage or at least allow this measure of Jewish difference to persist.

THE FUTURE OF AMERICAN JEWS

Ultimately, the critical question we put to our findings is to assess their implications for the American Jewish future. Or, to use terms the parents and grandparents of our respondents would easily recognize, are the developments that we have examined good or bad for the Jews?

Not surprisingly, we find this seemingly straightforward question exceedingly difficult to answer.

One complication concerns questions of fact, addressed at length below. What is really transpiring in American Jewish life? Are we seeing the transfer of energies and passion from one sphere to another? Or, alternatively, are we simply in the midst of the decline of the Jewish public sphere, with little compensation in the private lives of American Jews? Are we witnessing (merely) the abandonment of outmoded forms of communal organization? Or, more ominously, is a wholesale retreat in process, a withdrawal from all forms of collective Jewish expression? The evidence may be too sparse, and the trends too new, for any observer to make a clear inference from the evidence at hand. We will try to do so, with due caution, nonetheless.

The other complication concerns criteria and definitions. The choice of how to measure Jewish identity is inherently complex, and is complicated further by inevitable ideological considerations.

It is obvious that Judaism, Jewishness, and Jewish identity undergo unceasing transformation. Change in the essence and expression of these matters implies some change in the criteria we use to assess the strength of an individual's Jewish identity or the cultural vitality of a Jewish community. In other words, as Jews change the ways in which they express their Jewishness, analysts seem obliged to change the ways in which this Jewishness is measured. Participation in the temple sacrifice of ancient days, familiarity with Yiddish culture, and identification with the struggles of the Jewish working class have been central to being Jewish in previous times, but they are inappropriate measures of Jewish involvement in contemporary America. These measures are peculiar to Jews and peculiar to certain times and places.

The question is not whether our criteria should change, then, but how much they should change. Some indicators of Jewish engagement are largely neutral with respect to time, place, and group. Many of these can be applied to any cultural groups under almost any circumstances. The extent of in-group solidarity, marriage, friendship, institutional comprehensiveness, social differentiation (from the larger society), responsiveness to collective norms, and intragroup harmony (or divisiveness) are some examples. However, some of the more interesting individual and group measures are wrapped up in ideology specific to the group. How relevant and important are these in the United States today: possession of liturgical skills, involvement in leftist causes, involvement in conservative causes, engagement with traditional ritual practice, knowledge of Hebrew (or Yiddish or Ladino or Aramaic), support for Israel, or appreciation of Jewish humor? Ideologues of various stripes would provide different if not highly contrasting answers. As social scientists, even putting aside for the moment our own perspectives as committed Jews, we are compelled to make judgments that are inevitably ideologically tinged, if not ideologically driven. These include the degree to which our criteria and measures should be updated, as opposed to seeing Judaism as characterized by an unchangeable core of practice and belief.

One could put the issue this way: To what extent should analysts be *prescriptive*, using normative criteria reflective of established Jewish custom? To what extent should they (we) be *descriptive*, using criteria that emerge from an understanding of the present moment in Jewish life and history, as that moment is defined by the actions and omissions of Jewish actors? Prescription itself can follow more than one path: emphasizing long-standing practices and beliefs, or favoring adaptation and innovation —both in the name of continuity and survival. Most observers of American Jewish life, it seems fair to say, combine measures of prescription and description in their work. The preface to Sklare and Greenblum's classic volume contains an extended meditation on the subject (1967, pp. x–xi). Differences among scholars on this point seem a matter of degree rather than of kind. That is, they differ in the extent to which they apply descriptive or prescriptive criteria, not in the matter of their application. Our own assessment of the meaning of our findings and analysis for the future of American Jews inevitably hinges upon the mix of prescriptive and descriptive criteria that we are prepared to apply. We have tried to bend toward the descriptive pole throughout this study, and now, as we turn to speculation regarding the future, will try to make our prescriptive assumptions as explicit as possible.

Our basic take on the present situation, we repeat, disputes the oft-told tale of lessening religious belief and rising ethnic assimilation: a "straight-line theory" that is, our evidence suggests, both clichéd and outdated. The truth seems to us rather more complicated. For all that the focus on the Jewish self and the decline of the public dimension to Jewish identity are in our view unquestionable, we believe the jury is still out on what these developments portend for the Jewish future in America. Our suspicion is that neither development bodes particularly well for the future health of the community, for reasons we shall elaborate in a moment. But we find too many imponderables at work to venture a confident assessment.

One major issue, still unresolved, is whether the growth of private Jewish passion will turn out to be quantitatively and qualitatively equivalent to the decline in public Jewish commitment. Are we witnessing a falling away of public Judaism that leaves the level of Jewish practice in the private sphere of home and synagogue pretty much as it was before, all things considered? (Synagogue life can, of course, be seen as a very public venue of Jewish activity and expression, even if no one synagogue has the inclusiveness of community-wide or national organizations.) Alternatively, are we seeing new strength in the private realm that is compensating for, if not exceeding, the losses in the public realm? In addition, we wonder how one can measure the relative value of losses and gains in private and public Jewish life over time. The previous generation in American Jewry was marked by a steep decline in Yiddish cultural expression, but it gained the enormous cultural advantages of the state of Israel. Jews of the baby boomer generation are less emotionally attached to Israel than their parents' age-cohort, and care less about Jewish organizations. However, they are more open to religious belief, more engaged in home ritual observance, and often quite passionate about opportunities for serious Jewish learning.

One way to regard these developments is to see them as a very welcome adjustment to American postmodernity. All religious life has become more privatized. The larger society and culture sanction growth, experimentation, and fluidity in shaping personal identity. They militate against primordial ethnic attachments, especially among upper-middle-class whites of European origin. Contemporary attitudes view organized collectivities, or collectivist organizations based on ethnic affiliation, with great suspicion. The Jews we met seem to conform exactly to what one historian has termed the most common features of cultural pluralism in America:

> private celebration of cultural difference, public assimilation to puta-
> tively American behavioral norms, the presumption of every cultural
> group's shared commitment to tolerance, democracy, and human equal-
> ity, the recognition of the unique contributions of various cultural groups
> to American life and history, and some degree of cultural relativism.
> (Greenberg 1998, p. 57)

Hence, the move toward privatization and personalization, the quest for personal meaning coupled with nearly unqualified voluntarism among American Jews represents, to some observers, a healthy adaptation to America rather than a fateful surrender. In fact, so this argument goes, uniform and inflexible resistance to these powerful cultural trends by Jewish intellectuals, rabbis, educators, and communal leaders would consign American Judaism to the margins of society. A totally unadapted and unadaptable American Judaism would be doomed to irrelevance, and could not for long attract passionate supporters and adherents.

There is something to this, we believe, but we nonetheless cannot view the contraction, decline, and marginality of the public dimension of American Jewish life with equanimity. The public, institutional aspect to American Jewish life has been critical to the defense of Jewish interests. Its long-term atrophy would leave American Jewry less able to respond should their security or status ever be threatened again. As Michael Walzer has argued, what "gave the Jews place and standing in American society" was, "first, a strong internal organizational life, communal solidarity, reflected in institutions," and, second, legal protection, won with the help of these institutions, "in the form of friendly politicians and balanced tickets and equal access to public funds—which allows, in turn, for the strengthening of Jewish organizations." The result, he adds, is a model of "meat and potatoes multiculturalism" paralleled by the achievement of other religious groups—but not, at least not yet, by purely ethnic and racial groups (1998, pp. 92–93).

Perhaps more important, the panoply of organizations, charities, agencies monitoring antisemitism, and social services has provided Jews with important venues in which to act out their Jewishness. It is significant that just over half of American Jews still belong to a Jewish organization, and as many as 20 percent (on several surveys, not just ours) report serving on a board or committee. The experience of committee service is widespread in American Jewry, and is especially critical to Jewish communal leadership (which, by definition, largely fell outside the purview of our personal interviews). The shrinkage of organizations and the leadership positions they support would mean a shrinkage of opportunities for American Jews to act in ways that are peculiarly Jewish, and peculiarly American. (Jews in other societies, such as Israel, France, and the former Soviet Union, do not engage in as much voluntary, organized activity.) As Walzer observes, the "crucial institutions" of the community

> are not only places where highly specific services are provided; they are
> also places where Jews meet, socialize, help one another, observe the
> dietary laws, perform religious rituals, teach and learn, lecture about
> Jewish history or literature, organize dramatic productions, sing the tra-
> ditional songs, celebrate the holidays, comfort the sick, mourn the dead.
> . . . Cultures don't survive in people's heads. They need bounded spaces
> and organized activities of this kind. (1998, p. 93)

We could, perhaps, be persuaded that American Jewry can conduct a vibrant Jewish life in their homes, synagogues, schools, and JCCs, assuming all these grew in strength and in effect functioned as extensions of Jewish selves ("heads") and Jewish families. However, even if this were possible (and we are dubious), our ideological convictions lead us to view it as an unfortunate turn of events. Jewish participation in the public sphere has been a staple of Jewish life at least since the Babylonian Exile, coincident with the destruction of the First Temple in 586 B.C. Since then, Jews have established intricate infrastructures of communal organization that not only preserved Judaism, but also helped constitute its very essence. For centuries, an essential part of being Jewish has consisted of supporting, interacting with, and participating in the lives of organizational entities. Such activity, moreover, is mandated by major thrusts in Jewish religious tradition. The poor must be provided for. Tithes must be collected. Justice must be administered. Judaism has always focused on social matters of this sort, rather than on private contemplation or enlightenment.

The shrinkage of the American Jewish public sphere, then, would signify a weakened tie with the Jewish past and a significant loss of resources for the maintenance of religious and cultural traditions. It would also connote a weaker link with Jews around the world. Our research has demonstrated that attachment to Jewish peoplehood and to Israel is at least associated with, if not stimulated by, institutional involvement. American Jewish organizations maintain both the reality and the semblance (the latter is also important) of collective ties of Jews in America with those elsewhere. An American Jewry rich in institutional life is one with a greater similarity and connection to the Jewishness of other major Jewries. An American Judaism that is highly individualist, personalist, and voluntarist departs from that extant elsewhere, even though other Jewries may be moving in similar directions.

A further clue to the likely consequence of current trends is provided by the factors which brought moderately affiliated American Jews today to that, rather than a lower, level of Jewish commitment. Many of the Jews we met *have* chosen to join and attend synagogues, have undertaken more rituals of late, have embarked on serious programs of study to increase their knowledge of Jewish tradition, have visited Israel and pondered belief in God. Some are even open to—if not actually embracing—organizational involvements. What has brought them to higher levels of Jewish engagement? How have they overcome their fear of being "sucked in"? What led them to make the decision that more intense Jewish activity of some sort represents the fulfillment of the self, rather than its self-abnegation? The number of factors bearing on Jewish identity formation is, of course, extensive. The paths along which people walk toward and away from the community and Jewish tradition are extraordinarily diverse. The stories told by our subjects are highly individual. Yet, as we look back on this study, it seems worthwhile to note several sets of factors which have proved common to the journeys on which we have reported. The absence of these factors in the future, barring their replacement by others not yet apparent, would likely make the maintenance of current levels of activity unlikely, and achievement of higher levels improbable.

The first factor, of course, is *family*. Parents, whatever their attitudes toward being Jewish, matter enormously in the formation of adult identity and the stimulation of adult activity. So, too, do grandparents, whether they are actually Jewishly engaged or are idealized as such in the warm glow of memories from childhood. Spouses (almost all of whom were Jews in the population we interviewed) seem to have more influence than any one other individual. Even where both spouses were born Jewish, they nonetheless differ in their enthusiasm for Jewish behavior or their willingness to countenance it in their homes. Children, as we have noted, almost always stimulate more Jewish involvement.

It bears repeating that, whatever the influence of current families, our adult respondents largely have arrived at a level of Jewish involvement that could have been loosely predicted from their childhoods. After thoroughly reading the transcripts of the interviews several times, we divided our subjects into high and low levels of Jewish involvement, with all the problematics and imprecision that process entailed. We did so for their childhood and adolescent years and for their present situation. We learned that almost all were consistent (low-low or high-high). However, while the *level* of Jewish involvement remained roughly the same, the *form* of Jewish involvement in the adult years often differed markedly from that in the family of origin. No less important, the journeys to adult involvement have often been circuitous. These, like other matters of the heart and soul, are not straightforward—even if overall movement on the scale of activity has been far less than individual stories would lead us to believe.

We feel confident in inferring, therefore, that the current pattern of involvements will continue only if the positive influence of families is maintained. This cannot be accomplished by families alone, of course—if only because massive communal funding is required to provide the spaces and resources outside the home which make possible the activities in the home which American Jews find so meaningful.

Indeed, *communal institutions and professionals* were often cited by our respondents as major influences, negative and positive, on their behavior. We heard repeatedly of negative childhood experiences in Hebrew school and negative adult experiences with rabbis and congregations perceived as aloof, unwelcoming, or dogmatic. With the exception of a few individuals, none had anything very good to say about their local federations or about Jewish organizations generally. Synagogues, on the other hand, often elicited praise as a stimulus to greater commitment. So did several rabbis—particularly when the synagogue and the rabbi in question had offered adult education programs on a high level that their congregants found engaging.

Jewish institutions face a formidable task in this period of voluntarism and mobility. They must have a range of options available to every individual at every moment, so that when he or she is ready to seize hold of Jewishness or Judaism, the right option is there to be had. Jewish professionals more and more seem like the operators of a transit system. A bus must be ready and waiting at the bus-stop at the exact moment that the prospective Jewish rider appears. The fleet must be sufficiently large to be there whenever wanted, and it must be sufficiently diverse to take account of the diverse tastes and needs of its potential clientele. We are impressed by how well our interviewees believe the community is doing at present in providing the options they desire. They were, to be sure, a self-selected group. Those entirely alienated from Jewish community fell outside the range of our sample. Still, many whom we met had embarked on Jewish activity only recently, inspired by a rabbi, a program, or an experience—a "bus"—they found compelling.

The third factor promoting (and inhibiting) involvement, one that proved far more important than we ourselves recognized at the outset of our research, is *gender*. To a remarkable degree, the "action" where Jewish activity among the moderately affiliated is concerned now rests with women, who undertake such activity either with or without the assistance of male partners. Given the centrality of ritual to our subjects, and the fact that so much of Jewish ritual takes place in the home and involves children, the predominance of women in undertaking Jewish practice is not surprising. Women retain primary responsibility for child-rearing, even in two-career families. Home remains their domain, recognized as such by men and women alike.

Other forces too may be at work in this regard. The relatively new interest in spirituality in Judaism, for example, is a concern to which women are generally more open than men. Conversation about and experiences of transcendence come more easily to women than to men, if our interviews are a reliable indicator. And the visibility of women rabbis, lay leaders, and communal professionals has galvanized and legitimated re-interpretation of the tradition and re-direction of institutions, both of which in turn attract women who might otherwise have remained aloof. We suspect that the very language of search and quest presumes a hesitancy with which the men we met were often uncomfortable. As Molly put it, "The question about God is really a struggle. But life's been a struggle. That makes me feel better about it." The men we interviewed, even when similarly questing, tended to come across as more decisive.

We are not sure whether this factor is cause or effect (or both) of the current generation's move from the public to the private sphere, though it seems clear that women still play far less a role in the Jewish organizational world than they do in the synagogue, and far more a role than men in the home. Here, too, the future is uncertain; women could take on a larger share of responsibility and power in the public sphere, and move Jewish life in that direction; alternatively, though far less likely in our view, men could re-assert themselves in the synagogue and take on responsibilities in the home that, outside Orthodoxy, they seem at the moment to have resigned.

All of this makes for a large measure of uncertainty when it comes to limning the future, even the near future, of the American Jewish community. The final word on the Jew within, we believe, cannot yet be spoken. We are sadly confident, as Bellah and his colleagues warned about American society as a whole several years ago, that "the consequences of radical individualism are more strikingly evident than they were even a decade ago, when *Habits of the Heart* was published" (Bellah et al. 1996, p. xi). But it is also true that the current moment presents Jewish individuals and institutions with opportunities that might yet, if seized, radically transform Jewish selves and communities. The future hinges on whether the professional practice of rabbis, educators, social workers, and other communal activists can and will change in ways that take account of the increased sovereignty of self and the centrality of the search for personal meaning; whether they can and do find ways of overcoming the decreased appeal of institutions and the attenuated sense of Jewish peoplehood that these institutions have conveyed; whether Jews bent on the sovereign pursuit of fulfillment can be persuaded to seek and find that fulfillment inside revitalized communal frameworks and institutions.

Our interviewees, having recounted their personal journeys to us, nearly always looked forward to the next stage on the way with great anticipation. So do we, though in our case—pondering the community's collective journey—the sense of apprehension is no less acute. The emergence of the Jew within, it seems clear, will bear profound consequences—positive and negative—for Jews, Judaism, and Jewishness in the twenty-first century now upon us.

APPENDIX A: INTERVIEW GUIDE

[*Interviewer: Starred questions may be skipped if necessary. In addition, questions that are part of the same paragraph may be shortened or skipped if necessary and if answers to earlier questions have largely covered the same ground. Instructions to you are in caps and brackets.*]

INTERVIEW I

As I think I told you on the phone, two social scientists—Arnie Eisen of Stanford University and Steven Cohen of the Hebrew University—are writing a book on the meaning of being Jewish to American Jews. They're not at all interested in the views of professional Jews—rabbis, educators, and such. Rather, they and their associates are interviewing rank and file Jews all across the country to hear how such individuals describe their lives, their feelings, and their backgrounds.

I'll be recording our interviews and they will be transcribed. We promise you total anonymity. We will not use your name in the book, and when we use your words, we promise to disguise your identity.

Do you have any questions before we begin?

First, let's start with a bit of your basic biography—how old are you, what do you do professionally, and tell me a bit about members of your family.

Now, please tell me about your interests and activities. Outside of work and family, how do you spend your time?

What magazines do you read?

Are you involved in any organizations? sit on any committees or boards?

Do you do any other sort of volunteer work?

Do you have any interest in politics or social affairs? Any recent involvement in politics or in any social causes? [IF YES: Why? What attracted you to become active?]

Now, if we may, I'd like to run through your life—from childhood—and ask you to give me a running narrative that touches all the high points. [IF NOT MENTIONED, ASK ABOUT: parents, grandparents, college, graduate school, career]

Now let's go back and focus on the Jewish part of your biography. Again start with your childhood, your parents, and the types of Jewish things your family did.

With regard to your Jewish upbringing, what sorts of things most stick in your mind from your childhood? (Holidays, antisemitism, Hebrew school, summer camp, youth group, junior congregation, Israel, friends, friends' parents)

*What did it feel like, as a Jew, going to school?

When you were in high school . . . were your friends Jewish/not . . . did you date? who? . . . Jewish youth group, camp, Israel?

Tell me about how you met your [husband/wife]. Why did you decide to marry him/her? Was his/her way of being Jewish at all important to you then?

How would you say your husband's/wife's way of being Jewish differed from yours when you first got married? And how have you both changed since then?

What would you say were the key experiences or people that had the most decisive influence on the type of Jew you are today? Would you say that there was any particular turning point in your life where you became either decidedly more or less Jewishly involved than you were before?

*How did you decide on the names of your children?

What sort of Jewish schooling are you giving your children? Why? What other choices did you reject? Why? Do/did your husband/wife approach these issues about the same way you do/did?

Are you basically happy or unhappy with the way your children are developing as Jews? What would you change if you could, either in them or their environment or experiences?

What do you hope for your children? What kind of people should they be when they grow up? How would you like them to relate to being Jewish? How would you feel if they decided to marry non-Jews?

*Do you sense that your children approach being Jewish differently in any way? How? Why do you think that is?

In what ways is your husband's/wife's role as a Jewish parent different from yours? What types of things does he/she get involved in and what are you more likely to pick up on?

Do you have something to add about anything we've said? Anything you want to clarify? Is there anything I should have asked you that I didn't?

Thank you very much for you time . . .

[ARRANGE FOR NEXT INTERVIEW]

INTERVIEW II

Before we start this session, I'd like to ask you if you'd had any thoughts you'd like to share from our last interview?

I'd like to begin by asking you to review the holidays, telling me which you or your family celebrate, and how or why? [IF ASKED: Both Jewish and other holidays are fine.] Let's proceed through the twelve-month calendar from beginning to end. [IF ASKED: Jewish or "regular" calendar okay. R may pick either.]

What are some of the things you like about being Jewish?

What are some of the things that you find annoying, frustrating or disappointing about either Judaism or some Jews?

*Do you think of Judaism as a religion, an ethnicity, or what? Why?

Tell me about your friends. How many and which kinds are Jewish, which not? Do you have different sorts of relationships with Jewish and non-Jewish friends?

If I were to speak to your friends about you, how would you like them to describe you?

To what extent have you been involved in your synagogue/temple? Let's go over your involvement in the synagogue/temple. When did you first join? Why did you join? Why did you pick that particular synagogue/temple?

What do you get out of your involvement? How do you feel about going to services—Shabbat, High Holidays? Why do you go?

How has your involvement changed?

Aside from the synagogue, what other Jewish involvements would you say you have? [IF INVOLVED:] Why are you active? What do you get out of your involvement? Why did you pick that area to get involved in?

Have you ever been at all involved in any Jewish organizations? When? [Get history of involvement and reasons for joining, becoming active, dropping out]

*How do you feel about the Federation and other Jewish organizations?

What sort of causes or issues have you been involved in? Where do you give your charity? How much to where? Why there?

Do you see your involvement/interest in social justice causes in America as in any way connected with your being Jewish? How have your feelings about your connection to specifically Jewish causes and all other causes changed over the years?

How do you feel about God? What does God mean to you?

Do you feel you have a personal relationship with God? When do you think you pray to or talk with God?

Some people say they feel especially close to their religion or God during times of crises or personal difficulties. Has that ever been your experience? When? What happened?

*Do you think Jews are God's "chosen people?"

Have your feelings about God changed over the years? How? Why?

Would you call yourself a "spiritual" person? Why/why not?

[IF PARENT:] Do your children ever ask about God? What do you say? What do you really believe?

What about Israel? What are your impressions? Ever been? When? Why?/Why not? [IF NOT:] Want to go? How bad? Why? [IF BEEN:] What surprised you? What was your experience? Want to go back?

How have your feelings toward Israel changed over the years?

*How do you think the Holocaust has affected the way you relate to being a Jew? Do you derive any lessons from the Holocaust? Do you think that one day "IT" could happen here in America?

As a Jew, what sorts of obligations or responsibilities do you have? What are your responsibilities to yourself, your family, your local Jewish community, the larger society?

Do you think Jews have a special responsibility to be ethical? to be active in social causes?

Jews have been known as the "Chosen People." When you hear that expression, what does it mean to you?

Are Jews in any way different from other Americans? How?

What in your view is the most important thing a Jew should do as a Jew?

Do you think rabbis should perform marriages between Jews and Gentiles?

Aside from what we've spoken about, what other parts of Judaism or being Jewish are important to you?

Do you have something to add about anything we've said? Anything you want to clarify? Is there anything I should have asked you that I didn't?

APPENDIX B: THE SURVEY

Dear Panel Member,

Your household has been selected for a national survey about topics of importance to the American Jewish community. The information provided will contribute to the development of a unique profiling of the opinions, beliefs, and practices of contemporary American Jewry. All responses, of course, will remain anonymous and compiled together with hundreds of others in the form of statistical summaries. The statistical profile will be available to Jewish organizations and leaders, journalists, and academics interested in these issues. For the research to be valid, it is important that everyone selected complete the survey—not just those who feel they are "strongly Jewish."

IMPORTANT: Because we need a balanced number of replies from men and women, this questionnaire needs to be answered by a Jewish male in your household.

Cordially,

YOUR SENSE OF BEING JEWISH

1. In thinking about your sense of being Jewish, how important is each of the following?

	Extremely Important	Very Important	Somewhat Important	Not Important	Not Sure
a. Israel	33%	33	28	5	1
b. God	50%	25	17	7	1
c. The Holocaust	49%	36	12	2	1
d. The Torah	45%	31	18	6	1
e. Passover	39%	37	21	4	0
f. Rosh Hashana & Yom Kippur	50%	32	15	3	1
g. The Sabbath	22%	26	31	20	1
h. Jewish law	21%	24	38	14	3
i. American antisemitism	54%	30	12	3	2
j. The Jewish people	50%	34	14	2	1
k. The Jewish family	56%	28	13	3	1

ATTACHMENTS TO JEWISH INSTITUTIONS

2. To what extent do you feel attached to each of the following local Jewish groups and organizations?

	Extremely Attached	Very Attached	Somewhat Attached	Not Attached	Not Sure
a. A synagogue or temple	21%	17	28	34	0
b. A Jewish Community Center (or YMHA)	4%	7	25	64	1
c. The local Jewish Federation/UJA	3%	8	30	58	1
d. Another Jewish organization	7%	11	25	54	3

THE "GOOD JEW"

3. In your opinion, for a person to be a good Jew, which of the following items are essential, which are desirable, which do not matter, and which are undesirable (better not to do)?

	Essential	Desirable	Does Not Matter	Undesirable	Not Sure
a. Believe in God	52%	33	14	0	1
b. Contribute to Jewish philanthropies	11%	47	40	1	2
c. Support Israel	20%	51	28	1	1
d. Contribute to non-sectarian charities	6%	38	51	1	3
e. Belong to Jewish organizations	10%	41	47	1	1
f. Belong to a synagogue	24%	43	32	1	1
g. Belong to a Jewish Community Center	4%	27	67	1	2
h. Attend services on High Holidays	36%	38	24	1	1
i. Lead an ethical and moral life	67%	29	3	0	0
j. Have a kosher home	9%	18	67	5	1
k. Study Jewish texts	7%	35	54	2	2
l. Educate oneself about Judaism & Jewish history	24%	62	13	0	1
m. Have mostly Jewish friends	3%	17	67	12	1
n. Work for social justice causes	9%	41	45	3	3
o. Be a liberal on political issues	3%	18	65	9	4
p. Be a conservative on political issues	1%	10	69	14	6
q. Marry a Jew (or a convert to Judaism)	28%	39	30	2	1
r. Celebrate the Sabbath in some way	19%	42	38	1	1
s. Give one's children a Jewish education	48%	40	11	0	1
t. Feel attached to the Jewish people	41%	45	13	0	1
u. Visit Israel during one's life	18%	41	38	1	2

YOUR BELIEFS AND OPINIONS

4. Do you agree or do you disagree with each of the following statements?

	Agree Strongly	Agree	Disagree	Disagree Strongly	Not Sure
a. I am proud to be a Jew	68%	28	1	0	3
b. Being Jewish connects me with my family's past	51%	39	6	1	3
c. Being Jewish is a major part of how I live my life	30%	38	26	3	3
d. Jews are my people, the people of my ancestors	48%	46	4	1	2
e. Jews have had an especially rich history, one with special meaning for our lives today	48%	46	2	0	3
f. I look at the entire Jewish community as my extended family	14%	38	35	5	8
g. Jews have a permanent bond	23%	53	16	2	7
h. I feel I can count more on my Jewish friends than on my non-Jewish friends	8%	17	54	16	5
i. I relate easier to Jews than to non-Jews	9%	26	48	12	5
j. To me, being Jewish means having an ethnic identity as well as a religious identity	25%	55	14	2	4
k. My being Jewish doesn't make me any different from other Americans	25%	41	27	5	2
l. I feel that, as a Jew, there is something about me that non-Jews could never understand	14%	38	37	6	5
m. Jews are God's "Chosen People"	15%	35	30	6	14
n. As a Jew, I feel like somewhat of an outsider in American society	3%	16	55	22	3
o. I feel as moved by the oppression of non-Jews as by the comparable oppression of Jews	19%	56	16	2	8
p. I have a special responsibility to take care of Jews in need around the world	9%	38	39	5	9
q. Jews are widely disliked by Gentile Americans	3%	22	54	11	10
r. One day American Jews will probably face severe antisemitic persecution	6%	22	44	8	21
s. My feelings about the Holocaust have deeply influenced my feeling about being Jewish	21%	44	25	3	7

		Agree Strongly	Agree	Disagree	Disagree Strongly	Not Sure
t.	I really don't feel competent praying in synagogue	5%	26	40	22	7
u.	Most synagogue services are not interesting to me	6%	27	44	18	5
v.	I look forward to going to synagogue	12%	38	33	8	9
w.	Even if I don't observe every aspect of the Sabbath, I do try to make it a special day	11%	36	41	8	5
x.	A Jew can be religious even if he or she isn't particularly observant	29%	57	8	3	3
y.	I am a spiritual person	20%	43	23	3	11
z.	It bothers me when people try to tell me that there's a right way to be Jewish	41%	42	11	3	3
aa.	I have the right to reject those Jewish observances that I don't find meaningful	20%	54	16	6	5
bb.	Parents shouldn't try to impose a particular pattern of Jewish living on their children	10%	34	39	12	6
cc.	Having a Christmas tree would violate my sense of being Jewish	45%	24	18	11	2
dd.	Jews should marry Jews	27%	35	23	7	9
ee.	In-marriages (between Jews and Jews) tend to have fewer difficulties than intermarriages	15%	29	33	11	13
ff.	In synagogue, I feel closer to God	15%	39	31	6	9
gg.	Many Jews in synagogue or Jewish organizational life are hypocrites	10%	33	34	8	17
hh.	Jewish charities place too much emphasis on helping only Jews	4%	26	50	8	12
ii.	The organized Jewish community gives too much recognition to the wealthiest Jews	11%	34	36	4	15
jj.	I find Jewish organizations largely remote and irrelevant to me	6%	35	41	7	11
kk.	Orthodox Jews are the most authentic Jews	6%	9	48	30	7
ll.	Most Orthodox Jews are narrow-minded	13%	38	29	7	13
mm.	Orthodox Jews' feelings of superiority bother me	16%	36	32	6	9
nn.	I am grateful to Orthodox Jews for doing so much to maintain Jewish life	9%	30	36	11	13

	Agree Strongly	Agree	Disagree	Disagree Strongly	Not Sure
oo. I get upset when Orthodox Jews in Israel try to limit the practice of Conservative and Reform Judaism in Israel	44%	36	9	3	9
pp. Jews have a special intellectual style	9%	40	34	4	12
qq. Because I'm Jewish, I identify with the powerless, the vulnerable, and the underdog	6%	29	44	13	8
rr. Being Jewish means being especially compassionate	7%	34	42	6	11
ss. Generally, Jews are more materialist than other Americans	2%	12	57	20	9
tt. Generally, Jews are more charitable than other Americans	7%	34	39	6	14
uu. Israel is critical to sustaining American Jewish life	15%	37	29	5	14
vv. Israel is a dangerous place to visit	5%	28	40	16	11
ww. Israel doesn't really need American Jewish charity any more	2%	8	48	26	17

ISRAEL

5. How many times have you been to Israel?

Never	64%	Twice or more	15
Once	21%	I was born in Israel	1

6. How emotionally attached are you to Israel?

Extremely attached	9%	Not attached	27
Very attached	18%	Don't know	4
Somewhat attached	42%		

7. With respect to Israel's policies regarding Palestinians, the Land of Israel, and the Peace Process, which approach do you tend to favor more—that of Likud (the party of Benjamin Netanyahu and the late Menachem Begin), or that of Labor (the party of Shimon Peres and the late Yitzhak Rabin)?

Likud	20%	Other party	1
Labor	35%	Don't know	43
A religious party	2%		

YOUR BELIEFS ABOUT GOD

8. Do you believe that . . .

	Definitely Yes	Probably Yes	Probably Not	Definitely Not	Not Sure
a. There is a God	56%	27	7	3	8
b. God watches over you in times of danger	36%	32	16	5	12
c. God has a special relationship with the Jewish people	25%	27	24	7	17

INTERMARRIAGE AND OTHER MATTERS

9. If your child were considering marrying a non-Jewish person with no plans to convert to Judaism, would you . . .

Strongly encourage them to marry	4%	Oppose their marriage	15
Encourage them	6%	Strongly oppose	12
Be neutral/Not sure	64%		

10. What would you do about this marriage if it involved a conversion to Judaism?

Strongly encourage them to marry	9%	Oppose their marriage	2
Encourage them	39%	Strongly oppose	3
Be neutral/Not sure	47%		

11. To what extent do you feel . . .

	To a Great Extent	To Some Extent	Not at All	Not Sure
Close to other Jews	37%	55	6	2
Close to Israelis	8%	41	43	8
Close to non-Jewish Americans	15%	72	8	5

12. How important would you say religion is in your own life?

Very important	26%	Not very important	29
Fairly important	43%	Not sure	2

13. How important would you say being Jewish is in your own life?

Very important	47%	Not very important	13
Fairly important	39%	Not sure	1

YOUR JEWISH BACKGROUND

14. What is the main type of Jewish education you received as a child? (SELECT ONE ANSWER ONLY)

None	16%
Sunday School	22%
Hebrew School or other part-time Jewish school	48%
Yeshiva or Day School	7%
Private tutoring	5%
Any other type	3%

15. Referring to Jewish religious denominations, do you consider yourself to be . . . (SELECT ONE ANSWER ONLY)

Conservative	34%	Something else Jewish	2
Orthodox	7%	Just Jewish	18
Reform	35%	Secular	2
Reconstructionist	2%	Not Jewish	–

16. About how often do you personally attend any type of synagogue, temple, or organized Jewish religious service?

Not at all or only on special occasions (a Bar Mitzvah, a wedding)	33%
Only on High Holidays (Rosh Hashanah, Yom Kippur)	16%
A few times a year	26%
About once a month	10%
Several times a month or more	16%

17. Among the people you consider your closest friends, would you say that

None are Jewish	5%	Most are Jewish	36
Few are Jewish	16%	All or almost all are Jewish	10
Some are Jewish	33%		

18. Which of the following apply to you? (MARK EACH ITEM "YES" OR "NO")

		Yes	No
a.	During the Christmas season, does your household ever have a Christmas tree?	21%	79
b.	During Passover, do you usually attend a Seder?	87%	14
c.	Does your household usually light candles on Hanukkah?	90%	10
d.	Does your household use separate dishes for meat and dairy?	18%	82
e.	Do you fast on Yom Kippur?	64%	36
f.	Does your household usually light candles on Friday night?	28%	72
g.	Are you or any member of your household currently a member of a synagogue or temple?	49%	52
h.	Are you or anyone in your household a dues-paying member of a Jewish Community Center (JCC) or YMHA?	14%	86
i.	Have you or anyone in your household participated in any program or activity at a JCC or a YMHA within the past year?	27%	73
j.	Do you belong to any Jewish organizations other than a synagogue, temple, JCC, or YMHA?	32%	68
k.	In the past two years have you served as an officer or on the board or committee of a Jewish organization, synagogue, or temple?	19%	81
l.	Did you contribute to the UJA/Federation in the past year?	42%	58
m.	During the last 5 years have you engaged in regular study of Jewish subject matter such as in a class or in an informal study group?	25%	75
n.	Have you ever seriously considered living in Israel?	12%	88

19. Of the following people, who was raised Jewish, and who is Jewish now? (MARK THE "NA" BOX IF THAT QUESTION IS NOT APPLICABLE TO YOU.)

		Raised Jewish?			Jewish Now?		
		Yes	No	NA	Yes	No	NA
a.	You	95%	5		99	1	
b.	Your spouse	78%	22		80	20	
c.	The spouse of your youngest married child	55%	45		54	46	

20. (ANSWER IF YOU HAVE ANY MARRIED CHILDREN:) How old is your youngest married child?

32% have a married child
Average age of the married child: 37 (Range 21–58)

YOUR BACKGROUND

21. Are you:

Male   51%   Female   49

22. Are you (MARK ONE):

Married   77%   Divorced or separated   7
Never married   11%   Widowed   5

23. How many children have you had?

76% have children
1 child: 20%   2 children: 48%   3 or more children: 32%

24. What is your age?

Average age: 50 (Range 18–93)

25. With respect to your political views on most issues, do you regard yourself as (MARK ONE):

Very liberal   7%   Conservative   21
Liberal   28%   Very conservative   2
Moderate   43%

26. With regard to political party identification, do you regard yourself as:

A Democrat   64%
An Independent   20%
A Republican   16%

RAISING JEWISH CHILDREN

IF YOU HAVE HAD NO CHILDREN, SKIP THE REMAINING QUES-
TIONS AND RETURN YOUR COMPLETED QUESTIONNAIRE. THANK
YOU FOR TAKING THE TIME TO COMPLETE THIS SURVEY! OTHER-
WISE—IF YOU HAVE HAD CHILDREN—PLEASE CONTINUE.

27. Who would you say is/was more involved in your child(ren)'s Jewish
    upbringing—you or your spouse?

You	29%
Your spouse	17%
Both equally	50%
Not sure	4%

Please answer the questions below with respect to your oldest child:

28. How old is this child?

    Average age: 27 (Range 1–63)

29. Is this child male or female?

    Male   48%   Female   52%

30. Did this child ever attend . . .

		Yes	No
a.	A JCC pre-school	16%	84
b.	Another Jewish-sponsored pre-school	25%	75
c.	A full-time Jewish school (yeshiva or day school, grade 1 or higher)	11%	89
d.	A part-time Jewish school that met more than once a week	41%	59
e.	A Jewish Sunday School or other one-day-a-week program	50%	50
f.	A Jewish youth group	42%	58
g.	An overnight camp sponsored by a JCC	14%	86
h.	An overnight camp sponsored by another official Jewish agency such as a synagogue movement, or a Zionist organization	21%	79
i.	A Christian religious school	4%	96

THANK YOU FOR TAKING THE TIME TO COMPLETE THIS SURVEY!

BIBLIOGRAPHY

American Jewish Committee. 1998. *1998 Annual Survey of American Jewish Opinion*. New York: The American Jewish Committee.

Avruch, Kevin. 1981. *American Immigrants in Israel: Social Identities and Change*. Chicago: University of Chicago Press.

Bellah, Robert N. 1987. "Conclusion: Competing Visions of the Role of Religion in American Society." In *Uncivil Religion: Interreligious Hostility in America*, ed. Robert N. Bellah and Frederick C. Greenspahn. New York: Crossroad Press.

Bellah, Robert N., Richard Madsen, William M. Sullivan, Ann Swidler, and Steven M. Tipton. 1985. *Habits of the Heart: Individualism and Commitment in American Life*. New York: Harper and Row.

———. 1996. "Introduction to the Updated Edition: The House Divided." In *Habits of the Heart: Individualism and Commitment in American Life*. vii–xxxix. Berkeley: University of California Press.

Berger, Peter L. 1969. *The Sacred Canopy: Elements of a Sociological Theory of Religion*. Garden City, N.Y.: Doubleday.

———. 1980. *The Heretical Imperative: Contemporary Possibilities of Religious Affirmation*. Garden City, N.Y.: Doubleday.

Biale, David, Michael Galshinsky, and Susannah Heschel, eds. 1998. *Insider/Outsider: American Jews and Multiculturalism*. Berkeley: University of California Press.

Bock, G. 1976. "The Jewish Schooling of American Jews: A Study of Non-cognitive Educational Effects." Unpublished doctoral dissertation, Harvard University.

Buber, Martin. 1947. *I and Thou*. Edinburgh: T. and T. Clark.

Bubis, Gerald. 1992. "Jewish Dollars Drying Up." *Moment* (December): 28–33.

Carmichael, Stokely, and Charles V. Hamilton. 1967. *Black Power: The Politics of Liberation in America*. New York: Vintage Books.

Chanes, Jerome A. 1995. "Antisemitism and Jewish Security in America Today: Interpreting the Data—Why Can't Jews Take 'Yes' for an Answer?" In *Antisemitism in America Today: Outspoken Experts Explode the Myths*, ed. Jerome A. Chanes. New York: Birch Lane Press.

Clark, Wayne. 1949. "Portrait of the Mythical Gentile." *Commentary* 7, no. 6 (June): 346–349.

Cohen, Steven M. 1974. "The Impact of Jewish Education on Religious Identification and Practice." *Jewish Social Studies* (October): 316–326.

———. 1978. "Will Jews Keep Giving? Prospects for the Jewish Charitable Community." *Journal of Jewish Communal Service* (Fall): 59–71.

———. 1980a. "American Jewish Feminism: A Study in Conflicts and Compromises." *American Behavioral Scientist* (July): 519–559.

———. 1980b. "Trends in Jewish Philanthropy." *American Jewish Yearbook* 80: 29–51.

———. 1982a. "The American Jewish Family Today." *American Jewish Yearbook* 82: 136–154.

———. 1982b. "What American Jews Believe." *Moment* (July): 23–27.

———. 1983a. "The 1981–2 National Survey of American Jews." *American Jewish Yearbook* 83: 89–110.

———. 1983b. "Attitudes of American Jews toward Israel and Israelis." American Jewish Committee.

———. 1983c. *American Modernity and Jewish Identity.* New York: Tavistock.

———. 1984. "The Political Attitudes of American Jews." American Jewish Committee.

———. 1985a. "From Romantic Idealists to Loving Realists: The Changing Place of Israel in the Consciousness of American Jews." *Survey of Jewish Affairs 1985:* 169–182.

———. 1985b. "Outreach to the Marginally Affiliated: Evidence and Implications for Policy-makers in Jewish Education." *Journal of Jewish Communal Service* 62 (Winter): 147–157.

———. 1987. "Ties and Tensions: The 1986 Survey of American Jewish Attitudes toward Israel and Israelis." American Jewish Committee.

———. 1988. *American Assimilation or Jewish Revival?* Bloomington: Indiana University Press.

———. 1989a. "Alternative Families and the Jewish Community: Singles, Single Parents, Childless and Intermarried." American Jewish Committee.

———. 1989b. "Are American and Israeli Jews Drifting Apart?" American Jewish Committee.

———. 1989c. "The Dimensions of Jewish Liberalism." American Jewish Committee.

———. 1989d. "The Quality of American Jewish Life: Better or Worse?" In *Facing the Future: Essays on Contemporary Jewish Life,* ed. Steven Bayme. 23–49. Hoboken, N.J.: Ktav Publishing House.

———. 1989e. "Ties and Tensions: An Update—The 1989 Survey of American Jewish Attitudes toward Israel and Israelis." American Jewish Committee.

———. 1989f. "Undue Stress on Anti-Semitism." *Sh'ma* 19 (September): 1–3.

———. 1990. "Israel in the Jewish Identity of American Jews: A Study in Dualities and Contrasts." *Shofar: An Interdisciplinary Journal of Jewish Studies* 8 (Spring): 1–15. Reprinted in *Jewish Identity in America,* ed. David M. Gordis and Yoav Ben-Horin. 119–136. Los Angeles: Wilstein Institute of Jewish Policy Studies, University of Judaism, 1991.

———. 1991a. "After the Gulf War: American Jews' Attitudes toward Israel—The 1991 National Survey of American Jews." American Jewish Committee.

———. 1991b. "Content and Continuity: Two Bases for Jewish Commitment." American Jewish Committee.

―――. 1992. "Are American and Israeli Jews Drifting Apart?" In *Imagining the Jewish Future*, ed. David Teutsch. 119–133. Albany: State University of New York Press.

―――. 1994a. "Jewish Content versus Jewish Continuity." In *The Americanization of the Jews*, ed. Robert Seltzer and Norman Cohen. 395–416. New York: NYU Press.

―――. 1994b. "Why Intermarriage May Not Threaten Jewish Continuity." *Moment* (December): 54ff.

―――. 1995. "The Impact of Varieties of Jewish Education upon Jewish Identity: An Inter-generational Perspective." *Contemporary Jewry* 16: 68–96.

―――. 1996. "Did American Jews Really Grow More Distant from Israel? A Reconsideration." In *Envisioning Israel*, ed. Alon Gal. Detroit: Wayne State University Press, and Jerusalem: Magnus Press, Hebrew University.

―――. 1997a. "De-constructing the Outreach-Inreach Debate." *Conservative Judaism* (Winter): 26–33.

―――. 1997b. "Intermarriage and the Jewish Future." In *A Statement on the Jewish Future*. 10–19. American Jewish Committee.

―――. 1997c. "The Conversion Illusion." In *Jewish Identity and Religious Commitment*, ed. Jack Wertheimer. 29–35. Jewish Theological Seminary of America.

―――. 1998. "Religious Stability and Ethnic Decline: Emerging Patterns of Jewish Identity in the United States." New York: Jewish Community Centers Association.

―――. Forthcoming (a). "Assessing the Vitality of the Conservative Movement." In *The Jews in the Pews: Conservative Synagogues and Their Members*, ed. Jack Wertheimer.

―――. Forthcoming (b). "Camp Ramah and Adult Jewish Identity: Long-Term Influences on Conservative Congregants in North America." National Ramah Commission.

Cohen, Steven M., and Arnold M. Eisen. 1998. "The Jew Within: Self, Community, and Commitment among the Variety of Moderately Affiliated." Boston: Wilstein Institute of Jewish Policy Studies.

Cohen, Steven M., and Leonard Fein. 1985. "From Integration to Survival: American Jewish Anxieties in Transition." *Annals of the American Academy of Political and Social Science* (July): 75–88.

Cohen, Steven M., and Paula E. Hyman, eds. 1986. *The Jewish Family: Myths and Reality*. New York: Holmes and Meier.

Cohen, Steven M., and Charles S. Liebman. 1997. "Understanding American Jewish Liberalism." *Public Opinion Quarterly* 61 (Fall): 405–430.

―――. Forthcoming. "Israel and American Jewry in the 21st Century: A Search for New Relationships." In *North American Jewry and Israel: Beyond Survival and Philanthropy*, ed. Allon Gal and Alfred Gottschalk.

Cohen, Steven M., and Seymour Martin Lipset. 1991. *Attitudes toward the Arab-Israeli Conflict and the Peace Process among American Jewish Philanthropic Leaders, 1991*. Los Angeles: Wilstein Institute of Jewish Policy Studies, University of Judaism.

Cohen, Steven M., and Susan Wall. 1993. "Excellence in Youth Trips to Israel." Jewish Educational Services of North America.

Cowan, Paul, and Rachel Cowan. 1987. *Mixed Blessings: Marriage between Jews and Christians*. Garden City, N.Y.: Doubleday.

Cuddihy, John Murray. 1974. *The Ordeal of Civility: Freud, Marx, Levi-Strauss, and the Jewish Struggle with Modernity*. New York: Dell Publishing.

Dashefsky, Arnold, and Howard M. Shapiro. 1974. *Ethnic Identification among American Jews: Socialization and Social Structure*. Lexington, Mass.: Lexington Books.

Davidman, Lynn. 1991. *Tradition in a Rootless World: Women Turn to Orthodox Judaism*. Berkeley: University of California Press.

Dershowitz, Alan M. 1997. *The Vanishing American Jew*. New York: Little, Brown.

Douglas, Mary. 1966. *Purity and Danger*. New York: Praeger.

———. 1982. *In the Active Voice*. London: Routledge and Kegan Paul.

Durkheim, Emile. 1915. *The Elementary Forms of Religious Life*. New York: George Allen and Unwin.

Eisen, Arnold M. 1982. "Theology, Sociology, Ideology: Jewish Thought in America." *Modern Judaism* 2, no. 1: 91–103.

———. 1983. *The Chosen People in America: A Study in Jewish Religious Ideology*. Bloomington: Indiana University Press.

———. 1998a. *Rethinking Modern Judaism: Ritual, Commandment, Community*. Chicago: University of Chicago Press.

———. 1998b. "Israel at 50: An American Jewish Perspective." In *American Jewish Year Book 1998*. New York: American Jewish Committee.

Ezrahi, Yaron. 1996. *Rubber Bullets: Power and Conscience in Modern Israel*. New York: Farrar, Straus and Giroux.

Fackenheim, Emil. 1970. *God's Presence in History*. New York: Harper Torchbooks.

Fein, Leonard J. 1988. *Where Are We? The Inner Life of America's Jews*. New York: Harper and Row.

———. 1994. "Smashing Idols and Other Prescriptions for Jewish Continuity." New York: Nathan Cummings Foundation.

Fowler, J. W. 1981. *Stages of Faith: The Psychology of Human Development and the Quest for Meaning*. San Francisco: Harper and Row.

Friedman, Menachem. 1987. "Life Traditions and Book Traditions in the Development of Ultra-Orthodox Judaism." In *Judaism Viewed from Within and from Without*, ed. Harvey E. Goldberg. Albany: State University of New York Press.

Friedman, Murray. 1995. *What Went Wrong? The Creation and Collapse of the Black-Jewish Alliance*. New York: The Free Press.

Gans, Herbert J. 1958. "The Origins and Growth of a Jewish Community in the Suburbs: A Study of the Jews of Park Forest." In *The Jews: Social Patterns of an American Group*, ed. Marshall Sklare. New York: Free Press.

———. 1979. "Symbolic Ethnicity: The Future of Ethnic Groups and Cultures in America." *Ethnic and Racial Studies* 2: 1–20.

———. 1990. "American Jews and Non-Jews: Comparative Opinions on the Palestinian Uprising." *Jewish Political Studies Review* 2 (Spring): 178–179.

———. 1991. *Middle American Individualism: Political Participation and Liberal Democracy*. New York: Oxford University Press.

———. 1994. "Symbolic Ethnicity and Symbolic Religiosity: Towards a Comparison of Ethnic and Religious Acculturation." *Ethnic and Racial Studies* 17 (October): 577–591.

Glazer, Nathan. 1972. *American Judaism*. Chicago: University of Chicago Press.

Glazer, Nathan, and Daniel Patrick Moynihan. 1963. *Beyond the Melting Pot.* Cambridge, Mass.: MIT Press.

Goffman, Erving. 1967. "The Nature of Deference and Demeanor." In *Interaction Ritual: Essays on Face-to-Face Behavior.* New York: Pantheon Books.

Goldscheider, Calvin. 1986. *Jewish Continuity and Change.* Bloomington: Indiana University Press.

Goldstein, Sidney. 1992. "Profile of American Jewry." *American Jewish Year Book 92.*

Goldstein, Sidney, and Calvin Goldscheider. 1968. *Jewish Americans: Three Generations in a Jewish Community.* Englewood Cliffs, N.J.: Prentice-Hall.

Goodman, Allegra. 1996. "The Four Questions." In *The Family Markowitz.* 183–207. New York: Pocket Books.

Greeley, Andrew M. 1974. *Ethnicity in the United States: A Preliminary Reconnaissance.* New York: John Wiley and Sons.

Greenberg, Cheryl. 1998. "Pluralism and Its Discontents: The Case of Blacks and Jews." In *Insider/Outsider: American Jews and Multiculturalism,* ed. David Biale et al. 55–87. Berkeley: University of California Press.

Hartman, Moshe, and Harriet Hartman. 1996. *Gender Equality and American Jews.* Albany, N.Y.: State University of New York Press.

Heilman, Samuel C. 1976. *Synagogue Life: A Study of Symbolic Interaction.* Chicago: University of Chicago Press.

Heilman, Samuel C., and Steven M. Cohen. 1989. *Cosmopolitans and Parochials: Modern Orthodox Jews in America.* Chicago: University of Chicago Press.

Herberg, Will. 1955. *Protestant-Catholic-Jew: An Essay in American Religious Sociology.* Garden City, N.Y.: Doubleday.

Heschel, Abraham Joshua. 1951. *Man Is Not Alone.* New York: Farrar, Straus and Young.

———. 1966. *The Insecurity of Freedom.* Philadelphia: Jewish Publication Society of America.

———. 1986. *Quest for God: Studies in Prayer and Symbolism.* New York: Crossroad Publishing Company.

Himmelfarb, Harold S. 1974. "The Impact of Religious Schooling: The Effects of Jewish Education upon Adult Religious Involvement." Unpublished doctoral dissertation, University of Chicago.

———. 1975. "Jewish Education for Naught: Educating the Culturally Deprived Jewish Child." *Analysis* 51 (September). Washington, D.C.: Institute for Jewish Policy Planning and Research.

Hoffman, Lawrence. 1987. *Beyond the Text: A Holistic Approach to Liturgy.* Bloomington: Indiana University Press.

———. 1988. *The Art of Public Prayer.* Washington, D.C.: Pastoral Press.

Hoge, D. R. 1981. *Converts, Dropouts, and Returnees: A Study of Religious Change among Catholics.* New York: Pilgrim Press.

Hoge, D. R., B. Johnson, and D. Luidens. 1994. *Vanishing Boundaries: The Religion of Mainline Protestant Baby Boomers.* Louisville, Ky.: Westminster/John Knox Press.

Hollinger, David. 1995. *Postethnic America: Beyond Multiculturalism.* New York: Houghton and Mifflin.

Hyman, Paula. 1991. *The Emancipation of the Jews of Alsace: Acculturation and Tradition.* New Haven, Conn.: Yale University Press.

Israel, Sherry R. 1997. *Comprehensive Report on the 1995 Demographic Study*. Boston: Combined Jewish Philanthropies of Greater Boston.

Joselit, Jenna Weissman. 1994. *The Wonders of America*. New York: Hill and Wang.

Kaplan, Mordecai M. 1962. *The Meaning of God in Modern Jewish Religion*. New York: The Reconstructionist Press.

———. 1967a. *Judaism as a Civilization: Toward a Reconstruction of American Jewish Life*. New York: Schocken.

———. 1967b. *Judaism without Supernaturalism: The Only Alternative to Orthodoxy and Secularism*. New York: The Reconstructionist Press.

Katz, Jacob. 1961a. *Exclusiveness and Tolerance*. London: Oxford University Press.

———. 1961b. *Tradition and Crisis: Jewish Society at the End of the Middle Ages*. New York: Schocken.

———. 1972. *Emancipation and Assimilation: Studies in Modern Jewish History*. Farnborough, England: Gregg.

Kaufman, Debra Renee. 1991. *Rachel's Daughters: Newly Orthodox Jewish Women*. New Brunswick, N.J.: Rutgers University Press.

Kosmin, B., S. Goldstein, J. Waksberg, N. Lerer, A. Keysar, and J. Scheckner. 1991. *Highlights of the CJF 1990 National Jewish Population Survey*. New York: Council of Jewish Federations.

Laumann, Edward O. 1966. *Prestige and Association in an Urban Community: An Analysis of an Urban Stratification System*. Indianapolis, Ind.: Bobbs-Merrill.

———. 1973. *Bonds of Pluralism: The Forms and Substance of Urban Social Networks*. New York: John Wiley and Sons.

Lazerwitz, Bernard, J. Alan Winter, Arnold Dashevsky, and Ephraim Tabory. 1998. *Jewish Choices: American Jewish Denominationalism*. Albany: State University of New York Press.

Liebman, Charles S. 1990. "Ritual, Ceremony and the Reconstruction of Judaism in the United States." In *Studies in Contemporary Jewry*, vol. 6, ed. Ezra Mendelson. New York: Oxford University Press.

Liebman, Charles S., and Steven M. Cohen. 1990. *Two Worlds of Judaism: The Israeli and American Experiences*. New Haven, Conn.: Yale University Press.

———. 1996. "Jewish Liberalism Revisited." *Commentary* 102 (November): 51–53.

Liebman, Charles S., and Eliezer Don-Yehiya. 1983. *Civil Religion in Israel*. Berkeley: University of California Press.

Liebman, Charles S., and Elihu Katz, eds. 1997. *The Jewishness of Israelis: Responses to the Guttman Report*. Albany: State University of New York Press.

Luckmann, Thomas. 1967. *The Invisible Religion*. New York: Macmillan.

Markus, Hazel Rose, and Shinobu Kitayama. 1991. "Culture and the Self: Implications for Cognition, Emotion and Motivation." *Psychological Review* 98, no. 2: 224–253.

Medding, Peter Y., Gary Tobin, Sylvia Barrack Fishman, and Mordechai Rimor. 1992. "Jewish Identity in Conversionary and Mixed Marriages." *American Jewish Committee Yearbook* 92: 3–76.

Merton, Robert K. 1968. *Social Theory and Social Structure*. New York: Free Press.

Moore, Deborah Dash. 1981. *At Home in America*. New York: Columbia University Press.

Nash, D. 1968. "A Little Child Shall Lead Them: A Statistical Test of an Hypothesis

That Children Were the Source of the American 'Religious Revival.'" *Journal for the Scientific Study of Religion* 7: 238–240.

Nash, D., and Peter Berger. 1962. "The Child, the Family and the Religious Revival in Suburbia." *Journal for the Scientific Study of Religion* 2: 85–93.

Novak, Michael. 1971. *The Rise of the Unmeltable Ethnics*. New York: Macmillan.

Novick, Peter. 1999. *The Holocaust in American Life*. Boston: Houghton Mifflin.

Oyserman, Daphna, and Hazel Rose Markus. 1993. "The Sociocultural Self." In *Psychological Perspectives on the Self*. Vol. 4, *The Self in Social Perspective*. Ed. J. Suls. 187–220. Hillsdale, N.J.: Erlbaum.

Perel, Esther. 1990. "Ethnocultural Factors in Marital Communication among Intermarried Couples." *Journal of Jewish Communal Service* 66: 3.

Phillips, Bruce A. 1997. "Re-examining Intermarriage: Trends, Textures, and Strategies." Boston: Wilstein Institute, and New York: American Jewish Committee.

Pinkenson, Ruth S. 1987. "The Impact of the Jewish Day Care Experience on Parental Jewish Identity." Unpublished doctoral dissertation, Temple University.

Plaut, Guenther, ed. 1963. *The Rise of Reform Judaism*. New York: World Union for Progressive Judaism.

Prell, Riv-Ellen. 1989. *Prayer and Community: The Havurah in American Judaism*. Detroit: Wayne State University Press.

———. 1999. *Fighting to Become Americans: Jews, Gender, and the Anxiety of Assimilation*. Boston: Beacon Press.

Putnam, Robert. 1995. "Bowling Alone: America's Declining Social Capital." *Journal of Democracy* (January): 65–78.

Rappaport, Roy. 1979. *Ecology, Meaning, and Religion*. Richmond, Calif.: North Atlantic Books.

———. 1988. "Logos, Liturgy, and the Evolution of Humanity." Paper presented at the ICAES symposium "Evolutionary Ecology and the Human Condition." Zagreb.

———. N.d. "The Construction of Time and Eternity in Ritual." Department of Anthropology, University of Michigan, photocopy of unpublished manuscript.

Reisman, Bernard. 1977. *The Chavurah Movement: A Contemporary Jewish Experience*. New York: Union of American Hebrew Congregations.

Rieff, Philip. 1966. *The Triumph of the Therapeutic*. New York: Harper and Row.

Ringer, Benjamin B. 1967. *The Edge of Friendliness: A Study of Jewish-Gentile Relations*. New York: Basic Books.

Ritterband, Paul, and Steven M. Cohen. 1979. "Will the Well Run Dry? The Future of Jewish Giving in America." New York: National Jewish Conference Center.

Roof, Wade Clark. 1983. "America's Voluntary Establishment: Mainline Religion in Transition." In *Religion in America*, ed. Mary Douglas and Steven Tipton. Boston: Beacon Press.

———. 1993. *Generation of Seekers: The Spiritual Journeys of the Baby Boom Generation*. With the assistance of Bruce Greer et al. San Francisco: Harper San Francisco.

Roof, Wade Clark, and William McKinney. 1987. *American Mainline Religion: Its Changing Faith and Future*. New Brunswick, N.J.: Rutgers University Press.

Rosenzweig, Franz. 1964. *The Star of Redemption.* Boston: Beacon Press.

Roth, Philip. 1959. "Eli the Fanatic." In *Goodbye, Columbus.* Boston: Houghton Mifflin.

———. 1963. "The Jewish Intellectual and Jewish Identity." *Congress Biweekly* (September 16): 21, 39.

Rubinstein, Richard. 1966. *After Auschwitz: Radical Theology and Contemporary Judaism.* Indianapolis, Ind.: Bobbs-Merrill.

Sarna, Jonathan. 1990. "Reform Jewish Leaders, Intermarriage, and Conversion." *Journal of Reform Judaism* (Winter): 1–9.

Sharot, Stephen. 1997. "A Critical Comment on Gans' 'Symbolic Ethnicity' and 'Symbolic Religiosity' and Other Formulations of Ethnicity and Religion Regarding American Jews." *Contemporary Jewry* 18: 25–43.

Sklare, Marshall. 1972. *Conservative Judaism: An American Religious Movement.* New York: Schocken Books.

Sklare, Marshall, and Joseph Greenblum. 1967. *Jewish Identity on the Suburban Frontier: A Study of Group Survival in the Open Society.* New York: Basic Books.

Smith, Tom. 1991. *What Do Americans Think about Jews?* New York: American Jewish Committee.

Soloveitchik, Haym. 1994. "Rupture and Reconstruction: The Transformation of Contemporary Orthodoxy." *Tradition* 28, no. 4: 74.

Soloveitchik, Joseph B. 1983. *Halakhic Man.* Philadelphia: Jewish Publication Society of America.

Stanislawski, Michael. 1988. *For Whom Do I Toil: Judah Leib Gordon and the Crisis of Russian Jewry.* New York: Oxford University Press.

Stryker, Sheldon. 1987. "Identity Theory: Development and Extensions." In *Self and Identity: Psychosocial Perspectives,* ed. K. Yardley and T. Honess. London: John Wiley and Sons.

Swidler, Ann. 1999. Remarks at a conference of Jewish educators sponsored by the Whizin Institute, Los Angeles, Inc.

"Symbols of a Desert Exile Bloom in Jews' Backyards." *New York Times* (October 14, 1995).

Taylor, Charles. 1989. *Sources of the Self: The Making of Modern Identity.* Cambridge, Mass.: Harvard University Press.

Wall, Susan Segal. 1994. "Parents of Pre-schoolers: Their Jewish Identity and Its Implications for Jewish Education." Unpublished DHL dissertation, the Jewish Theological Seminary of America.

Walzer, Michael. 1998. "Multiculturalism and the Politics of Interest." In *Insider/Outsider: American Jews and Multiculturalism,* ed. David Biale et al. 88–98. Berkeley: University of California Press.

Warner, R. Stephen. 1993. "Work in Progress toward a New Paradigm for the Sociological Study of Religion in the United States." *American Journal of Sociology* 98, no. 5 (March): 1044–1093.

Waters, Mary C. 1990. *Ethnic Options: Choosing Identities in America.* Berkeley: University of California Press.

Waxman, Chaim I. 1992. "All in the Family: American Jewish Attachments to Israel." In *A New Jewry? America since the Second World War—Studies in Contemporary Jewry.* 134–149. New York: Oxford University Press.

Weissler, Chava. 1989. *Making Judaism Meaningful: Ambivalence and Tradition in a Havurah Community.* New York: AMS Press.

Wertheimer, Jack. 1987. *The American Synagogue: A Sanctuary Transformed.* Hanover, N.H.: Brandeis University Press.

———. 1993. *A People Divided: Judaism in Contemporary America.* New York: Harper-Collins.

———. 1997. "Current Trends in American Jewish Philanthropy." *American Jewish Yearbook* 97: 3–92.

Wertheimer, Jack, Charles S. Liebman, and Steven M. Cohen. 1996. "How to Save American Jews." *Commentary* 101 (January): 47–51.

Winer, Mark L., Sanford Seltzer, and Steven J. Schwager. 1987. *Leaders of Reform Judaism.* Research Task Force on the Future of Reform Judaism. New York: Union of American Hebrew Congregations.

Woocher, Jonathan S. 1986. *Sacred Survival: The Civil Religion of American Jews.* Bloomington: Indiana University Press.

Wuthnow, Robert. 1988. *The Restructuring of American Religion.* Princeton, N.J.: Princeton University Press.

———. 1989. *The Struggle for America's Soul: Evangelicals, Liberals, and Secularism.* Grand Rapids, Mich.: Wm. B. Eerdmans.

———. 1994. *Sharing the Journey: Support Groups and America's New Quest for Community.* New York: Free Press.

———. 1998. *After Heaven: Spirituality in America since the 1950's.* Berkeley: University of California Press.

———. 1999. *Growing Up Religious: Christians and Jews and Their Journeys of Faith.* Boston: Beacon Press.

Yerushalmi, Y. H. 1982. *Zakhor: Jewish History and Jewish Memory.* Seattle: University of Washington Press.

Zborowski, Mark, and Elizabeth Herzog. 1952. *Life Is with People: The Culture of the Shtetl.* New York: Schocken.

INDEX